**Prentice-Hall
Contemporary Topics in Accounting Series**

KATHERINE SCHIPPER, SERIES EDITOR

BEAVER, *Financial Reporting: An Accounting Revolution, 2/E*

DYCKMAN AND MORSE, *Efficient Capital Markets and Accounting:
A Critical Analysis, 2/E*

JAEDICKE AND SPROUSE, *Accounting Flows: Income, Funds, and Cash*

HOPWOOD, *Accounting and Human Behaviour*

LEV, *Financial Statement Analysis: A New Approach*

LIBBY, *Accounting and Human Information Processing: Theory and
Applications*

REVSINE, *Replacement Cost Accounting*

WATTS AND ZIMMERMAN, *Positive Accounting Theory*

Financial Reporting: An Accounting Revolution

second edition

Financial Reporting: An Accounting Revolution

WILLIAM H. BEAVER
Stanford University

Prentice Hall, Englewood Cliffs, New Jersey 07632

Library of Congress Cataloging-in-Publication Data

Beaver, William H.
   Financial reporting : an accounting revolution/William H. Beaver.
     p. cm.
   Includes bibliographies and index.
   ISBN 0-13-316993-6
   1. Accouting—United States. 2. Financial statements—United States. I. Title.
HF5616.U5B36 1989
657′.3′0973—dc19   88-29246
                                               CIP

Editorial/production supervision and
  interior design: **Lisa Schulz Garboski**
Manufacturing buyer: **Ed O'Dougherty**

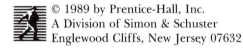
© 1989 by Prentice-Hall, Inc.
A Division of Simon & Schuster
Englewood Cliffs, New Jersey 07632

Printed in the United States of America

10 9 8 7 6 5 4 3 2 1

ISBN 0-13-316993-6

Prentice-Hall International (UK) Limited, *London*
Prentice-Hall of Australia Pty. Limited, *Sydney*
Prentice-Hall Canada Inc., *Toronto*
Prentice-Hall Hispanoamericana, S.A., *Mexico*
Prentice-Hall of India Private Limited, *New Delhi*
Prentice-Hall of Japan, Inc., *Tokyo*
Simon & Schuster Asia Pte. Ltd., *Singapore*
Editora Prentice-Hall do Brasil, Ltda., *Rio de Janeiro*

To Sue, Marie, Sarah, and David.

Contents

PREFACE TO THE FIRST EDITION   **xi**

PREFACE TO THE SECOND EDITION   **xv**

ACKNOWLEDGMENTS   **xvii**

chapter one

THE REVOLUTION   **1**

chapter two

INFORMATION   **22**

chapter three

EARNINGS UNDER CERTAINTY   **49**

chapter four

EARNINGS UNDER UNCERTAINTY   **77**

chapter five

THE EVIDENCE   **104**

chapter six

MARKET EFFICIENCY   **130**

chapter seven

REGULATION   **176**

INDEX   **199**

Preface
to the First Edition

The material that follows represents an attempt to synthesize security price research, in which I have participated, and institutional knowledge of the financial reporting environment based in part on my experience as a member of the SEC Advisory Committee on Corporate Disclosure. The result is a distinctive and hopefully interesting perspective on the nature of the financial reporting environment.

Each of the seven chapters is oriented toward concepts rather than procedures. The chapters are based on materials which have partially appeared in previous publications, but a major portion is taken from my class notes of an elective, second-year financial accounting MBA course at Stanford. The focus on concepts rather than procedures seems appropriate for several reasons. First, the financial reporting rules and standards are growing at an unprecedented rate. As a result, it becomes increasingly difficult to provide a comprehensive treatment. Second, the estimated life of any given rule is short and is growing shorter. As a result, a treatment of the current menu of regulations is likely to become quickly out-of-date. The estimated useful life of a book that is concepts-oriented is likely to be much longer than one that is procedures-oriented. Third, many persons have a vital interest in the financial reporting environment who are not and do not intend to become accountants.

These individuals include analysts, regulators, and managers, among others. For example, most of the students who take the elective financial reporting courses at Stanford do not intend to become accountants or auditors. Yet they have a demand for a financial reporting course beyond the "nuts and bolts" level because they are likely to become participants in the financial reporting environment as preparers, consumers, or regulators of financial reports.

Although the emphasis is on concepts, specific illustrations are provided throughout. Some familiarity with financial accounting is presumed. When these materials are used in my course, they are further supplemented with specific financial reporting issues. However, there is no attempt to provide an exhaustive treatment, which would be difficult for the reasons cited above. The specific issues are chosen as illustrations of the concepts and will change from year to year.

The book is a personal one in several respects. It primarily reflects my perspective on the financial reporting environment based upon two major sources of experience—research and institutional knowledge. There has been no attempt to provide a comprehensive treatment of other perspectives, but there has been no conscious attempt to preclude them either. In a related vein, the source materials referenced show a strong "Beaver" bias. For the most part, the previous articles referenced contain a detailed bibliography of other works.

The sequence of the materials is somewhat arbitrary, and I anticipate other sequences may seem more appropriate, given the context in which the materials are being assigned. As a result, some redundancy is deliberately built into the chapters (e.g., Chapter 7). Hopefully, this redundancy will not impair the effectiveness of the presentation.

The length of some of the chapters may appear excessive. At one stage I considered dividing Chapter 2 into two parts. The single-person–multi-person analysis provides a natural separation. Similarly, Chapter 4 could have been split into one chapter on perfect and complete markets and another chapter on an imperfect, incomplete market setting. However, some long chapters (3 and 6) would still remain, and there appeared to be no natural separation for these chapters. The longer chapters remain intact, and the separation decision is left as a matter of personal choice, which it is, in any event.

There are several obvious extensions of this perspective to specific accounting topics. At the outset, I drew up topical outlines for one chapter each on materiality, forecasting, and accounting for inflation (based on extensions of the Illinois paper). I also prepared an outline on the role of financial accounting research. It adds the researcher as a major constituency to the financial reporting environment and views research from an informational, multi-person perspective. None of these topics progressed beyond the outline stage because I decided to devote scarce resources to improving the chapters presented here. As a result, there are some obvious "omissions". Similarly, the reader may feel that the book ends rather abruptly. I had considered adding a "wrap up" chapter but I could see no point in merely summarizing the previous chapters. Nor did I see any merit to essentially paraphrasing Chapter 1, which is the synthesizing chapter. Having rejected these two approaches, I was not clear as to what the contents of the wrap up chapter would be. If a wrap up is desired, Chapter 1 could be reread. Presumably, it will appear in a different light from what it did on first reading.

I visualize several potential uses for the book other than for the course for which the materials were originally developed. Such courses would include accounting theory courses (at an advanced undergraduate level, masters level, and doctoral level), financial statement analysis courses, and certain finance courses in which financial reporting plays an important role (e.g., investments courses). However, such delusions of an author are best not elaborated, and usage is better left for "market forces" to decide.

William H. Beaver
Stanford, California

Preface
to the Second
Edition

In the revision, there were two obvious options—either a major or minor revision. Any intermediate ground was clearly nonoptimal. There is only so much tinkering that can be done before one better off to start from scratch. I have chosen the route of minor revision. This decision was made easier by the introduction of Watts and Zimmerman's *Positive Accounting Theory* and by the revisions of George Foster's *Financial Statement Analysis* and Dyckman and Morse's *Efficient Capital Markets and Accounting*, all occurring since the publication of the first edition in 1981. The existence of these excellent texts meant the second edition did not have to be as self-contained and did not have to provide detailed discussions of recent developments in the areas covered by these three books. There are two principal differences between the first and second editions—greater discussion of contracting theory and the supporting evidence and an update of the empirical evidence that has occurred since the first edition.

Another reason in favor of minor revision is that the first edition met my expectations and, in fact, exceeded them. I have been surprised, amazed, and pleased at the variety of courses in which the text has been used, ranging from undergraduate accounting theory seminars to masters level courses to introductory doctoral seminars. I am grateful to those of you who have seen fit to use the text and for the extremely helpful feedback you have provided. Were I to spend resources in a major textbook effort, it would more likely be in a different text rather than a major revision of this text. But that is another story.

William H. Beaver
Stanford, California

Acknowledgments

This manuscript would not have been possible without the contributions of many teachers, colleagues, and friends. My debts are too numerous to cite exhaustively. However, some debts are too great not to mention. I apologize for those I have inevitably but unintentionally omitted. I am indebted to Paul Conway of Notre Dame for being a role model and for first suggesting an academic career.

The philosophy in this book reflects my training by and discussions with the many outstanding individuals whom I met at the University of Chicago. Most prominently, I am indebted to George Sorter, my thesis advisor and mentor, whose support and encouragement were invaluable. Other major contributors were Sidney Davidson, Nick Dopuch, and David Green. I also benefited from a gifted group of individuals who were doctoral students at Chicago, including Ross Archibald, Ray Ball, Philip Brown, Mel Greenball, Orace Johnson, Jack Kennelly, Fred Neumann, William Voss, and Ross Watts, among others.

A special debt is owed to Joel Demski and Charles Horngren, my colleagues and friends, with whom I have shared the Chicago and Stanford experiences. Over the past eighteen years they have been instrumental in my developing the philosophy of the text. They also provided detailed suggestions on earlier versions of the manuscript. Detailed comments on specific chapters were provided by George Foster, Jim Patell, and Mark Wolfson. I also benefited from general discussions with Amin Amershi, Paul Griffin, David Ng, and Bill Wright.

A debt of gratitude is also owed to several doctoral students at Stanford, from whom I have learned considerably, including Mary Barth, Bob Bowen, Jerry Bowman, Andrew Christie, Pete Dukes, Rick Lambert, Wayne Landsman, Larry Lookabill, Jim Manegold, Dale Morse, Stephen Ryan, D. Shores, and Michael Van Breda.

I have been fortunate enough to have been surrounded by an extraordinary group of talented individuals. Any merits this book may have are largely attributable to these associations. However, limitations herein are to be attributed to my inability to take full advantage of the situation. In any event, I am sure these individuals have no intention of sharing the blame.

Portions of Chapter 6 heavily draw upon portions of my previous publications, "The Implication of Security Price Research for Disclosure Policy and the Analyst Community" (proceedings of the *Duke Symposium on Financial Information Requirements for Security Analysis*), (Duke University, December, 1976), 67–81; "Reflections on Market Efficiency," *Annual Accounting Review: 1980* (Harwood Academic Publishers: New York, 1980 and "Market Efficiency," *Accounting Review,* (January, 1981). I am indebted to Tom Keller of Duke University, to Michael Walker and Stanley Weinstein, editors of the *Annual Accounting Review,* and Steve Zeff, editor of the *Accounting Review,* respectively, for granting permission to extract the excerpts.

Most of all, I wish to thank my family, especially my wife, Sue, whose love and understanding were essential to my undertaking and completing this project.

chapter one

The Revolution

The Financial Accounting Standards Board (FASB) and the Securities and Exchange Commission (SEC) have been issuing additional financial reporting requirements at an unprecedented rate.[1] Notwithstanding this activity, Congress and the courts, among others, have expressed concern that the current reporting system is inadequate.[2] In an era of deregulation of our economy, legal liability for financial reporting and calls for additional regulation are at an all-time high.[3]

[1] The SEC is an independent agency of the federal government created by the Securities Acts of 1933 and 1934. It is empowered to ensure "full and fair" disclosure by corporations. The nature of its activities is described in an excellent text by Skousen (1983). The FASB is a private sector organization which determines the financial accounting standards to be used in the preparation of annual reports to shareholders. The generic term, *financial reporting*, will be used to include financial statements and financial disclosures.

[2] The activities of the committee chaired by Congressman Dingell is described in Berton and Ingersoll (1985). Congressman Wyden has introduced proposed legislation entitled the "Financial Fraud Detection and Disclosure Act of 1986" which would substantially increase the responsibility of the financial reporting system for the detection and disclosure of fraud. The level of legal liability for financial reporting is vividly described by Schares (1984).

[3] The paradox of increased demand for financial reporting in the presence of deregulation economy-wide is not as anomalous as is often suggested. In many cases, the result of deregulation has been an increase in risks borne by the firm and its management.

1

Rapid growth in additional financial reporting requirements and rapid changes in existing requirements are likely to continue to be permanent features of the financial reporting environment.

The result is a bewildering increase in financial data for the user to interpret. Beneath this turbulence, a major evolution is occurring with respect to the philosophy of financial reporting. This evolution, which has been called a *financial reporting revolution*, is the main subject of this book.[4]

This introductory chapter provides a brief historical perspective on the purposes of financial reporting, with a special emphasis on the objectives of financial statements. A stewardship view of management and the concept of economic income, which dominated financial accounting theory until the mid-1960s, are briefly summarized. The informational approach is then introduced, and the role of accrual accounting from an informational perspective is discussed. The financial reporting environment is described in terms of the major constituencies and the economic consequences of financial reporting. In presenting this framework, several trends in financial reporting are identified. Key features of the environment are its complexity, diversity, and its impact on the preferences of the constituencies for financial reporting.

The selection among financial reporting systems by management or by the financial reporting regulators is a substantive choice, which involves making tradeoffs with respect to the effects on the different constituencies. A particular financial reporting requirement is the outcome of a political (or social choice) process.

This chapter provides the basis for understanding the nature of the financial reporting revolution and provides a perspective for the remaining chapters, which are briefly summarized at the close of this chapter.

1-1. HISTORICAL PERSPECTIVE

The stewardship function of management was dominant in early views of the purpose of financial statements. Under this view, management is the steward to whom capital suppliers (i.e., shareholders and

---

When unexpectedly unfavorable events are the outcome of such risk, litigation and allegations of financial reporting deficiencies typically arise.

[4] Sidney Cottle of FRS Associates suggested that these changes constituted a "revolution." The initial reaction was surprise at such a dramatic description of these changes. However, conversations with Sid convinced me that these changes constitute a major alteration in the way policy makers and users view financial reporting.

creditors) entrust control over a portion of their financial resources. In this context, the purpose of financial statements is to provide a report to capital suppliers to facilitate their evaluation of management's stewardship. A variety of reporting systems could conceivably fulfill this purpose. However, in financial accounting it has long been presumed that merely reporting cash flows is inadequate and that some form of accrual accounting is appropriate.

This basic faith in the superiority of accrual accounting is epitomized in Paton and Littleton's (1940) monograph, which focuses on the *matching concept*. This monograph has recently been called one of the most important contributions to financial accounting of the twentieth century.[5] The matching concept states that revenues and expenses should be recorded such that efforts and accomplishments are properly aligned. Reporting cash receipts and cash disbursements will not properly match, and some form of accrual accounting is called for. Accrual accounting is viewed to be essential to proper financial reporting. However, it is apparent that the nature of the accrual process is ambiguous and not well-defined. For example, for virtually every major event that could affect the financial statements of a firm, there exists a variety of alternative methods for matching costs and revenues. LIFO versus FIFO methods of inventory valuation and straight-line versus accelerated methods of depreciation are two prominent examples within the framework of historical cost accounting. Departures from historical cost accounting, such as various forms of current cost and market value accounting, further increase the alternatives available. The question then arises as to which accrual method is "best." This question has been viewed as essentially a normative one (i.e., the search for the superior method of reporting.)

One approach to evaluating alternative accrual methods is to attempt to infer criteria from general definitions, such as *net income*. Net income can be defined as the difference between revenues and expenses (plus or minus gains and losses). This is tautologically correct, but it is not particularly insightful. Attempts to dig deeper by exploring various definitions of *revenues* and *expenses* suffer from the same problem. An expense is typically defined as an *expired cost*, but the definition is silent on the basis for determining expiration. For example, consider the definition of *depreciation*, which has been described as the allocation of the original cost over the estimated useful life. Again this is tautologically correct, but it provides no insight into what criteria to use in selecting an allocation method from among a large number of possibilities.

---

[5] American Accounting Association Committee on Concepts and Standards for External Financial Reports (1977) and Hakansson (1978).

Another approach is to ask, "What properties should the 'ideal' net income have?" Accounting alternatives would then be evaluated in terms of these "desirable" criteria. When a "desirable" properties approach is pursued, financial accounting theorists have usually adopted an *economic income* approach. Under this approach, accounting alternatives are evaluated in terms of their perceived proximity to this "ideal." It is assumed that economic income is a well-defined concept, and in most cases certainty is assumed or uncertainty is treated in a casual manner. In a multiperiod setting the discounted present value of future cash flows is usually adopted as the valuation model for the firm and its securities. *Economic income* is defined as the change in the present value of the future cash flows, after proper adjustments for deposits (e.g., additional common stock issues) or withdrawals (e.g., dividends).

As will be shown in Chapter 3, this concept is virtually unassailable under conditions of perfect and complete markets. For example, it not only reflects the effects of management's actions on current year's operations (e.g., current cash flows), but it also incorporates the future effects into this year's measure of net income. Hence, from a stewardship perspective, economic net income has appealing qualities.

This perspective can be traced to the early classics of Paton (1922), Canning (1929), and Alexander (1950). It has been applied to the comparison of specific accounting alternatives, such as depreciation methods, lease accounting, and the treatment of long-term receivables and payables. This approach also motivates proposals for market value or current cost approaches to financial reporting which appear in Edwards and Bell (1961), Chambers (1966), and Sterling (1970).

1-2. INFORMATIONAL PERSPECTIVE

In the late 1960s the perspective shifted from economic income measurement to an "informational" approach. This is reflected in financial accounting research in the areas of information economics, security prices, and behavioral science. It is also reflected with increasing emphasis in authoritative statements on the purpose of financial statements, such as in Accounting Principles Board Statement No. 4 (1970) and the *Report of the Study Group on the Objectives of Financial Statements* [AICPA (1973)]. The shift in emphasis culminated in the FASB's Conceptual Framework Project and is reflected in its *Statement of Financial Accounting Concepts No. 1 (1978)*, which states:

> Financial reporting should provide information that is useful to present and potential investors and creditors and other users in assessing the amounts, timing, and uncertainty of prospective cash receipts . . . Since investors'

and creditors' cash flows are related to enterprise cash flows, financial reporting should provide information to help investors, creditors, and others assess the amounts, timing, and uncertainty of prospective net cash inflows to the related enterprise. (page viii)

Perhaps the notion that financial statement data ought to provide useful information on the assessment of future cash flows appears to be relatively innocuous. However, if taken seriously, the informational perspective has several dramatic implications for financial statement preparation and interpretation.[6] Chapter 2 will explore the informational approach and its implications.

There are at least two reasons for this shift in emphasis. (1) The concept of economic income is not well-defined when there are imperfect or incomplete markets for the assets and claims related to the firm. For example, in the simple case of certainty, the value of the firm is described in terms of the present value of the future cash flows. The present value model effectively collapses the multiperiod cash flows into a single number called the *present value*. Perfect and complete markets are sufficient to permit the vector of cash flows to be adequately described by a single number. Without perfect and complete markets, the properties of such a collapsing operation are not clear. Given that many of the assets and claims reported on the financial statements are represented by imperfect or incomplete markets, the concept of economic income is not well-defined. Hence, the "ideal" that financial statement data are attempting to represent is not clear conceptually. (2) Moreover, even in situations in which the relevant markets for claims exist (e.g., marketable equity securities) there seems to be an inability to reach a consensus of the "best" method of reporting. There appears to be more at stake in the setting of financial accounting standards than is evident when adopting an economic income approach. Various groups or constituencies, such as shareholders, creditors, financial analysts, regulators (e.g., the FASB and the SEC), management and auditors, are affected by the choice of the financial reporting requirements. Hence, they have interests in which requirement is chosen. These interests are not incorporated within the framework of an economic income approach. In any event, the economic income perspective does not lead to a consensus on what financial standards should be, and the reasons for the lack of consensus are obscured by this perspective.

Financial reporting data play two distinct, but related informational roles. The first role is to facilitate decision makers, such as investors, in

---

[6] Armstrong (1977) reported substantial opposition to adopting an informational perspective. Stewardship was cited most often as the preferred alternative. However, according to the FASB (1976b), stewardship is subsumed under the informational perspective.

selecting the best action among the available alternatives, such as alternative investment portfolios. The second role is to facilitate contracting between parties, such as management and investors, by having the payment under the contract defined in part in terms of financial reporting data. Management incentive contracts defined in part in terms of the firm's accounting net income would be an example. The first role is often called the *pre-contracting role* while the second is often called the *post-contracting role*. Both roles aid in the understanding of why management and financial reporting regulators perceive the choice of accounting method to be a substantive issue. This perspective also helps us understand why the standard-setting is the result of a political process. Chapter 2 describes both roles in greater detail.

1-3. ACCRUAL ACCOUNTING IN AN INFORMATIONAL SETTING

Although the informational perspective potentially represents a dramatic shift with respect to the purpose of financial statements, the FASB concluded that accrual accounting with its attendant net income number is still superior to cash flow accounting with respect to the "new" purpose—information about future cash flows. This future cash flow orientation has been interpreted by many as implying that accrual accounting may not be superior to cash flow accounting after all. However, according to the FASB (1978),

> Information about enterprise earnings based on accrual accounting generally provides a better indication of enterprise's present and continuing ability to generate cash flows than information limited to the financial aspects of cash receipts and payments.   (page ix)
> *The primary focus of financial reporting is information about earnings and its components.*   (page ix) (emphasis added)

Even though there has been a shift in philosophy, the FASB still retains a basic faith in the superiority of accrual accounting and accounting earnings over a system of cash flow reporting.

Notwithstanding the assurances of the FASB, there has been some questioning of the efficacy of the accrual system.[7] Hawkins (1977, 1978) has noted a trend in security analysis away from earnings oriented valuation approaches to discounted cash flow approaches. Deficiencies in current financial reporting rules are given as a primary reason. Current

---

[7] In addition to the specific cases cited here, FASB (1976c) briefly discusses other criticisms or alleged abuses of accrual accounting.

FASB standards for reporting research and development expenditures (FAS No. 2), foreign currency translations (FAS No. 8), and reliance on historical cost in an inflationary economy are cited as examples. Stern (1972) has been a vocal critic of an "excessive" emphasis on earnings. Ijiri (1978) also has expressed concern over the importance of accruals. He suggested that financial statements be based upon a cash flow orientation, and he offered several reasons for this recommendation: (1) There is a direct logical link between past cash flows and future cash flows (i.e., they are of a similar nature or character). (2) Cash flows offer a more primitive system. By the principle of Occam's razor (a principle approximately 700 years old), the simpler method should be used until the more complex one has proven that it adds something. (3) Cash flow is less misleading in the sense that it does not have the same connotations that earnings do (i.e., often viewed as an indicator of economic income).

Of course, to challenge the accrual process strikes at the heart of financial accounting and financial statements as they are currently structured. It is not surprising that the FASB chose to reaffirm the importance of accrual accounting. Accrual accounting represents one way of transforming or aggregating cash flows, as illustrated in Figure 1-1. Accrual accounting reflects information in addition to cash receipts and disbursements. For example, information on the aging of receivables may be reflected in the allowance for estimated uncollectible accounts. Inventory, under a lower of cost or market rule, may reflect information on salability of inventory. More generally, the accruals reflect management's expectations about future cash flows and are based on an information system potentially more comprehensive than past and current cash flows. Accruals can be said to involve some implicit or explicit prediction of the future, and accrual accounting can convey information not contained in cash receipts and disbursements. As suggested by the FASB, accrual accounting may transform cash flows in order to provide a better indicator of future cash flows and dividend-paying ability than current cash flows do.

However, the efficacy of accrual accounting is an open issue. It is

FIGURE 1-1

The Accrual Process

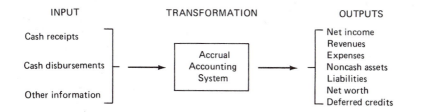

related to the broader issue of aggregation of financial data [Ijiri (1975), Sorter (1969)]. For example, why prepare financial statements (e.g., summaries) at all? Why not merely place the underlying source data in the public domain? One issue is the comparative costs of processing the data. To the extent that data items would be processed (e.g., aggregated) by investors in a relatively uniform manner, it may be cost-effective to have the corporation perform the process once instead of having the process performed several times over by analysts and investors. Of course, there may be no consensus on the method of aggregation, and generally there is a loss of information when aggregating. Hence, when presented with aggregated data, users may incur costs in an attempt to restore the lost information. So the cost of processing may not be related to the level of aggregation in any simple fashion. Moreover, in addition to the cost issues, there are other consequences of nondisclosure due to aggregated data. Hence, the appropriate level of aggregation is not a trivial issue, and income determination can be viewed as one special case. In this context, accrual accounting can be viewed as one potentially cost-effective compromise between merely reporting cash flows and a more ambitious system of fuller disclosure. These issues are discussed more fully in later chapters.

1-4. THE FINANCIAL REPORTING ENVIRONMENT

The shift toward an informational perspective can be better understood in light of the current financial reporting environment. This environment consists of various groups or constituencies who are affected by and have a stake in the financial reporting requirements of the FASB and the SEC. These groups include investors, information intermediaries, regulators, management, and auditors, among others.[8]

The investment process, a central feature of the financial reporting environment, involves the giving up of current consumption for securities, which are claims to future, uncertain cash flows. The claims to

---

[8] Unless otherwise indicated, the term *investors* will refer to common shareholders. This usage is consistent with that of the FASB quotation cited earlier. The primary user orientation of both the FASB and the SEC is the common stock investor. This orientation is natural given the intent of the Securities Acts of 1933 and 1934. Other groups include creditors and labor. Neither will be given explicit treatment here. Creditors are a form of investor (i.e., a supplier of capital). Although their interests may not be the same as those of the stockholders, many of the general statements made with respect to investors also apply or could be easily extended to creditors. As a result, creditors will not be treated here as a separate constituency. The reason is parsimony of exposition and does not imply that creditors are unimportant. In the United States labor has played a relative minor role in the financial reporting environment. However, in many countries of Western Europe labor plays a more active role, and it may eventually do so in the United States as well.

uncertain future cash flows are of value because they represent command over future consumption. Hence, investment is the giving up of current consumption for future, uncertain consumption. The investor must decide how to allocate wealth between current consumption and investment and how to allocate funds set aside for investment among the various securities available. The investor naturally has a demand for information that will aid in assessing the future cash flows associated with the securities and the firms that offer those securities.

However, the investor is not acting in isolation but within a larger investment environment. This environment consists of several characteristics: (1) Investors, some perhaps with limited financial and accounting training, have the opportunity to avail themselves of the services of financial intermediaries, such as investment companies, to whom they can defer a portion of the investment process. (2) Investors, some perhaps with limited access to and ability to interpret financial information, have the opportunity to avail themselves of the services of information intermediaries, such as analysts, to whom they can defer a portion or all of the information gathering and processing function. (3) Investors have the opportunity to invest in a number of securities and to diversify out of some of the risks associated with a single security. (4) Information intermediaries compete with one another in gathering and interpreting financial information. (5) Managements, competing with one another for the investors' funds, have incentives to provide financial information to the investment community. (6) Investors and intermediaries have information available that is more comprehensive and perhaps more timely than the annual report to shareholders or the SEC filings. (7) Security price research suggests that security prices reflect a rich, comprehensive information system. (8) The flow of financial information to the investment community is regulated by a dual regulatory structure that consists of the private sector FASB and the public sector SEC.

Investors

Investors are a heterogeneous group in many ways. For example, they may differ with respect to tastes or preferences, wealth, beliefs, access to financial information, and skill in interpreting financial information. These factors can affect their demand for financial information. In general, the demand for information will be a function of the investor's wealth, tastes (e.g., attitudes toward risk), and beliefs about the future. Since these attributes differ across investors, their demand for financial information can also naturally differ. In addition, investors may also differ with respect to their access and ability to interpret financial information. As a result, the information demands of professional users (i.e., the financial and information intermediaries) may differ from that of the nonprofessional users (e.g., individual or non-institutional investors).

Nonprofessional investors can also differ in many respects. Such investors may not operate in an unaided fashion and have a variety of investment strategies available. These options illustrate some reasons for heterogeneity among investors with respect to demand for financial information: (1) direct management of portfolio versus deferral of investment function to an intermediary, (2) use versus nonuse of information intermediaries, (3) diversified versus undiversified portfolio policies, and (4) active versus passive portfolio management.

If an individual investor defers a portion of the investment process to a financial intermediary, there may be a reduced direct demand for financial information by that individual.[9] To the extent that the individual relies upon the analysis and recommendations of an information intermediary, the direct demand for financial information may also be reduced.[10] The individual, perhaps because of limited access and ability to interpret financial information, may choose to defer such functions to an intermediary. The individual is substituting the analysis and recommendations (i.e., the information) of the intermediary for the financial information. In this sense, they constitute competing sources of information. In both of the cases (deferral to a financial intermediary and deferral to an information intermediary), there may be an indirect demand for financial information by the individual investors.

Apart from options involving the extent to which the individual investor can defer to intermediaries, investors may also differ with respect to portfolio strategies. One dimension of this investment choice is the extent to which the investor chooses to be diversified. For example, mean-variance portfolio theory [Sharpe (1978)] indicates that individual securities are relevant to the investor only in so far as they affect the risk (variance of return) and expected return associated with the portfolios. Under this view, the objects of interest to the investor are the risk and expected return of the entire portfolio. Individual securities are means by which different portfolios can be constructed. From this perspective, interactions or correlations among the returns of securities are of interest, as well as the expected return and variability of return of the individual security. In fact, for well-diversified portfolios, some as-

---

[9] The term *financial intermediary* as used here includes those involved in investing the funds of others. Specifically, it includes mutual funds, closed end investment companies, investment trusts, and pension funds, among others.

[10] The term *information intermediary* as used here includes those involved in the gathering, processing, analyzing, and interpreting of financial information. It includes financial analysts, bond rating agencies, stock rating agencies, investment advisory services, and brokerage firms, among others.

pects of individual security return behavior may be relatively unimportant because they can be diversified away (e.g., the so-called unsystematic risk). Portfolio theory stresses the importance of diversification which can reduce much of the uncertainty or risk associated with holding a single security. For example, there may be considerable uncertainty as to the return on a single security, yet through diversification much of this risk (unsystematic or diversifiable risk) can be eliminated at the portfolio level.

As a result, the demand for financial information may be a function to the extent to which the investor chooses diversity. The investor is concerned with financial information only in so far as it is useful in assessing the attributes of the portfolio return. For the well-diversified investor, factors such as unsystematic risk may be relatively unimportant, and financial information which helps assess such risk may not be of value. However, for the less diversified investor, such information may be perceived to be extremely valuable.[11]

In a similar vein, the demand for financial information can be influenced by the extent to which the investor adopts an "active" versus a "passive" trading strategy. Under a passive trading strategy, the investor essentially buys and holds a security and anticipates little trading until liquidation for consumption purposes. In the limit, the investor would simply purchase a well-diversified cross section of securities (e.g., an "index" fund) and the direct demand for firm-specific financial information would be essentially nonexistent.[12] By contrast, an "active" trader has a speculative demand for information. In other words, an active policy involves continually seeking information that will permit the detection of mispriced securities and continually trading on such information. By definition, the turnover of the active portfolio will be greater than that implied by a passive policy. In many cases, an active trading policy is attempting to take advantage of perceived short-term aberrations in security prices and expects to open and close the speculative position in a relatively short time period. Here, information which helps predict short-run movements in security prices is of interest to the active trader, but it would not be of interest to the investor who follows a passive policy and tends to adopt a longer-term perspective.

These classifications by no means exhaust the possibilities and they are not mutually exclusive. They do, however, illustrate a fundamental point. Investors are heterogeneous, and their demand for financial information can be heterogeneous. Moreover, they operate in an envi-

---

[11] For a further discussion, see Beaver (1974).
[12] The use of index funds is described in Ehrbar (1976).

ronment in which they can rely on financial and information intermediaries and in which they can adopt portfolio strategies that can substantially
alter their direct demand for financial information.[13]

Information Intermediaries

The information intermediaries can be viewed as an industry whose
factors of production include financial information and other types of
data and whose product is analysis and interpretation. The output of
the information intermediaries is also a form of information. The intermediaries take primitive information and transform it into another
type of information, which reflects their ability to understand, synthesize,
and interpret the raw data. As indicated earlier, the nonprofessional
user may have less direct demand for financial information if that user
relies upon the information provided by an intermediary.

More specifically, information intermediaries can be viewed as per-
forming three information-related activities: (1) the search for information that is not publicly available (hereafter called *private information
search*), (2) the analysis, processing and interpretation of information for
the purpose of prediction (hereafter called *prospective analysis*), and (3) the
interpretation of events after-the-fact (hereafter called *retrospective analysis*).

As a result, the relationship between financial reporting and the
information intermediary is not simple. At one level, public financial
reporting provides one source of input factors for the intermediaries.
However, if part of the function of the intermediary is to obtain more
comprehensive and more timely information, financial reporting can be
a competing source of information to that provided by the information
intermediary. Moreover, information intermediaries compete with one
another in the gathering and interpretation of financial information.

Information intermediaries engage in private information search.
This private sector information system is large and active. For example,
by recent estimates there are over 14,500 financial analysts.[14] Management has incentives to provide information to analysts, and analysts have
incentives to seek out and to disseminate such information. It was reported that JC Penney logged in over 1,000 interviews with analysts in
one year [Axelson (1975)]. This does not appear to be unusual for a
company of JC Penney's size.[15] In fact, it has been argued that the

---

[13] Obviously, the investors may have an *indirect* demand for financial information
and can be indirectly affected by the financial reporting system.
[14] This is the membership in the Financial Analysts Federation, as reported in the
May–June 1986 issue of the *Financial Analysts Journal*.
[15] The informal information network is documented in SEC (1977).

informal information network may be the mechanism which permits security prices to promptly reflect a comprehensive information system. [Bernstein (1975)]. The competition among analysts for disclosures and for the interpretation of disclosures may result in security prices that reflect a broad information system. Statements of legislative intent at the time of the enactment of the Securities Acts indicate that at least some were relying upon the competition within the professional investment community to interpret the SEC filings and to effect an "efficiently" determined market price.[16] Chapter 6 will discuss further the relationship between security prices and financial information.

The role of the information and financial intermediaries in the financial reporting environment has been receiving increasing recognition by the financial reporting regulators. The recognition of the professional user as a prime target for the financial reporting system is reflected in the following ways:

(1) Information intermediaries, such as analysts, are viewed as major representatives of investor demand for additional financial reporting. As a result, the FASB and the SEC look to this community as a source of ideas for further disclosures. As long as the financial reporting policy makers rely upon information intermediaries, their preferences will be an important barometer of future financial disclosure requirements. Analysts' interest in segment or divisionalized reporting and in management forecasts are prominent examples.[17]

(2) The nature of the financial reporting requirements assumes that the user has a greater sophistication and technical skill to interpret the data reported than has previously been assumed. The FASB's standards on foreign currency translation (FAS No. 8) and accounting for the effects of changing prices (FAS No. 33) are two prominent examples of financial reporting requirements that require a considerable amount of expertise in interpretation.

(3) There is greater emphasis on the reporting of so-called "soft" data, such as future-oriented disclosures and current cost data. Burton (1981) describes the emerging trend toward such data as reflected in SEC requirements with respect to management discussion and analysis and in FASB requirements with respect to changing prices.

[16] Consider the following statement by Justice William O. Douglas (1933), who at the time was teaching at Yale: "Even though an investor has neither the time, money, or intelligence to assimilate the mass of information in the registration statement, there will be those who can and who will do so, whenever there is a broad market. The judgment of those experts will be reflected in the market price."

[17] The financial analyst community has made several suggestions for increased financing reporting [see Duff and Phelps (1976) and Financial Analysts Federation (1977)].

(4) There is greater emphasis on disclosure and less emphasis on a single earnings number. Supplemental disclosures are used to report financial aspects of certain events without an attempt to prescribe exactly how those disclosures are to be used to arrive at "the" net income or earnings for the firm. FAS No. 33 on the effects of changing prices is a prime example of the use of supplemental disclosure instead of attempting to prescribe the "best" way to report the effects of changing prices. This shift away from a single "best" measure of earnings affords users a greater opportunity to structure the analysis of financial disclosures in a manner they perceive is appropriate. This is particularly important to the extent that users are heterogeneous in their demand for and analysis of financial information.

Financial Reporting Regulators

A prominent feature of the financial reporting environment is the regulation of the flow of financial information to investors. The primary regulators are the FASB and the SEC, although Congress and the independent regulatory agencies can also influence financial reporting requirements.

The SEC and the FASB share a concern over the effects of the financial reporting on investors [FASB (1976b, Chapter 2) and SEC (1977, Introduction)]. The investor orientation is natural given the intent of the Securities Acts of 1933 and 1934. This orientation appears to be partially motivated by a concern over the welfare of investors, the "fairness" of the markets in which they buy and sell securities, and the prevention of perceived adversities and inequities that may befall investors due to informational deficiencies, such as a failure to disclose material financial information. However, the policy makers also appear to be concerned with the effects of financial reporting on resource allocation and capital formation.

A distinctive feature of the regulatory system is its dual structure. The relationship between the FASB and SEC has not been clearly defined, although a similar perspective on the purposes of financial reporting has been suggested for both. The SEC Advisory Committee on Corporate Disclosure [SEC (1977)] suggested a purpose of corporate disclosure similar to the FASB's statement of purpose cited earlier. The Advisory Committee states that the SEC's objective in corporate disclosure is:

> to assure the public availability in an efficient and reasonable manner on a timely basis of reliable, firm-oriented information, material to informed investment, and corporate suffrage decision making.   (page D-8)

This similarity of objectives further blurs the historically fuzzy distinction between the two aspects of financial reporting: disclosure and financial accounting. This distinction has been previously invoked to define the jurisdictional lines between the FASB and the SEC. In principle, the jurisdiction of the FASB was said to be the setting of financial accounting standards, while the jurisdiction of the SEC was said to be disclosure. Yet the distinction has never been well-defined, and, as a practical matter, the distinction is not operational. The standards of the FASB typically also include disclosure requirements. In fact, some standards, such as the standard on segment reporting (FAS No. 14), are viewed by many as primarily disclosure standards. Similarly, the SEC influences financial accounting standards, as has been well documented by Horngren (1972, 1973) and Armstrong (1977). The SEC Accounting Series Release (ASR) No. 190 on replacement costs deals with a central accounting issue of asset valuation and expense recognition. ASR No. 190 effectively preempted the FASB efforts in price level accounting at that time. The SEC's rejection of the FASB standard on accounting in the oil and gas industry (FAS No. 19) is still another example.

Since both organizations have adopted an informational perspective, the jurisdictional boundaries are unclear. Moreover, no private sector (e.g., FASB) accounting standard has prevailed without the support of the SEC. Chapter 7 explores these issues further and provides a framework for viewing the FASB–SEC relationship.

Management

Managements, competing with one another for investors' funds, have incentives to provide financial information to the investment community [(Watts 1977)]. Moreover, management can be viewed as an agent to whom investors have entrusted control over a portion of their resources. This stewardship view implies that management has a responsibility to act in the interests of the investors. Management plays many roles including productive agent, risk bearer, and supplier of information. A prime responsibility of management is financial reporting, which can help to evaluate the stewardship of management. This financial reporting responsibility is reinforced by the legal liability of management under the Securities Acts of 1933 and 1934. Financial reporting by management can influence the terms on which management can obtain additional financing and can affect the competitive position of the firm, among other effects. Hence, management clearly has a stake in the financial reporting environment and plays an important role as the preparer of the financial statements and a supplier of financial information.

Auditors

The incentives of management with respect to financial reporting are an open issue, and their reports are subject to "monitoring" or certification by an auditor. The concept of the "independence" of the auditor from management is a part of the auditor's professional ethics [AICPA (1978)] and underscores the responsibility of the auditor to users (e.g., investors) of the financial statements. As with management, this responsibility is reinforced through the legal liability of the auditor under the Securities Acts. Auditors, in addition to also being risk bearers, are major suppliers of information and have an obvious stake in the financial reporting environment.

Summary of Environment

The financial reporting environment consists of the five major constituencies discussed above, although other groups may be involved to some extent. The role and the interests of each of these constituencies differ. Moreover, each group is not homogeneous. The constituencies and possible subgroups are summarized in Table 1-1. As a result of the diversity and complexity of the environment, financial reporting can induce a variety of economic consequences and the various constituencies may not be affected by these consequences in a similar way.

TABLE 1-1

Constituencies in the Financial Reporting Environment

I. Investors

    A. Diversified vs. Undiversified
    B. Active vs. Passive
    C. Professional vs. Nonprofessional

II. Information Intermediaries

    A. Financial Analysts
    B. Bond Rating Agencies
    C. Stock Rating Agencies
    D. Investment Advisory Services
    E. Brokerage Firms

III. Regulators

    A. FASB
    B. SEC
    C. Congress

IV. Management

    A. Large vs. Small Firms
    B. Publicly vs. Closely Held Firms

V. Auditors

    A. National vs. Local Firms
    B. SEC Practice vs. Non-SEC Practice

1-5. ECONOMIC CONSEQUENCES AND SOCIAL CHOICE

There are a number of potential economic consequences of financial reporting, including the effects on the following: (1) the distribution of wealth among individuals, (2) the aggregate level of risk and allocation of risk among individuals, (3) the aggregate consumption and production (e.g., effects on the rate of capital formation), (4) the allocation of resources among firms, (5) the use of resources devoted to the production, certification, dissemination, processing, analysis, and interpretation of financial information, (6) the use of resources in the development, compliance, enforcement, and litigation of regulations, and (7) the use of resources in the private-sector search for information. These are summarized in Table 1-2 and are discussed more fully in Chapter 2.

Because these consequences may affect the various constituencies differently, the selection of a financial reporting system is a social choice. There may be no consensus among the constituencies on what financial reporting system is "best." The selection among financial reporting systems by the FASB and the SEC involves making tradeoffs among consequences *and among constituencies.* Moreover, it involves tradeoffs within constituencies. For example, well-diversified investors may not have the same preferences for a financial reporting system as less diversified investors would. Similarly, investors with passive portfolio strategies may not have the same preferences for financial reporting systems as would investors with active portfolio strategies. The section on investors hinted at the reasons why these diversities might induce heterogeneous preferences for financial reporting systems.

Debates over the "best" financial accounting standard not only emphasize traditional "technical" issues, such as which method produces the "best" matching of cost and revenues, but also focus on the economic consequences. Recent examples are accounting for the investment credit, accounting for research and development expenditures, financial disclosures by the banking industry, the successful efforts versus full costing

TABLE 1-2

Economic Consequences of Financial Reporting

Wealth Distribution
Aggregate Risk Incurred and Risk Allocation
Aggregate Consumption and Aggregate Production
Resource Allocation
Resources Devoted to Publicly Available Information
Resources Devoted to Regulation
Resources Devoted to Private Search for Information

controversy in the oil and gas industry, and accounting for the effects of inflation.

There is considerable controversy over which economic consequences and constituencies should be considered by the financial reporting policy makers [Armstrong (1977), Rappaport (1977), and Zeff (1978)]. To address such issues requires a framework that recognizes the role of information in a multiperson setting (Chapter 2) and the rationale for regulation as an institutional solution to resolving social choice questions (Chapter 7).

1-6. CURRENT TRENDS IN FINANCIAL REPORTING: A CHAPTER SUMMARY

This chapter identifies several trends in financial reporting which are summarized in Table 1-3. The chapter also provides a historical perspective within which to view these trends and it provides a description of the financial reporting environment within which the trends are occurring. A key feature of the environment is its complexity and its diversity. This feature can affect preferences for financial information across and within the major constituencies (investors, information intermediaries, regulators, managements, and auditors). A variety of consequences can result from a financial reporting policy and can affect the constituencies in diverse ways. As a result, there may be a lack of consensus on the "best" reporting system. The selection among financial reporting systems can be viewed essentially as an issue of social choice involving tradeoffs among constituencies. Under this view, standard-setting is the outcome of a political process.

TABLE 1-3

Current Trends in Financial Reporting

I. General

    A. Shift in financial accounting from an economic income to an informational perspective

    B. Increased emphasis on complex nature of the financial reporting environment and the professional user of financial information

    C. Recognition of social choice nature of selection among financial reporting systems

II. Specific

    A. Rapid growth in reporting requirements and rapid change in existing requirements

    B. Less emphasis on earnings and more emphasis on disclosure

    C. Emphasis on disclosures that require a greater expertise to interpret

    D. Emphasis on "soft" data

    E. Increased debate over economic consequences

1-7. SUMMARY OF REMAINING CHAPTERS

Because the FASB and the SEC, among others, have adopted an informational perspective to financial reporting, Chapter 2 explores in some detail and depth the nature of information in a single-person and multiperson setting. The chapter discusses the potentially dramatic implications of adopting an informational perspective and examines the potential economic consequences of financial reporting.

Even though the FASB has adopted an informational perspective, it has indicated that the prime focus of financial reporting is still information about earnings and its components. As a result, Chapters 3 and 4 explore in detail the concept of earnings under conditions of certainty and uncertainty. The chapters discuss the relationship of earnings to the valuation of securities and indicate why earnings information is of potential value to investors in conducting security analysis. The chapters also examine how the nature of earnings differs under an economic income perspective as opposed to an informational perspective. Chapter 5 reviews the empirical evidence regarding the relationship between earnings and security prices. The evidence indicates that security prices behave as if earnings are an important source of information but only one such source.

Security prices play an important role in the financial reporting environment, and security price research has been a major area of financial reporting research. Chapter 6 explores in detail the relationship between prices and information and its implications for the various constituencies in the financial reporting environment.

A prominent feature of the financial reporting environment is that the flow of financial information to the investment community is regulated by a dual regulatory apparatus. Chapter 7 explores the potential economic rationale for the regulation of financial information. It also discusses the relationship between the financial reporting policy makers under the dual regulatory apparatus.

BIBLIOGRAPHY

ACCOUNTING PRINCIPLES BOARD. *Statement No. 4: Basic Concepts and Accounting Principles Underlying Financial Statements of Business Enterprises* (October 1970).

ALEXANDER, S. *Five Monographs on Business Income*. New York: Study Group on Business Income, AI(CP)A, 1950.

AMERICAN ACCOUNTING ASSOCIATION COMMITTEE ON CONCEPTS AND STANDARDS FOR EXTERNAL FINANCIAL REPORTS. *Statement on Accounting Theory and Theory Acceptance*. Sarasota, Fla: AAA, 1977.

AMERICAN INSTITUTE OF CERTIFIED PUBLIC ACCOUNTANTS. *Report of the Study Group on the Objectives of Financial Statements*. New York: AICPA, 1973.

ARMSTRONG, MARSHALL. "Disclosure: Considering Other Views." *Financial Executive* (May 1976), 36–40.

———— "The Politics of Establishing Accounting Standards." *Journal of Accountancy* (February 1977), 76–79.

AXELSON, K. "A Businessman's View of Disclosure." *Journal of Accountancy* (July 1975), 42–46.

BEAVER, W. "Implications of Security Price Research for Accounting." *Accounting Review* (July 1974), 563–571.

———— "The Implications of Security Price Research for Disclosure Policy and the Analyst Community." *Proceedings of the Duke Symposium on Financial Information Requirements for Security Analysis*. Duke University, December 1976, 67–81.

BERNSTEIN, L. "In Defense of Fundamental Investment Analysis." *Financial Analysts Journal* (January–February 1975), 57–61.

BERTON, L., AND B. INGERSOLL. "Representative Dingell to Take Aim at Accountants, SEC in Hearings on Profession's Role as Watchdog." *Wall Street Journal* (February 19, 1985), 4.

BURTON, J. "Emerging Trends in Financial Reporting." *Journal of Accountancy* (July 1981), 54–66).

CANNING, J. *The Economics of Accountancy*. New York: Ronald Press, 1929.

CHAMBERS, R. *Accounting, Evaluation and Economic Behavior*. Englewood Cliffs, N.J.: Prentice-Hall, 1966.

DOUGLAS, W. "Protecting the Investor." *Yale Review* (1933), 523–24.

DUFF AND PHELPS. *A Management Guide to Better Financial Reporting* (a report prepared for Arthur Andersen & Co., 1976).

EDWARDS, E., AND P. BELL. *The Theory and Measurement of Business Income*. Berkeley: University of California Press, 1961.

EHRBAR, A. "Index Funds—An Idea Whose Time Is Coming." *Fortune* (June 1976), 145–154.

FINANCIAL ACCOUNTING STANDARDS BOARD. *Tentative Conclusions on Objectives of Financial Statements of Business Enterprises*. Stamford, Conn.: FASB, December 2, 1976a.

———— *Scope and Implications of the Conceptual Framework Project*. Stamford, Conn.: FASB, December 2, 1976b.

———— *Statement of Financial Accounting Concepts No. 1*. Stamford, Conn.: FASB, November 1978.

FINANCIAL ANALYSTS FEDERATION, CORPORATE INFORMATION COMMITTEE. "Response to SEC's Advisory Committee on Corporate Disclosure." *Financial Analysts Journal* (March–April 1977), 12.

HAKANSSON, N. "Where We Are in Accounting: a Review of 'Statement on Accounting Theory and Theory Acceptance,' " *Accounting Review* (July 1978), 717–725.

HAWKINS, D. "Toward an Old Theory of Equity Valuation," *Financial Analysts Journal* (November–December 1977), 49–52.

———— AND W. CAMPBELL. *Equity Valuation: Models, Analysis, and Implications.* New York: Financial Executive Institute, 1978.

HORNGREN, C. "Accounting Principles: Private or Public Sector," *Journal of Accountancy* (May 1972), 37–41.

———— "The Marketing of Accounting Standards." *Journal of Accountancy* (October 1973), 61–66.

IJIRI, Y. *Theory of Accounting Measurement.* Studies in Accounting Research No. 10. Sarasota, Fla.: American Accounting Association, 1975.

———— "Cash Flow Accounting and Its Structure." *Journal of Accounting, Auditing and Finance* (Summer 1978), 331–348.

KRIPKE, H. "The Myth of the Informed Layman." *The Business Lawyer* (January 1973), 631–638.

PATON, W. *Accounting Theory.* Chicago: Accounting Studies Press, Ltd., 1962 (originally published in 1922).

———— AND A. LITTLETON. *An Introduction to Corporate Accounting Standards.* Columbus, Ohio: American Accounting Association, 1940.

RAPPAPORT, A. "Economic Impact of Accounting Standards—Implications for the FASB." *Journal of Accountancy* (May 1977), 89–98.

SCHARES, G. "Shareholders Sue as Stock Prices Fall." *San Francisco Chronicle* (April 30, 1984), 5.

SECURITIES AND EXCHANGE COMMISSION. *Report of the SEC Advisory Committee on Corporate Disclosure.* Washington, D.C.: U.S. Government Printing Office, November 1977.

SHARPE, W. *Investments.* Englewood Cliffs, N.J.: Prentice-Hall, 1978.

SKOUSEN, K. F. *An Introduction to the SEC*, 3d ed. Cincinnati, Ohio: South-Western Publishing Company, 1983.

SORTER, G. "An 'Events' Approach to Basic Accounting Theory," *Accounting Review* (January 1969), 12–19.

STERLING, R. *Theory of the Measurement of Enterprise Income.* Lawrence, Kan.: University of Kansas Press, 1970.

STERN, J. "Let's Abandon Earnings per Share." *Wall Street Journal* (December 18, 1972), 8.

WATTS, R. "Corporate Financial Statements. A Product of Market and Political Processes." *Australian Journal of Management* (April 1977), 53–75.

ZEFF, S. "The Rise of Economic Consequences." *Journal of Accountancy* (December 1978), 56–63.

chapter two

Information

The purpose of this chapter is to explore the implications of the notion that the purpose of financial statement data is to provide information useful to investors, creditors, and others. The discussion begins with the context of an individual user of financial statement data and the analysis is then extended to a multiperson setting. Each setting will be general, characterizing the role of any type of information, of which financial reporting is one example. For illustrative purposes, the user context chosen here will be that of the common stock investor (hereafter, simply investor).[1]

The chapter consists of two major parts: (1) information in a single-person setting in which the investor is used to illustrate the role of information, and (2) information in a multi-person setting in which other investors and other constituencies are also considered.

The single-person setting is a natural prelude to the multi-person

---

[1] The investor's decision is a primary orientation of the FASB [FASB (1978)] and the Securities Acts of the 1933 and 1934 [SEC (1977)]. Other users include creditors, bondholders, potential acquiring firms (e.g., takeovers), labor and governmental organizations, consumers, and "public interest" groups, among others.

setting. Many of the intuitive notions about the value of financial information appear to be based upon a single-person setting (e.g., if additional disclosure is costless, more is at least as good as less). It provides a benchmark for showing how the role of information changes or expands when a multi-person context is adopted.

The chapter begins by illustrating the role of information for a single investor. A simple illustration is provided, and implications are discussed. As an extension of the single-investor setting, two-parameter portfolio theory is introduced as the decision context, and the potential role of information in this setting is examined. A key feature is that the value of information is personal and subjective and can vary across investors as their personal characteristics differ. This can lead to a heterogeneity in the demand for financial information across investors.

A multi-person setting introduces several additional aspects or effects of information. Initially, a pure exchange setting in which no effects on production are present is considered, and then production effects are introduced. This splitting facilitates an orderly treatment of the effects of information in a multi-person setting. In a multi-person setting, a key feature is that the economic consequences of a financial information system may affect the constituencies in different ways. The chapter closes with viewing the selection among financial reporting systems as a social choice, involving tradeoffs among the various constituencies.

2-1. INFORMATION IN A SINGLE-PERSON SETTING

Before the role of information can be understood, the nature of the decision context in which the information is to be used must be described. Decision making under uncertainty is typically characterized as choosing that act which maximizes the expected utility of the decision maker. The decision making process involves the following components: (1) acts, (2) states, (3) consequences, (4) a preferences function for consequences, (5) a probability distribution across states, and (6) an objective function.

Acts

Acts refer to the various alternative choices available to the decision maker. In an investment setting, the available acts could be described as the various portfolios available.

States

Uncertainty is described in terms of a set of mutually exclusive and collective exhaustive possible occurrences (or events) called *states*. A description of each state is sufficiently rich so that no uncertainty about consequences is implied by that state.

Consequences

A set of consequences to the decision maker is associated with each state. In general, the description is sufficiently rich to capture all aspects of the states that are of importance. In a simple investment setting, the consequences are often described in terms of the future cash flows (e.g., interest, dividends, cash proceeds from the sale of the security) received.

Preferences

The desirability of each set of outcomes is described in terms of the decision maker's preferences. Decision making is characterized as if the investor were maximizing a preference function. It is also further assumed that the preference function can be divided into two elements— a belief function and a preference function for certain (as opposed to uncertain) consequences. The preference function is denoted $U(\cdot)$, to represent the investor's *utility function*.

Beliefs

The decision maker's beliefs refer to a set of probabilities assigned to each state. Beliefs are personal and subjective. They are based upon the cumulative experience of the investor, including training, education, and prior investment experience. Beliefs are also influenced by what information the investor has. This information could not only include financial reports, but also analysts' reports, newspaper articles, and other publicly available information. *Beliefs are the critical element of the decision process, because the role of information is its potential to alter beliefs and hence alter decision making behavior.*

The Objective Function

The objective function typically is characterized as the maximization of the expected utility, where expected utility is the "average" utility associated with the consequences of each state weighted by the probability of occurrence of each state. Maximization merely implies the decision maker chooses the act that is associated with the highest or "best" expected utility. It can be shown that under fairly general conditions decision-making behavior under uncertainty can be characterized *as if* the decision maker were choosing the act that maximized expected utility. The theory does not imply that the decision maker literally forms probability assessments and preferences for outcomes. It merely states that if the decision maker obeys some general axioms of consistency, choice behavior can be described *as if* the decision maker were solving such an optimization problem [Savage (1972)].

The investor will select that portfolio and current consumption that has the greatest expected utility. In general, the optimal portfolio is a function of the investor's wealth, preferences, beliefs, and the securities' prices. Stated in simplest terms, the decision maker chooses that portfolio which is most preferred. The underlying objects of choice are the individual securities, and the choice among different portfolios can be characterized by the amount of each security held.

The investor setting thus far is quite general. Under appropriate additional assumptions, the familiar mean-variance portfolio theory can be derived.[2] In this special setting investor behavior can be described as selecting the portfolio whose combination of expected return and risk (defined as the variance of the portfolio's return) is optimal given the investor's preference function for wealth at the end of one period. The role of information in a two-parameter context is explored in later subsections.

Illustration of a Simple Investment Setting

Assume that the investor is risk indifferent with respect to end-of-year wealth and further assume that only two securities, A and B, are available. The current price for each is $50. The expected value of the price at the end of the year is $60, as derived in Table 2-1. Assume that the amount to be invested is fixed ($10,000) and the only decision is how much to allocate between the two securities. Given risk indifference, let U equal the market value of the portfolio at the end of the year. Assume that no dividends are paid and ignore income tax considerations. In this case, the investor is indifferent among portfolio strategies in that all strategies offer an expected utility of 12,000 (10,000/50 × 60). However, suppose that earnings per share for the year is not yet known and knowledge of such information could potentially alter the decision.

---

[2] The assumptions are: (1) There exists a surrogate preference function for wealth at the end of one period that is state-independent, (2) the relevant attributes of any portfolio are completely described by two parameters, its expected return and its variance, and usually (3) the investor is risk averse. Multivariate normality of individual security returns would be sufficient to induce condition (2). Assumption (3) is not necessary for a two-parameter characterization. However, assuming risk indifference, the second parameter is irrelevant. Conversely, risk preference is thought to be not descriptively valid of investor and capital market behavior. For a further discussion, see Sharpe (1978).

TABLE 2-1

Simple Investment Setting

State	Probability of State	End-of-Year Price Security A	Security B
1	.5	$80	$40
2	.5	$40	$80
Expected End-of-Year Price[a]		$60	$60

[a]$60 = .5($40) + .5($80)

Role of Financial Information

In this setting the role of information is to alter the probability that future states will occur. This will be illustrated in the context of use of earnings per share (hereafter EPS) in the investment decision setting described immediately above. The value of information is derived in a series of steps.

Step 1: Consider all possible signals.
For simplicity, assume that there are two possible EPS signals for securities A and B. Either firm A will report EPS of $6.00 and B will report EPS of $4.00 (signal 1) or firm A will report EPS of $4.00 and B will report EPS of $6.00 (signal 2).

Step 2: Assess the probability of state conditional upon each signal.
The pre-information probabilities of states 1 and 2, as reported in Table 2-1, are .5 and .5, respectively. Conditional upon the knowledge of signal 1, the probabilities of states 1 and 2 are .9 and .1, respectively, as reported in Table 2-2. Similarly, if signal 2 occurs, the conditional probabilities of states 1 and 2 are .1 and .9, respectively. This will lead to revisions in the expected value of end-of-year prices conditional upon each signal, as reported in Table 2-2. The probability of each signal is .5.

Step 3: Optimize the portfolio decision for each signal.
Assume that $10,000 is available for investment and that the *current prices of securities A and B remain the same as they were in the pre-information case.*[3] If signal 1 is observed by the investor, the optimal portfolio is to invest 100 percent in security A, which has an expected utility of 15,200 (10,000/50 × 76). Similarly, if signal 2 is observed, the optimal portfolio is a 100 percent investment in security B, which also leads to an expected utility of 15,200.

---

[3] This assumption can be motivated in at least two ways. (1) The EPS figures are privately revealed to the investor. (2) The EPS figures are publicly announced. Due to heterogeneous interpretations of the data, there is no effect on the price.

TABLE 2-2

Effect of Information in Simple Setting

Signal	Security A	Security B	Conditional Probabilities[a] State 1	State 2	Expected End-of-Year Price Security A	Security B
1	$6.00	$4.00	.9	.1	.9($80) + .1($40) = $76	.9($40) + .1($80) = $44
2	$4.00	$6.00	.1	.9	.1($80) + .9($40) = $44	.1($40) + .9($80) = $76

[a] $p_s = \sum_{y=1}^{2} p(s|y)p_y$, where $p(s|y)$ is the probability of state s given signal y and p_y is the probability of signal y.

For each state, $p_s = .5 = .9 \cdot .5 + .1 \cdot .5$, where $p_v = .5$.

Step 4: Compute the expected value of the conditional expected utilities across all possible signals.

The investor does not know in advance which signal will be reported. Hence, the expected utility of having access to the information system is determined by "averaging" the conditional expected utilities by the probability each signal will be observed. In this particular numerical example it is trivial since *each* conditional expected utility is 15,200 and the expected value across signals is also 15,200 regardless of the probability of each signal. However, in general, the conditional expected utility will vary across signals.

In this simple setting, in which prices are invariant to the signals, the expected utility associated with a *costless* information system can never be less than the expected utility associated with the pre-information setting. Moreover, expected utility associated with the information system can be higher, as it is in the numerical illustration. In such a case, access to the information system is valuable. In fact, the value of the information system (e.g., access to EPS data) can be defined as the difference in the level of expected utility in the post- and pre-information decision setting. More generally, the value to the investor of having one information system versus another can be defined in terms of the level of expected utility associated with each. Thus, expected utility conditional upon an information system will rank alternative information systems according to their value to the investor. *The investor will always prefer that information system which is associated with the highest expected utility. Such an information system is "best" for that investor.* While the illustrations have been specific, the latter point is quite general.

The non-negative value of costless information arises because the decision maker is able to adjust the optimal choice to the revision of beliefs caused by the signal. In the pre-information case, the action must be taken before the receipt of the signal and hence the same action must be taken regardless of the signal. In effect, the post-information case represents a less constrained optimization problem. In particular, the decision is taken after the receipt of a signal. Since the action chosen is "optimal" given the signal, it can never be worse than the pre-information action and it can be better. This non-negativity holds for each possible signal. In other words, the expected utility of the post-information action based upon the conditional probabilities must be at least as great as the expected utility of the pre-information action based upon those same conditional probabilities. Because the non-negativity holds for each signal, it also holds for any average across signals. In particular, it holds for the expected value of the differences in utility in which the probability of each signal is used as the weight.

The demand for information, such as financial reporting, is inherently personal and subjective, depending upon the personal attributes of the investor.[4] There is no "intrinsic value" of an information system existing apart from the user and a specific decision context. Moreover, personal value can vary across individual investors. Hence, the demand for financial information can also vary across investors and decision contexts.

Portfolio Theory and Financial Reporting

Portfolio theory provides one decision context within which to view financial information. If the purpose of financial reporting is to provide information for investor decision making, the investor decision context is a critical aspect of financial reporting. One period, mean-variance portfolio theory is one such decision context. As indicated earlier, it is a special case of a more general investor setting in the sense that sufficient restrictions are placed on the preferences and beliefs of the investor so that the decision behavior can be described as if the investor were choosing among portfolios based solely upon two parameters, the expected one-period return and the variance of that return. However, it is still general in the sense that it can embrace a variety of types of investors. For example, diversified, nondiversified, active, and passive investors are all consistent with this theory. In other words, the theory is sufficiently general so that it can be used to illustrate the role of financial information in an individual investor setting broader than the previous illustration. Moreover, portfolio theory enjoys considerable usage in the investment community [Sharpe (1978)].

Implications of Portfolio Theory

The mechanics of portfolio theory will not be discussed, but several excellent descriptions are available.[5] Instead, the discussion will focus on implications of portfolio theory for financial reporting. Three aspects of portfolio theory are worth noting. (1) The consequences of concern of the investor are characterized as the expected return (also called

---

[4] For example, there is no notion of an objective or "true" set of probabilities. Information can be said to be "false" or "misleading" only in terms of the beliefs and behavior it induces, relative to that induced by a finer information system. From the perspective of an information system that is the finest among three systems, there is no assurance that the information system of intermediate fineness is less "misleading" or less "false" than the system which is least fine. An information system A is finer than system B if and only if observing a signal from A permits the decision maker to infer what signal would be reported by B, and the converse does not hold. This is discussed more fully in Demski and Feltham (1976).

[5] Excellent discussions appear in FASB (1976), Sharpe (1978), and Foster (1986). The nature of the demand for financial information in a portfolio theory context is also discussed in Hakansson (1976).

reward) and the variance of return (also called risk) of the portfolio. The attributes of the returns of individual securities are relevant only in so far as they contribute to the expected return or risk of the portfolio. (2) A portion of the variance of individual securities' returns can be diversified away, and therefore the variance of the portfolio return is not merely an average of the variances of the securities' returns that comprise it. (3) The security-specific parameters of interest to the investor, and the investor's demand for security-specific information (e.g., financial reporting) will vary in a manner related to the portfolio strategy chosen.

The role of financial information is to alter the beliefs of the investor. In this setting the relevant investor beliefs are the expected return and variance of return for each of the portfolios.[6] These two parameters are in turn a function of the expected return on the individual securities, the variance of return on the individual securities, and the covariance or correlation among returns of the individual securities.[7] The role of information is potentially to alter these parameters of the investor's beliefs.

A convenient characterization of a security's return is the market model. Here a security's return is viewed as the sum of a systematic and an unsystematic component. The systematic component reflects that portion of security return that is linearly related to the return on a "market" portfolio.[8] The unsystematic return is a "residual" portion of the security return that remains after taking out the systematic component.[9] Under

---

[6] The one-period return is defined as the dividends received during the period plus any price appreciation (or less any price decline) divided by the market value at the beginning of the period. More formally, the expected return and variance of return of the portfolio are denoted $E(R_p)$ and $\sigma^2(R_p)$, respectively.

[7] The security-specific parameters are expected return, $E(R_i)$, variance of returns, $\sigma^2(R_i)$, and the covariance among returns, $\sigma(R_i, R_j)$, and the correlation among returns, ρ_{ij}, respectively. The correlation can be viewed as the covariance "standardized" by the standard deviations of two securities' returns [i.e., $\rho_{ij} = \sigma(R_i, R_j)/\sigma(R_i)\sigma(R_j)$]. Both concepts reflect the extent to which the returns of two securities are affected by common events (e.g., economy-wide or industry events). These events cause the prices of the securities to move together.

[8] Conceptually, this could include all capital assets. Operationally, the return on the market portfolio is usually the percentage change in an index reflecting a comprehensive group of stocks (e.g., *Standard and Poor's Composite Index*).

[9] More precisely,

$$R_i = \alpha_i + \beta_i R_m + u_i$$

where

R_i = return on security i;
R_m = return on a market portfolio;
u_i = unsystematic or residual portion of return (or simply unsystematic return);

this construction, the systematic and unsystematic components will be uncorrelated with one another. The systematic portion of the security return is perfectly correlated with the return on the market portfolio because it is a linear function of the market portfolio. The unsystematic portion, by contrast, is uncorrelated with the return on the market portfolio. Hence, the systematic portion of returns across securities is perfectly correlated. The unsystematic portion of returns may be correlated across securities due to factors such as common industry effects. Beja (1972) and Fama (1973) have shown that such a decomposition is quite general.

An intuitive motivation for the market model is that a portion of securities returns is commonly affected by economy-wide events, such as inflation, interest rate changes, and changes in GNP, among other factors. Under this description, the relevant investor beliefs are the expected return on the market portfolio, the variance of return on the market portfolio, the intercept and slope terms of the security's linear relationship with the market return (called alpha and beta, respectively), the variance of unsystematic returns (called unsystematic risk), and the covariance or correlations among the unsystematic returns.[10] Beta is also known as the systematic (relative) risk of the security. In this setting the role of financial information is to alter these parameters of the investor's beliefs. The first two are economy-wide parameters; the remaining are security-specific parameters.

Financial Information in a Portfolio Theory Context[11]

The role of financial reporting information is to alter investor beliefs about security-specific parameters. An investor's ability to diversify out of unsystematic risk has potentially dramatic implications for the investor's *direct* demand for security-specific information, such as financial reporting data. While the undiversified investor has a demand for assessing unsystematic risk, the well-diversified investor does not.

α_i = intercept of linear relationship;
β_i = slope of linear relationship; and
$\alpha_i + \beta_i R_m$ = systematic portion of return.

[10] More precisely, the relevant parameters are $E(R_m)$, $\sigma^2(R_m)$, α_i, β_i, $\sigma^2(u_i)$, and $\sigma(u_i, u_j)$, respectively. Note that

$$\beta_i = \frac{\sigma^2(R_i, R_m)}{\sigma^2(R_m)}$$

[11] These comments are being made from the perspective of a single investor. They are offered as intuitively plausible implications in this setting.

The role of security-specific financial information reduces to altering assessments of the parameters, alpha and beta.[12]

In general, portfolio theory does not assume that alpha and beta bear any necessary relationship to one another. However, investor behavior is likely to be affected by the relationship perceived between these two parameters. For example, suppose that the investor perceives the expected returns on securities have the property that alpha is directly related to beta such that securities with the same beta also have the same alpha and hence the same expected returns.[13]

For the investor who has such beliefs and who considers only diversified portfolios, the portfolio choice problem reduces to choosing the beta level of the portfolio. In this context, the only security-specific parameter of interest is beta, the systematic risk of the securities. In the most extreme form, the investor may consider only holding an index fund combined with borrowing and lending. In other words, the index fund is the only common stock portfolio considered and the desired beta level for the entire portfolio is attained by levering the portfolio up or down by borrowing or lending.[14] For this class of portfolio strategies, there is no direct demand for security-specific information.

Therefore, the direct demand for financial information would appear to depend upon the class of portfolio strategies considered. Certainly, after-the-fact investors can be observed as preferring one of these categories. However, this begs the issue as to why the investor would act as if the portfolio strategy chosen were restricted to a particular class.

Why does an investor choose to be undiversified? Given the apparent

---

[12] Why an investor would be motivated to prefer only well-diversified portfolios will be discussed shortly. For a diversified portfolio,

$$E(R_p) = \alpha_p + \beta_p E(R_m)$$
$$\sigma^2(R_p) \simeq \beta_p^2 \sigma^2(R_m)$$

where

$$\alpha_p = \sum_{i=1}^{N} w_i \alpha_i$$

w_i = proportion of portfolio invested in security i;

$$\beta_p = \sum_{i=1}^{N} w_i \beta_i.$$

[13] For example, $\alpha_i = E(R_z)(1 - \beta_i)$, where $E(R_z)$ is the expected return on the minimum variance zero-beta portfolio. See Sharpe (1978) for further discussion.

[14] An "index" fund is a portfolio whose return is highly correlated with percentage changes in the stock price indexes. It consists of a comprehensive diversified group of securities and is intended to be a cost-effective substitute for literally holding the market portfolio. The use of index funds is described in Ehrbar (1976). The riskless security version of the Capital Asset Pricing Model represents one situation in which investors would consider such a strategy. Hakansson (1976) explores other cases in which holding the market portfolio could be optimal.

effectiveness of diversification in reducing a major source of risk (i.e., unsystematic risk), what would lead an investor to perceive that an undiversified portfolio is best? There are many possible reasons, such as transactions costs. However, one reason is the nature of the investor's beliefs regarding the structure of security returns. An investor may choose to be undiversified because of the perception that a few securities offer an expected return sufficiently high to compensate the investor, not only for the systematic risk (which is not diversifiable) but also for the unsystematic risk (which is potentially diversifiable) [Treynor and Black (1973)].

The investor may be motivated to incur unsystematic risk when "mispriced" securities are perceived. A security is perceived to be mispriced when it is felt that the price of the security does not "fully reflect" the beliefs of the investor. In particular, the investor may perceive that the information upon which the investor's beliefs are based is not fully reflected in the price of the security. The extent to which information is fully reflected in prices is known as *market efficiency*. Alternatively stated, the optimal portfolio chosen by the investor will depend upon the investor's perceptions of market efficiency. This perception can also influence the investor's demand for financial information, and the financial reporting system can influence the investor's perceptions of market efficiency. The definition and the implications of the concept will be discussed at greater length in Chapter 6.

The perceived relationship between financial information and security prices can be a major source of diversity among investors with respect to the direct demand for financial information. However, once we focus on the relationship between information and security prices, it strains the discussion to keep the level of analysis confined to the single-person setting.

The portfolio chosen is not only a function of the investor's beliefs and information but also the beliefs and information the investor perceives as implicit in the *consensus* beliefs and information reflected in prevailing security prices. The prevailing price depends upon the beliefs and information of other investors. By contrast, the illustration provided earlier assumes that the current security prices remains the same before and after the receipt of the signal. In particular, the example assumes other investors' behavior, at least as reflected in stock prices, is unaffected by the public availability of those signals or is unaffected by other investors' knowledge that a particular investor has asymmetrical access to some information.[15] Neither assumption is plausible. Prices arise in a multiperson setting in which securities are issued and traded, which naturally leads to a multiperson perspective.

---

[15] For example, others' willingness to trade is not affected by the information de-

2-2. INFORMATION IN A MULTI-PERSON EXCHANGE SETTING

Financial information is not produced in a setting in which there is only one investor. Additional aspects of financial information arise when a multi-person setting is considered. In order to separate the consequences of providing information, initially it is assumed that financial data are being used in an exchange economy. Later the consequences of information on production are introduced.

Analysis of the role of information in a multi-person setting is an important, but a relatively recently explored, area.[16] As a result, many aspects of the issue are still not well understood. This research offers considerable promise for increasing our insight into financial reporting, and for this reason, some aspects of this literature are presented here. However, because of the embryonic nature of the work, discussing the implications is a tenuous process. The discussion in this section is intended to illustrate some of the possible effects of financial reporting in a multi-person environment. Hopefully, the discussion gives a flavor for the richness and complexity of the problem and provides a framework within which to view the potential consequences of financial reporting.

Financial statement information not only plays a role in altering beliefs (called a pre-decision role) but also affects the trading or contracting opportunities available to investors (called a *post-decision role*). The post-decision role was introduced by Radner (1968), and the dual role in the financial reporting context has been explored by Demski (1974). The investor may not have access to some state-contingent claims to consumption simply because that attribute of the state may not be observable to the rest of the market. The inability to obtain some forms of insurance is an obvious case. The ability of both buyer and seller to observe some states can alter the trading and contracting opportunities. The introduction of an information system can permit the observability of some states that otherwise would have been unobservable. Hence, the richness or completeness of the trading and contracting opportunities is increased. In the context of the securities market, investors can trade contingent upon the public disclosure of a signal (such as EPS). This increases the set of feasible trading strategies relative to what is available without the signal. In a single-period setting the distinction between the pre-decision and the post-decision role of information is clearcut. In a

---

cisions of the investor. Similarly, there is no attempt by others to infer what information the investor may have from the investor's behavior. Obviously, however, others' behavior must be affected by the investor's actions in the sense that the securities must be purchased from someone.

[16] An excellent review of this literature appears in Hirshleifer and Riley (1979).

multi-period setting both roles blend together. In other words, a signal which is playing a post-decision role for a decision made at time $t - 1$ may be playing a pre-decision role for a decision made at time t.

Pre-Decision Role of Information

The discussion of information in a multi-person setting initially focuses on the pre-decision role of information. While some interesting issues arise when everyone has the same information, a primary concern of regulators, among others, arises under conditions of *information asymmetry*. Two situations are relevant: (1) information asymmetry among investors, and (2) information asymmetry between management and investors.

More Informed Versus Less Informed Investors

A more general setting is provided by describing the information asymmetry in terms of *more* informed and *less* informed investors. The exchange market for securities provides a ready example. In this setting the more informed investors may be either holders or nonholders of the security and may be either potential sellers or buyers. In other words, at some price (a bid price) an investor is willing to buy shares and at some price (an ask price) is willing to sell shares. The distinction is based upon the information possessed by the individual, not whether the individual is a holder or nonholder, a buyer or a seller.

In this setting the more informed have incentives to engage in "active" trading in order to reap expected abnormal returns from trading with the less informed. However, the less informed investors have other options available.

(1) They can refuse to trade with the more informed and insulate themselves from the more informed via a buy-and-hold portfolio strategy. This passive policy will minimize trades and thereby reduce the ability of the more informed to extract benefits of their information via abnormal returns.[17]

(2) The less informed can attempt to infer information from the behavior of the more informed. For example, the less informed may

---

[17] This leaves the "more informed" to trade among themselves. Treynor (1979) has developed a trading model whereby prices are solely determined by "active" investors, each of whom possesses some inside information. The less informed investors effectively play no role in the price-setting process because they follow a "passive" buy-and-hold portfolio policy designed to insulate themselves from trading with the more informed investors.

attempt to infer the information of the more informed from the prices the more informed are willing to pay for the securities. This constitutes a form of "learning from prices" and has been studied by Grossman (1976) and Grossman and Stiglitz (1975), among others. In other words, the actions of the more informed may reveal some of their information to the less informed. As a result, prices may partially reflect and in the limit fully reflect the information.

(3)   The less informed can attempt to obtain the information of the more informed by hiring information intermediaries either directly or through a financial intermediary.

Of course, the more informed are aware of the motives and incentives of the less informed. For example, the more informed may attempt to thwart the efforts of the less informed to infer information from their actions. The relationship between more informed and less informed investors can be described as a game of asymmetrical information in which each player is aware of the potential strategies available to the other and assumes that the other players will act in an "optimal" manner. This may cause the more informed to act *as if* they were "throwing away" some of their information by adopting a *mixed strategy*. A mixed strategy involves some form of randomization of behavior (i.e., randomization of response to observing a given signal). The mixed strategy may be dictated when a pure strategy (i.e., a predictable, certain response to observing a given signal) would permit the less informed to extract the information from the actions of the informed. Moreover, the less informed are aware that it may be optimal for the more informed to follow a mixed strategy and construct an optimal response to the actions of the more informed incorporating that possibility.[18]

However, the investors may have incentives to want to remove the information asymmetries, which leads to the preemptive role of public disclosure.

Preemptive Role of Public Information

Information asymmetries among investors provide another role for the provision of publicly available information, namely, preempting the opportunity for abnormal returns due to inside information. In the Hirshleifer analysis, potentially there are enormous gains from private access to information. Hence, the private value and the demand for private information can be enormous. However, in the setting described above the social value of publicly disclosing that information might be zero or negative. Costless private search for information is a zero-sum game in terms of real resources from the viewpoint of the entire set of

---

[18] An example is proved in Demski (1980), Chapter 6.

investors. If the private search for information is costly (e.g., fees paid to financial analysts for private search), in terms of real resources it is a negative-sum game for investors (i.e., due to the wealth accruing to those paid for the private search). Hence, investors might prefer to mutually agree not to privately search for information to save the expenditure of real resources consumed in the private search process. However, such a contract would be difficult (i.e., costly) to enforce and there would be natural incentives to cheat. In this context one potential role for the regulation of financial reporting is to effect such a contract. This could be accomplished by inducing a penalty (i.e., liability) for obtaining private information which itself is a costly process involving detection and litigation cost. Alternatively, it might be cost-effective to preempt private search activities by placing the data in the public domain.[19] This rationale will be discussed further in Chapter 7.

More Informed Management and Less Informed Investors

It is often assumed that management is more informed about the firm than the investors are. In this situation, two phenomena can occur, *adverse selection* and *moral hazard*.

Adverse Selection

A related aspect of asymmetrical information among investors is the self-selection that may occur on the part of those offering securities for sale, a phenomenon known as *adverse selection*. It has been illustrated in the market for used cars in a seminal article by Akerlof (1970). In a security market setting, information asymmetry means that securities of different "quality" can sell for the same price. To maintain the analogy with the used car market, assume that security holders (e.g., potential issuers and sellers) have superior information (i.e., a strictly finer information system) than nonholders (e.g., potential buyers). The superior information can be thought of as inside information (known only to holders) plus what is publicly known. The inferior information system is simply what is publicly known to buyers and seller alike. There are several potential consequences.

(1) The holders of the higher-quality securities may be "forced" to hold a greater amount of those securities than would be the case if the information asymmetry were removed. Such investors may hold a less diversified portfolio and hence incur more unsystematic risk than

---

[19] The preemptive role of public disclosure is discussed in Beaver (1973, 1978).

they would if the superior information were publicly available. In general, this can lead to nonoptimal risk sharing relative to the more complete information setting.

(2) Holders of high-quality securities will attempt to alleviate the information asymmetry by some form of "signaling" behavior.[20] In general, signaling involves undertaking some action that would be irrational unless they were in fact holders of higher-quality securities. Specifically, they have incentives to publicly disclose the information to potential buyers that leads them to believe that their securities are underpriced. It may be costly to do so, and there is the question of the credibility of the evidence. For example, the effectiveness will be affected by the ability of holders of lower-quality securities to imitate the signaling behavior (e.g., lie about the information they have).[21]

(3) Effectiveness could also be affected by the ability to have the information "certified" in some sense and hence improve the credibility of the information. Other options include offering insurance or warranties, under which the holders promise to pay a penalty or reimbursement to the buyer if in fact the security is judged subsequently to be of lower quality. However, certification and warranties are costly and the latter can also lead to an "excessive" shifting of risk.

(4) The prospective purchasers are aware of the information asymmetry and will not act in a naive fashion (e.g., as if no information asymmetry existed). They know that the prospective sellers have access to a superior information system, but they do not know which signal from the system has been observed. They may attempt to infer the "average" quality of the securities offered for sale and to reflect it in their offering price. However, at any offering price, there will be some degree of adverse selection, unless there is a natural floor on the quality. In the limit, the information asymmetry may lead to no trading at all (i.e., the market simply shuts down). In fact, the meaning and existence of equilibrium in a market with asymmetrical information are open issues and the subject of extensive current research.[22]

It has been assumed in this example that potential issuers and sellers of the security have access to a superior information system. The markets for used cars and the issuance of new securities provide possible examples. The Securities Act of 1933, which provides for disclosure reg-

---

[20] Ross (1979) examines the implications of the signaling literature for financial reporting.

[21] Obviously, such imitative behavior may be discouraged by economic sanctions, such as legal liability under the anti-fraud provision of the Securities Acts.

[22] This literature is discussed more fully in Hirshleifer and Riley (1979).

ulation in connection with the issuance of securities, is motivated by concern that the issuer (e.g., management) may possess superior information relative to the potential buyers.

Stewardship, Moral Hazard, and Agency Theory

One of the consequences of information is its effect on the relationship between management and investors. Previously, this relationship has been described in terms of the stewardship theory. The economics literature treats this as a problem of moral hazard and is of primary concern to agency theory.[23]

In an agency setting a moral hazard problem arises because of an informational asymmetry. Typically, the agent is assumed to have access to superior information. In particular, it is assumed that the principal cannot observe the agent's behavior. Hence, there is a general concern that the agent will use the position of superior information to maximize the agent's self-interest at the expense of the principal. This is the moral hazard problem. Moral hazard not only includes such acts as fraud and shirking, but it also includes other actions that are not in the best interests of the principal, such as risk-reward tradeoffs made in project selection. The parallel to the management-shareholder relationship is direct and obvious, and several responses to the moral hazard problem are possible.

(1) One response is to provide an incentive contract for management so as to more closely align the interests of management and the shareholders. Profit-sharing agreements and stock options are examples of incentive schemes that could play this role. However, such schemes can also have some potentially undesirable properties. In such a setting management may not only become insurers against deficiencies in their own behavior but also insurers of unfavorable outcomes due to environmental factors beyond the control of management. Hence, management becomes involved in risk sharing with the principal in a way that may be nonoptimal, relative to the risk sharing that would occur in the absence of a moral hazard problem.

(2) Another option to alleviate the moral hazard problem is to provide for public disclosure of the firm's information so as to remove the superior information position of management. Hence, the information asymmetry that leads to the concern over moral hazard is re-

---

[23] Recent studies that have applied agency theory to the relationship between managers and owners include Stiglitz (1974), Jensen and Meckling (1976), Watts and Zimmerman (1986), Harris and Raviv (1979), and Demski and Feltham (1978).

moved. Further, one can imagine hiring an independent "monitor" to come into the firm and inspect the information system and to render a "certification" that no material information has been withheld by management in its reporting to shareholders.[24]

This approach, therefore, gives rise to a demand for auditing services, and it offers a potentially rich area for future research into the nature of the demand for audit services. One of the intriguing aspects of the agency research is its recognition that it can be mutually beneficial to both parties to have public disclosure and an audit. The merits for the shareholder have long been acknowledged in the accounting literature. However, the agency approach highlights the fact that management benefits as well. The absence of public disclosure or an audit may require the use of an incentive scheme that induces an undesirable risk sharing. In the limit, if the concern over moral hazard is sufficiently great, the principal may be unwilling to enter into a contract with the agent. Hence, the demand for the agent's service may increase with the agreement to provide the additional information. As a result, management may be willing to pay for audits.

Alleviating the moral hazard problem via disclosure is one aspect of the investors' demand for financial information. The agency theory perspective is consistent with the FASB (1976) position that the stewardship role of financial information is part of the general investor informational approach.

Post-Decision Role on Information

The discussion of adverse selection and moral hazard has suggested that the less informed investor would have a demand for information that would *monitor* the behavior of the more informed manager. Audits would be one form of such information. A demand would also exist to have the contract between the investor and management defined in terms of some observable aspects of the state. Management incentive contracts defined in terms of net income is a prominent example. Both examples constitute a *post-decision* role for financial reporting data.

The issue of information asymmetry can be more comprehensive than those issues involving management and investors. One class capital

---

[24] Signaling behavior may also arise. In this setting, managers signal they have nothing to hide by undertaking certain acts that would be nonoptimal for them otherwise. This is discussed in greater detail in Chapter 7. Examples of the signaling literature are discussed in Ross (1979) who applies the signaling literature to financial reporting issues. Obviously, the strategies, similar to those discussed in the adverse selection situation, may also be considered in an analysis of the moral hazard problem.

suppliers (e.g., bond holders) may be concerned about information asymmetries with respect to another class (e.g., common stock investors, whose interests are represented by management). In this case, contracts between these classes of suppliers of capital (e.g., bond covenants) can be structured in terms of accounting data. A bond covenant that imposes a minimum times interest earned ratio (income before interest divided by interest payments) is a prominent example. If our laws are viewed as forms of explicit or implicit contracts between the government and the firm's owners, these "social contracts" are also often defined in terms of accounting data. Explicitly, the provisions of the Internal Revenue Code are defined in terms of accounting data. More subtly, the anti-trust provisions of our law can be thought of as implicit contract; accounting data may be used by the Anti-Trust Division of the Department of Justice to detect violations of the law. In regulated industries, regulators impose constraints on firm behavior that is defined in terms of financial data. Capital adequacy ratios imposed by federal banking regulators would be one prominent example. Watts and Zimmerman (1986) develop in depth the notion that many of the firm's contracts are defined in terms of financial reporting data.

The contracting perspective has at least two important implications. First, it provides a basis for understanding why management and regulators, among others, regard the choice of accounting method as a substantive issue, even in situations where there would be no difference in information provided from an investor, pre-decision perspective. The reason is that the *form* of the disclosure can affect some of the contracts and have an economic impact on the parties involved. Wyatt (1983) provides several excellent examples. Second, the contracting perspective helps explain why management spends a firm's resources lobbying before the financial reporting regulators on behalf of form of accounting versus another, and why management contends that a financial reporting regulation can have adverse economic consequences upon the value of the firm. Such adverse consequences were alleged in the controversy over the FASB's Standard, FAS No. 19, accounting for intangible drilling costs. Such effects were offered as an interpretation of the adverse security price effects at the time the standard was proposed. The demand for off-balance sheet financing, particularly in regulated industries such as banking, can be better understood from a contracting perspective.

In order for the contracting perspective to be plausible, the costs of contracting (or recontracting) must be material. Much of the motivation for adopting this perspective arises because explicit, private contracts are not only defined in terms of accounting numbers, but also define those numbers subject to *Generally Accepted Accounting Principles* (GAAP). When the FASB proposes to change GAAP, it is tantamount to altering the terms of the private contracts. At least two questions arise. (1) Why don't the parties, at the outset, define the contract in terms of an explicit set of accounting methods, rather than be subject to the regulatory risk induced by changing GAAP after the inception of the contract? (2) Why don't the parties simply recontract when GAAP is changed in order to restore themselves to the original position? In both cases, the answer must be that the costs of doing so are large, relative to the "costs" imposed by having the terms of the contract changed.

These contracting costs not only involved the direct "out of pocket" costs of negotiating and drafting the contract but also indirect costs that include effects on the production and financing decisions of management. These latter costs are often alleged to be substantive and systematic across firms.

There are several illustrations of potential economic consequences of financial reporting on the production sector.[25]

(1)   Opponents of the deferral treatment of the investment tax credit argued that such treatment would act as a deterrent to capital formation. Congress passed a law preventing any group (such as the FASB or the SEC) from requiring a corporation to use the deferral treatment.

(2)   From 1968 to 1971 the FASB and SEC considered requiring the inclusion of bad debt provisions in the net income of commercial banks. Bankers argued that such disclosure would erode confidence in the banking system and such erosion would be detrimental to the economy.

(3)   The FASB's standard, FAS No. 2, required the expensing of major types of research and development expenditures. It was alleged to be a deterrent against further research and development investment by corporations.

(4)   The FASB's standard, FAS No. 19, required the "successful efforts" method of accounting for intangible drilling costs in the oil and gas industry. It was cited as contributing to increased concentration in the industry, because it favored large corporations and would harm small corporations. In fact, the anti-trust division of the Department of Justice testified before the SEC against FAS No. 19 on the basis that the standard was anti-competitive and would lead to a elimination of smaller corporations.

---

[25] These and other examples are documented in Horngren (1972, 1973), Armstrong (1977), Rappaport (1977), and Zeff (1978).

2-3.   SUMMARY OF ECONOMIC CONSEQUENCES
OF FINANCIAL INFORMATION

(1)   Financial information can affect the distribution of wealth among investors. This consequence involves issues of equity or fairness. Differential access to the information may permit more informed investors to increase their wealth at the expense of the less informed. Information asymmetry is perceived by Congress and the SEC to be unfair and is one motivation for the securities legislation governing disclosure.

(2)   Financial information can affect the aggregate level of risk incurred and can affect the distribution of the risk among the constituencies. For example, the incentive contracts between investors and management, in response to concern over moral hazard, also determine how risk is shared between them. Similarly, legal liability imposed on management for unfavorable outcomes can influence the risk-reward tradeoffs made by management in project selection and can affect the aggregate level of risk taking in the economy.

(3)   Financial information can affect the rate of capital formation in the economy with a resulting reallocation of society's wealth between consumption and investment.

(4)   Financial information can also affect how investment is allocated among firms. Disclosure may alter investors' beliefs about the relative rewards and risks associated with particular securities. Consider the recent analyses of the effects of inflation on corporate profits. It has been stated that failure to disclose the effects of inflation, among other things, may be contributing to a misallocation of resources toward industries or groups of firms showing illusory profits. To the extent that disclosure does alter investor perceptions of relative rewards and risks, investors will shift toward more desirable investment opportunities. In general, this shift may be reflected in the manner in which new capital is allocated among firms.

(5)   Financial information can affect the amount of resources devoted to the production, certification, dissemination, processing, analysis, and interpretation of disclosures.

(6)   Financial information involves the use of resources in the development, compliance, enforcement, and litigation of disclosure rules. These will be termed the costs of regulation because they exist in addition to the direct costs of disclosure.

(7)   Financial information can alter the amount of resources used by the private sector to search for nondisclosed information. Corporations have an incentive to provide such information, and analysts have an incentive to search for and to disseminate such information. This activity constitutes private-sector information production and permits

the investment activity, as well as the resulting security prices, to reflect a broader information set than the formal documents of the corporation.

These consequences are summarized in Table 1-2. There are obviously other ways in which the consequences could be described [e.g., Foster (1986)]. For example, information could alter the incentives of management to undertake certain projects. Disclosure could reduce the ability of the firm to reap the benefits of innovative activities, such as oil exploration, product development, and research and development. This is often called the *competitive disadvantage* aspect of disclosure. Similarly, disclosure of information can alter the risk-return tradeoffs that management is willing to make. Consider the requirement to publicly disclose management's forecasts of earnings. If management perceives that greater legal liability is associated with forecasts that have large forecast errors, it may alter the nature of the projects accepted so that earnings will be more stable and more predictable. Hence, the risk-return tradeoffs may be affected. Obviously, management may also alter its forecasting behavior to reduce the risk of legal liability of an incorrect forecast. Disclosure of financial information may also deter "undesirable" forms of management behavior, such as fraud—one form of the moral hazard problem. However, effects such as competitive disadvantage and legal liability (often viewed as "costs" of disclosure) as well as the deterrence of fraud can be described as having an impact on one or more of the seven categories listed above.

Furthermore, the list of potential consequences does not include security price effects. Financial information can affect security prices. These security price effects in turn can result in one or more of the consequences listed above. For example, the security prices determine the wealth of the investor and the command the investor has over consumption goods and other investments. Security prices affect the terms on which new securities are offered, and as a result they are related to the rate of capital formation and resource allocation. The importance of prices will be discussed in greater detail in Chapter 6. At present, the purpose is to provide a description of primitive consequences of financial information, rather than a description of intermediate effects on security prices, which may be related to these consequences.

2-4. SOCIAL VALUE AND FINANCIAL INFORMATION

A major implication of a multi-person view of financial reporting is that there may be a lack of consensus among individuals on the value of any particular financial reporting system. The discussion has brought out a number of potential consequences of information. The constituencies can be affected in diverse ways by particular financial accounting standards or corporate disclosure requirements.

As the previous chapter indicated, financial accounting theory has long had a predominantly normative flavor (i.e., oriented toward which accounting method is "best"). The multi-person viewpoint suggests that it may be difficult to pursue that perspective by staying strictly within the bounds of technical accounting expertise. Since these various constituencies may be affected by the consequences of information in different ways, there may be no consensus on what the "best" accounting method is.

A standard approach to such an issue is to assess the "cost" and the "benefits" of a policy decision requiring the provision of additional information. The notion is that the policy maker (i.e., the FASB or the SEC) should select those policies in which the benefits exceed the costs. However, whether a particular consequence is a benefit or a cost will depend upon which constituency's perspective is adopted. The setting for choosing among financial reporting systems is thus a political one in the sense that it involves an issue of social choice. In a setting with diverse constituencies, the notion of a single, overall objective function, such as a social welfare function, is not a well-defined concept. Such issues have long been the subject of welfare economics and are dealt with in greater detail in a financial reporting context by Beaver and Demski (1974). A choice among financial reporting systems inevitably involves a choice among which set of consequences is most desirable. This in turn involves value judgments or tradeoffs among the welfare or interests of the various constituencies affected. Such judgments can certainly be made. However, they typically involve considerations of a normative nature which are beyond the purview of technical aspects of accounting. Social choices involve issues of equity, such as altering the distribution of wealth among individuals in our society. No amount of accounting expertise alone is going to resolve such an issue, because such an issue also involves value judgments.

To reinforce this point, consider only the investor interests in information production. It has already been noted that professional investors may differ from nonprofessional investors in their assessments of the value of an information system. Similarly, the interest of a well-diversified investor may differ from that of an undiversified investor. Generally, the demand for financial information will naturally differ across investors. As indicated earlier, the private demand for information by any given individual will depend upon its costs and personal attributes of the investor, such as wealth, tastes, and beliefs. It is reasonable to suspect heterogeneity in the preferences for information. When exchanges among investors are introduced, other aspects arise in the form of redistributional effects that induce a further source of divergence among investors regarding the value of an information system.

A direct extension of a political, social choice view of selecting financial reporting systems is to predict what position the various constituencies will take on various financial accounting proposals. Watts and Zimmerman (1978) attempt to predict which groups will support or oppose financial accounting standards based upon an analysis of the groups' self-interests.

Viewing the selection among financial reporting systems as a social choice does not necessarily imply that some form of regulation of financial reporting is called for. Markets offer one mechanism for social choice, and an issue is whether some form of "market failure" is present that could be remedied via regulation [e.g., Gonedes and Dopuch (1974)]. The regulation of financial reporting systems is dealt with in greater detail in Chapter 7.

2-5. CONCLUDING REMARKS

The chapter has focused upon a number of potential consequences of financial reporting. These effects are diverse and affect various groups in diverse ways. Hence, the search for the "best" method of financial reporting is inherently a social choice issue. This is an inevitable conclusion if one adopts the view of treating financial reporting information in a multi-person setting. As a result, there are some nonobvious and rather dramatic implications of the FASB adopting an informational perspective.

However, little has been said about the exact content of financial information. The treatment has been intentionally general. It has focused upon the potential economic consequences of information, where financial disclosures and financial statement data are but two sources of information among the total available to investors in making their decisions. The next chapter turns to the issue of the concept of earnings, the primary output of an accrual accounting system, and explores the concept of economic income in some detail. The analysis of earnings begins with the case of certainty (Chapter 3) and then moves to uncertainty (Chapter 4). In order to better appreciate the implications of such a movement, it is critical to have first explored the general nature of financial information.

BIBLIOGRAPHY

AKERLOF, G. "The Market for 'Lemons': Quality Uncertainty and the Market Mechanism." *Quarterly Journal of Economics* (August 1970), 488–500.

ARMSTRONG, M. "The Politics of Establishing Accounting Standards." *Journal of Accountancy* (February 1977), 76–79.

BEAVER, W. "What Should Be the FASB's Objectives?" *Journal of Accountancy* (August 1973), 49–56.

———. "Current Trends in Corporate Disclosure." *Journal of Accountancy* (January 1978), 44–52.

——— AND J. DEMSKI. "The Nature of Financial Accounting Objectives: A Summary and Synthesis." *Studies on Financial Accounting Objectives*, supplement to the *Journal of Accounting Research* (1974), 170–182.

BEJA, A. "On Systematic and Unsystematic Components of Financial Risk." *Journal of Finance* (March 1972), 37–46.

DEMSKI, J. "The Choice Among Financial Reporting Alternatives." *Accounting Review* (April 1974), 221–232.

——— *Information Analysis*. 2d ed. Reading, Mass.: Addison-Wesley, 1980.

——— AND G. FELTHAM. *Cost Determination: A Conceptual Approach.* Ames, Iowa: Iowa State University Press, 1976.

——— "Economic Incentives in Budgetary Control Systems." *Accounting Review* (April 1978), 336–359.

EHRBAR, A. "Index Funds—An Idea Whose Time Is Coming." *Fortune* (June 1976), 145–154.

FAMA, E. "A Note on the Market Model and the Two-Parameter Model." *Journal of Finance* (December 1973), 1181–1186.

FINANCIAL ACCOUNTING STANDARDS BOARD (FASB). *Tentative Conclusions on Objectives of Financial Statements of Business Enterprises*. Stamford, Conn.: FASB, October 1976.

——— *Statement of Financial Accounting Concepts No. 1*. Stamford, Conn.: FASB, November 1978.

FOSTER, G. *Financial Statement Analysis*. 2d ed. Englewood Cliffs, N.J.: Prentice-Hall, 1986.

GONEDES, N., AND N. DOPUCH. "Capital Market Equilibrium, Information Production, and Selecting Accounting Techniques: Theoretical Framework and Review of Empirical Work." *Studies on Financial Accounting Objectives: 1974*, supplement to *Journal of Accounting Research* (1974), 48–129.

GROSSMAN, S. "On the Efficiency of Competitive Stock Markets Where Traders Have Diverse Information." *Journal of Finance* (May 1976), 573–585.

——— AND J. STIGLITZ. "On the Impossibility of Informationally Efficient Markets" presented at the Econometric Society meetings, December 1975.

HAKANSSON, N. "Information Needs for Portfolio Choice" presented and published as part of the *Proceedings of the Duke Symposium on Financial Information for Security Analysis*. Duke University (December 1976), 18–46.

HARRIS, M., AND A. RAVIV. "Optimal Incentive Contracts with Imperfect Information." *Journal of Economic Theory* (April 1979), 231–259.

HIRSHLEIFER, J., AND J. RILEY. "The Analytics of Uncertainty and Information—An Expository Survey." *Journal of Economic Literature* (December 1979), 1375–1421.

HORNGREN, C. "Accounting Principles: Private or Public Sector?" *Journal of Accountancy* (May 1972), 37–41.

_____"The Marketing of Accounting Standards." *Journal of Accountancy* (October 1973), 61–66.

JENSEN, M., AND W. MECKLING. "Theory of the Firm: Managerial Behavior, Agency Costs and Ownership Structure." *Journal of Financial Economics* (October 1976), 305–360.

RADNER, R. "Competitive Equilibrium Under Uncertainty." *Econometrica* (January 1968), 31–58.

RAPPAPORT, A. "Economic Impact of Accounting Standards—Implications for the FASB." *Journal of Accountancy* (May 1977), 89–98.

ROSS, W. "Disclosure Regulation in Financial Markets: Implications of Modern Finance Theory and Signaling Theory." *Key Issues in Financial Regulation* (1979), 177–201.

SAVAGE, L. *The Foundations of Statistics*, 2d rev. ed. New York: Dover Publications, 1972.

SECURITIES AND EXCHANGE COMMISSION. *Report of Advisory Committee on Corporate Disclosure*. Washington, D.C.: U.S. Government Printing Office, 1977.

SHARPE, W. *Investments*. Englewood Cliffs, N.J.: Prentice-Hall, 1978.

STIGLITZ, J. "Risk Sharing and Incentives in Sharecropping." *Review of Economic Studies* (April 1974), 219–255.

TREYNOR, J. "Trading Cost and Active Management." *Proceedings of Seminar on Investment Management: The Active/Passive Decisions*. Menlo Park, Calif.: FRS Associates, September 23–26, 1979, iv–94 through iv–107.

_____ AND F. BLACK. "How to Use Security Analyses to Improve Portfolio Selection." *Journal of Business* (January 1973), 66–86.

WATTS, R. AND J. ZIMMERMAN. "Towards a Positive Theory of the Determination of Accounting Standards." *Accounting Review* (January 1978), 112–134.

_____ *Positive Accounting Theory*. Englewood Cliffs, N.J.: Prentice-Hall, 1986.

WYATT, A. "Efficient Market Theory: Its Impact on Accounting." *Journal of Accountancy* (February 1983), 56–65.

ZEFF, S. "The Rise of Economic Consequences." *Journal of Accountancy* (December 1978), 56–63.

chapter three

Earnings Under Certainty

The purpose of Chapters 3 and 4 is to explore the relationship between accounting earnings and the value of the firm and its common stock.[1] As indicated in the introductory chapter, accounting earnings are a primary product of the accrual process. No other figure in the financial statements receives more attention by the investment community than earnings per share. The relationship between accounting earnings and security prices is probably the single most important relationship in security analysis, and its prominence is reflected in the attention given to price-earnings ratios. A considerable amount of empirical research has been conducted on the relationship between earnings and security prices. This research will be the topic of Chapter 5.

The setting in this chapter is perfect, complete markets and certainty. The setting of uncertainty and incomplete markets will be examined in Chapter 4.

---

[1] The terms *earnings* and *net income* are used interchangeably throughout. However, it is important to distinguish between *economic* earnings and *accounting* earnings, assuming the former is well-defined. Usually the context of the discussion will make it clear which concept is being referred to. However, often the distinction will be made explicit in order to reinforce the importance of the distinction.

3-1. PERFECT, COMPLETE MARKETS
AND CERTAINTY

The concept of *perfect markets* means that (1) trading of commodities and claims take place at zero transactions costs, (2) no firm or individual has any special advantage or opportunity to earn abnormal returns on its investments, and (3) prices are invariant to the actions of any individual or firm. The concept of *complete markets* means that markets exist for *all* commodities or claims, and hence the market price for any commodity or claim is publicly observable. Of particular interest here is the valuation of "cash flows" over time. Two critical aspects are the completeness of the market with respect to claims to future cash flows (hereafter intertemporal claims) and the ability to costlessly trade in these claims in any desired combination.[2] For example, consider a simple economy in which there are three points in time: now ($t = 0$), one period from now ($t = 1$), and two periods from now ($t = 2$). A complete market for claims to future cash flows would permit the opportunity to (1) invest now and receive \$1 at $t = 1$, (2) invest now and receive \$1 at $t = 2$, (3) invest now and receive \$1 each at $t = 1$ and $t = 2$, (4) contract now to invest at $t = 1$ and receive \$1 at $t = 2$ (i.e., a futures market exists), and (5) know now that at $t = 1$ a market will open for one-period claims to \$1 to be received at $t = 2$ (i.e., future spot markets will be available). Moreover, claims can be traded in any multiple, and fractions of claims are available. In other words, a complete market for claims to future cash flows is simply a very "rich" market that permits whatever trading that is desired by investors.[3]

The assumption of certainty means that all expectations are realized and investors know that they will be realized. Hence, the future prices of any claim are known with certainty. Given the assumption of zero

---

[2] The chapter will adopt the terminology of claims to "cash flows" to ease the transition to traditional valuation theory, which is typically characterized in terms of future cash flows. However, no "money illusion" is being assumed here. Obviously, claims to consumption are of ultimate concern to investors. However, with known prices for commodities at each point in time, the cash flow characterization is merely a convenient way to summarize the implied purchasing power over goods and services. Alternatively, the claims could be expressed in terms of some "numeraire" commodity, such as a bushel of corn. The insight would be the same since the cash flow and corn characterizations are merely alternative and substantively equivalent ways of describing the multi-period economy. In fact, since the existence of several consumption commodities is not of immediate concern, the economy can be thought of as a single good economy without any loss of insight for the purposes here. See Hirshleifer [(1970) Chapter 2] for further discussion.

[3] While the text refers to investment (i.e., lending opportunities) analogous borrowing opportunities are also implied. Default risk is not an issue here because of the certainty assumption. Note that in equilibrium the opportunities listed in (1) through (5) are redundant. In particular, the existence of a futures market (4) obviates the existence of a future spot market (5). While such a market is potentially available, there would be no activity in such a market because of the activities at $t = 0$ in the futures market.

transactions costs, the setting implies that there must be certain relationships between the prices of intertemporal claims. These relationships give rise to the familiar present value formulation. Perfect and complete markets permit a costless, riskless arbitraging of intertemporal claims and hence require the pricing of the claims to behave such that a present value formulation is attainable.

For example, the price of any one-period claim will depend upon the one-period interest rate. Suppose that the interest rate in the first period (i.e., from $t = 0$ to $t = 1$) is 8 percent and the rate in the second period (i.e., from $t = 1$ to $t = 2$) is 12 percent. The price at $t = 0$ for a one-period claim to receive $1 at $t = 1$ is $.926 [i.e., $(1 + .08)^{-1}$]. Similarly, at $t = 1$ the price of a one-period claim to receive $1 at $t = 2$ is $.893 [i.e., $(1 + .12)^{-1}$]. Arbitrage implies that the price of a claim at $t = 0$ to receive $1 at $t = 2$ will be $.827 (i.e., $.926 × $.893). If the price were higher, riskless and costless arbitrage profits would be available by borrowing in the two-period market and investing the proceeds in the successive one-period markets.[4] If the price were lower, riskless and costless arbitrage profits could be made by purchasing two-period claims and financing the purchase by borrowing in the successive one-period markets.[5] In equilibrium, such *money pump* situations would not exist because prices of the claims would be bid so that such situations could not occur.

In the most general case, both interest rates and amounts to be received will vary over time. However, without loss of insight and with the added convenience of illustration, the interest rate (r) is hereafter assumed to be constant over time. Let C_t denote the cash flow to be received at time t for $t = 1, T$. $_0P_t$ is the present value (or price) as of now ($t = 0$) for a claim to receive $1 at time t. Then,

$$_0PV_T = \sum_{t=1}^{T} \frac{1}{(1 + r)^t} C_t = \sum_{t=1}^{T} {_0P_t}C_t$$

where $_0PV_T$ is the present value or price of the compound claim as of now ($t = 0$) for a T-period compound claim of nonconstant amounts.[6]

---

[4] For example, suppose that the price were $.90. The proceeds of the borrowing would be $.90 and could be invested to obtain a terminal wealth at $t = 2$ of $1.089 (i.e., $.90 × 1.08 × 1.12) before paying off the loan. After paying off $1, there is a pure arbitrage profit of $.089.

[5] For example, suppose that the price were only $.80. Borrow $.80 in the one-period market and buy (i.e., lend in) the two-period market. At $t = 1$, $.864 must be repaid but borrow in the second one-period market to pay off the first loan. At $t = 2$, $.968 must be repaid but $1 is received from the two-period investment, leaving a pure arbitrage profit of $.032.

[6] With $r_t = r$ for all t (i.e., with the interest rate constant),

$$_0P_t = {_0P_1} × \cdots × {_{t-1}P_t} = \frac{1}{1 + r} × \cdots × \frac{1}{1 + r} = \frac{1}{(1 + r)^t}$$

The compound claim can be viewed as a bundle of simple claims, and the price of the bundle is the sum of the prices of the simple claims that comprise the bundle. Each T-period compound claim represents T valuable claims. The analogy to commodities in an atemporal setting is obvious. In perfect and complete markets the value of any bundle of claims (commodities) is merely the sum of the value of claims (commodities) it represents. This value additivity property follows from the fact that arbitrage profits must be zero in this setting. If value additivity did not hold, arbitrage profits could be earned, as illustrated earlier for the two-period simple claim.

The present value characterization permits a vector of future cash flows $(C_1, C_2, \ldots, C_T)$ to be converted into a scalar, the present value of those cash flows. Moreover, this single number has several important properties. The cash flow stream that has the highest present value is the most preferred by investors. This statement can be made regardless of the personal characteristics of investors, such as the exact nature of their initial endowment of intertemporal claims or their preference function for intertemporal cash flows. It merely requires that they prefer (or at least do not oppose) more cash flow to less in any given time period. Because of the richness of the market for intertemporal claims, any two streams can be evaluated regardless of their individual cash flow patterns. Obviously, cases in which one stream strictly dominates another are simple to evaluate. For example, consider the case in which the cash flow for stream A is at least as large as the cash flow for stream B at each and every point in time and is strictly larger for at least one point. However, the present value mechanism permits a comparison of cash flow streams which initially cannot be evaluated in terms of a strict dominance criterion. The market assumptions underlying the present value model (i.e., perfect and complete markets) permit any arbitrary cash flow stream to be expressed as an infinite number of other cash flow streams of equivalent present value (i.e., "alter ego" cash flow streams). This flexibility guarantees that any cash flow stream that has a higher present value than another cash flow stream has at least one "alter ego" cash flow stream that strictly dominates the cash flow stream with the lower present value. Hence, as long as the marginal utility of additional

---

Note $_0P_1 = {}_1P_2 = {}_{t-1}P_t = \dfrac{1}{1+r} = (1+r)^{-1}$. With r_t nonconstant, in the general case, the present value as of time n for future cash flows to be received through $t = T$ is

$$_nPV_T = \sum_{t=n+1}^{T} {}_nP_tC_t = \sum_{t=n+1}^{T} \left(\prod_{j=n+1}^{t} {}_{j-1}P_j \right) C_t$$

cash flows is non-negative (positive), the cash flow stream with the higher present value will be at least as good as (strictly preferred to) the cash flow stream with the lower present value.

Alternatively stated, regardless of the initial endowments of an investor and regardless of the preference function for intertemporal cash flows, in equilibrium investors will trade in the markets for intertemporal claims to reach that point where their utility is maximized. This utility maximizing point has an important property. The relative marginal utility for intertemporal cash flows will be equal to the relative prices of the intertemporal claims and hence the relative marginal utility of intertemporal cash flows will be the same for every investor.

Therefore, the present value of future cash flows strictly ranks all simple and compound claims to future cash flows in spite of investors' diversity with respect to initial endowments and preferences. In equilibrium, ranking claims according to their present values is equivalent to ranking them according to the preferences of each and every investor. Moreover, this unanimity of preference is fully reflected in the price. The price of any compound claim to future cash flows *is* the present value of that claim. Finally, the present value rule gives the management of firms a basis for project selection. Management can select projects that maximize the firm's present value and hence maximize the utility of each of the owners.

The dominant position of the present value model in managerial accounting with respect to capital budgeting decisions also has its origins in this economic setting. Of course, at equilibrium, since prices fully reflect the value of the cash flow streams, arbitrage profits will be zero and pure profits (e.g., the "excess" present value) of firms will be zero. Preference for future cash flows is fully reflected in the price that must be paid to purchase such claims, and in this sense there are "no bargains." Before turning to a discussion of economic income, it is worth stressing again that such convenient properties occur because of the nature of the markets assumed, not because of certainty *per se*.

3-2. ECONOMIC EARNINGS UNDER CERTAINTY

This section explores the concept of economic income under conditions of certainty of future cash flows. It is the simplest setting and approximates the setting accounting theorists had in mind in their early developments of accounting earnings concepts. Moreover, the economic concept of earnings in this setting is well defined. As a result, it is a natural starting point for the discussion of the economic earnings concept. Throughout this section the illustrations will refer to an all-equity

TABLE 3-1

Assumptions

I. *Assumptions About the Economy*

    A. Certainty
        1. All expectations are realized
        2. All future prices of assets and claims are known
    B. Perfect and complete markets
        1. Zero transactions costs
        2. No abnormal earnings opportunities
        3. No arbitrage profits
        4. Prices are invariant to actions of individuals or firms
        5. Markets are very "rich"
    C. Interest rate is 10 percent per year
        1. It is constant over time
        2. It is also the earnings rate (i.e., internal rate of return) on all multi-period assets and claims

II. *Assumptions About the Firm*

    A. Single-asset firm
    B. All equity—no debt
    C. Cash flows occur discretely at end of each year
    D. All cash flows from operations are paid out as dividends
        1. No cash is retained in firm
        2. At each balance sheet date only the single asset is shown (i.e., there is no cash balance)

III. *Assumptions About the Asset*

    A. Useful life is two years
    B. Salvage value is zero
    C. Cash flow pattern:

Year	1	2
Amount	$600	$550

    D. Acquisition price at end of year 0 (now) is $1000
    E. Economic depreciation is used
    F. Depreciation is recorded at end of year

---

firm.[7] The firm's net income will also be the earnings available to common shareholders. Because there is no debt, the total assets of the firm will equal shareholders' equity at any point in time. The concept of earnings is explored in two contexts: (1) a single-asset firm in which the cash flows have a finite life and (2) a multi-asset firm in which the cash flow stream is treated as having an infinite life. The assumptions about the economy and the firm are summarized in Table 3-1.

Single-Asset Firm

Consider the simple setting of a single-asset firm, as illustrated in Table 3-2. The assumptions about the asset are summarized in Table

---

[7] Given the assumptions of certainty and perfect and complete markets, this is not a restrictive assumption.

TABLE 3-2

Economic Earnings for a Single-Asset Firm

	Year	
	1	*2*
Net Cash Flow	$600	$550
Present Value (PV) of Asset, Firm, and Equity at Beginning of Each Year[a]		
PV of year 1 flow	$545	
PV of year 2 flow	455	$500
	$1000	$500
Economic Depreciation		
Beginning present value	$1000	$500
Ending present value	500	0
Decline in present value	$500	$500
Economic Net Income of Asset and Firm	$600	$550
Net cash flow		
Less: economic depreciation	⟨500⟩	⟨500⟩
Economic net income	$100	$50
Return on Investment	$\frac{\$100}{\$1000} = 10\%$	$\frac{\$50}{\$500} = 10\%$
Economic Net Income of Shareholders		
Dividends received	$600	$550
Decline in present value of equity	⟨500⟩	⟨500⟩
Net income	$100	$50
Permanent Earnings		
Present value at beginning of year	$1000	$500
Times: interest rate	.10	.10
Permanent earnings	$100	$50
Beginning Market Value of Asset, Firm, and Equity[b]	$1000	$500
Beginning Market Price per Share[c]	$10	$5
Earnings per Share[c]	$1	$.50
Price-Earnings Ratio	10X	10X

[a]$545 = \dfrac{600}{1.1}$; $455 = \dfrac{550}{(1.1)^2}$; $500 = \dfrac{550}{(1.1)}$.

[b]Because of assumptions about the economy, present value equals market value. In other words, net value equals entry value equals value in use.

[c]100 shares are outstanding.

3-1. The asset has a two-year life, an estimated salvage value of zero, and an acquisition cost of $1000. The after-tax cash flows are $600 and $550, and the discount rate is 10 percent.[8]

---

[8] The assumption of perfect and complete markets implies that the earnings rate on all assets will be equal to the cost of capital, which is the interest rate. The definition

The present value of the asset at the time of acquisition is $1000, as shown in Table 3-2. The present value of $1000 represents the present value of $600 to be received in one year (i.e., at the end of year 1) and of $550 to be received in two years. Because of the assumptions made about the economy, the present value must be equal to the market value at the time of acquisition. One year later, the present value of the asset is only $500, representing the present value of $550 to be received in one year (i.e., at the end of year 2). Of course, at the end of year 2 the present value is zero. All cash flows received are immediately paid out as dividends (see Table 3-1), and the present value of the two-year asset is also the present value of the cash flows of the firm. Because the firm is all-equity, the present value of the asset's remaining cash flows is equal to the present value of the cash flows of the equity. Economic depreciation is defined as the change in the present value of the remaining cash flows at two points in time. The present value of the asset will decline by $500 per year. Hence, economic depreciation is $500 per year in this example, which happens to be equal to the amount of depreciation that would have been recorded using a straight-line method.

From the perspective of the firm, economic income in any given year is defined as the cash flows received in that year less the reduction in the present value of the asset's remaining cash flows (i.e., cash flow less economic depreciation). This would produce economic earnings of $100 and $50 respectively for each of the two years as shown in Table 3-2.

From the perspective of the shareholders, economic net income is the amount of cash dividends received in that year less any change in the market value of their holdings (i.e., any capital gain or loss). As Table 3-2 shows, this also produces the same net income figures. Hence, economic net income for the firm is equal to the economic net income to the shareholders. Further, the present value of the asset is equal to its market value at any point in time.[9] Moreover, the market value (present

---

of the *earnings rate (r*)* is that rate which will discount the asset's future cash flows to a present value equal to the acquisition cost of the asset. It is also known as the *internal rate of return* or the *time adjusted rate of return*. More formally, r^* has the property that

$$\text{acquisition cost} \equiv \sum_{t=1}^{T} \frac{C_t}{(1 + r^*)^t}$$

In the example,

$$\$1000 = \frac{\$600}{(1 + .10)} + \frac{\$550}{(1 + .10)^2}$$

[9] The entry price of the assets (i.e., what it would cost to purchase the asset) is equal to its exit price (i.e., what it could be sold for), which in turn is equal to its value in use

value) of the asset is equal to the market value (present value) of the firm is equal to the market value (present value) of the firm's equity.

With 100 shares outstanding, the market price per share is $10 as of the beginning of year 1, and the earnings per share (EPS) is $1. The price-earnings ratio is 10 times. In year 2 the beginning market price would be $5 and the EPS would be $.50. Again the price-earnings ratio would be 10 times, and it is equal to the reciprocal of the interest rate of 10 percent.

In this simple context there would be little dispute about the attributes of this measure of net income, and it would have the "desirable" properties discussed in Chapter 1. In any given time period, more net income is preferred to less. In evaluating management's stewardship function, a more preferred management action will result in a higher net income than a less preferred management action. In year 1 the implications for management's stewardship with respect to this asset are reflected in the cash flows of year 2 and in their present value. Hence, the net income of year 1 reflects the impact of management's actions in the subsequent year. Not only is this measure of net income virtually unassailable in the context of this simple setting, but no notions of accrual accounting were required in order to generate this number. Economic earnings is a valuation concept, not an accounting concept, as has been eloquently argued by Treynor (1972), among others. It could have been generated with a modicum of knowledge about the present value model, but it does not require knowledge of financial accounting.

However, various financial accounting proposals on how to measure *accounting* net income have been evaluated in terms of their proximity to the measure of economic net income. For example, if straight-line depreciation were applied to the asset described above, accounting net income would be equal to economic net income. The book value of the asset at any point in time (i.e., its acquisition cost less accumulated depreciation) would be equal to the market value of the asset and to the present value of its remaining cash flows. This is illustrated in Table 3-3. As a matter of fact, there exists extensive literature in financial accounting called *depreciation theory* that evaluates the relative merits of various depreciation schemes in precisely this manner.[10] In this setting, net income is a well-defined concept and is a byproduct of the valuation process. However, such a characterization is redundant and the merits of computing earnings are unclear.

(i.e., its present value). Hence, there is no ambiguity about the definition of the market value of the asset at any point in time.

[10] This literature is discussed and bibliographic references are given in Beaver and Dukes (1973, 1974).

TABLE 3-3

Financial Statements for a Single-Asset Firm

	Year	
	1	2
Cash Flows	$600	$550
Less: Straight-Line Depreciation	(500)	(500)
Accounting Net Income	$100	$ 50
Book Value of Asset at Beginning of Year:		
Original Cost	$1000	$1000
Less: Accumulated Depreciation	0	500
Net Book Value of Asset	$1000	$ 500
Book Value of Firm and Equity	$1000	$500
Accounting Return on Investment:		
$\dfrac{\text{Accounting Net Income}}{\text{Beginning Book Value of Firm}}$	$\dfrac{\$100}{\$1000} = 10\%$	$\dfrac{\$50}{\$500} = 10\%$
Accounting Return on Equity:		
$\dfrac{\text{Net Income Available for Common}}{\text{Beginning Book Value of Equity}}$	$\dfrac{\$100}{\$1000} = 10\%$	$\dfrac{\$50}{\$500} = 10\%$
$\dfrac{\text{Market Value of Equity}}{\text{Accounting Net Income}}$	$\dfrac{\$1000}{\$100} = 10X$	$\dfrac{\$500}{\$50} = 10X$

A Multi-Asset (Infinite-life) Firm

Now consider a firm that purchases an asset identical to the one described in the previous illustration once each year. In a "steady state" the firm will report the financial results depicted in Table 3-4. The financial results will be the same for each year in perpetuity. For simplicity, the financing of the additional investment in assets of $1000 per year is assumed to be provided via internal equity financing (i.e., via the retention of a portion of cash flows from operations).

In this simple "no-growth" case, the annual net cash flow from operations is $1150, the sum of the cash flows from the two assets held. At the beginning of each year the firm is assumed to have just purchased a new asset. As a result, at the start of each year the firm has one asset new (i.e., with a two-year life) and one asset one-year old (i.e., with one year remaining). At the end of that year the new asset will produce cash flows of $600 and the one-year old asset will produce cash flows of $550. Each asset has an economic depreciation of $500, as illustrated in the single-asset example, and total depreciation for both assets is $1000. Economic net income is $150 (i.e., $1150 less $1000).

Each year the firm purchases an additional asset with an acquisition cost of $1000, which is financed out of the cash flows from operations.

TABLE 3-4

Multi-Asset Firm
(No-Growth)

Net Cash Flows ($600 + $550)	$1150
Less Economic Depreciation ($500 + $500)	⟨$1000⟩
Economic Net Income ($100 + $50)	$150
Dividend ($1150−$1000)ᵃ	$150
Present Value of Dividend	$\dfrac{\$150}{.10} = \$1500$
Stream (i.e., PV of Equity)	
Market Value of Firm and Equity	$1500
Permanent Earnings	$1500 × .10 = $150
Market Price per Share	$15
Economic Earnings per Share	$1.50
Price-Earnings Ratio	10X
Dividend per Share	$1.50
Payout Ratio	
$\dfrac{\text{Dividend per Share}}{\text{Earnings per Share}}$	$\dfrac{\$1.50}{1.50} = 100\%$

ᵃCash flows of $1150 less the additional investment required to keep the firm in "steady-state."

As a result, each year the firm pays out a dividend of $150 ($1150 less $1000). The present value of the perpetuity of $150 (assuming an interest rate of 10 percent) is $1500 (i.e., $150/.10).[11] Of course, the market value of the firm and its equity will equal the present value of that perpetual dividend stream and hence also is $1500. With 100 shares outstanding, the market price per share will be $15 and the economic net income per share is $1.50. The ratio of market price to economic earnings per share will be 10 times, the reciprocal of the interest rate of 10 percent (i.e., $1/.10 = 10$ times). The payout ratio with respect to economic earnings is 100 percent (i.e., $1.50/$1.50).

The analysis can be easily extended to a "growth" case by the retention of a portion of economic earnings (i.e., by paying a smaller dividend than economic earnings). Consider a second firm identical to the one above, except that the second firm follows a policy of paying out dividends equal to 60 percent of its economic earnings. Specifically, at the beginning of a year in which its economic earnings are $150, the payout ratio is 60 percent (instead of 100 percent) of $150 (and subsequent economic earnings). This implies an amount invested of $60 more than if all of economic earnings are paid out. As a result, economic earnings will grow by 4 percent per year. For example, the additional

---

[11] The present value of a perpetual annuity of $X per year at a discount rate of r is X/r.

$60 available for investment will earn at a rate of 10 percent, which means that next year's economic earnings will be higher by $6. Economic earnings will increase from $150 in one year to $156 in the next year, which is a growth rate of 4 percent. The dividend paid out in the next year will be $93.60 (i.e., $156 times .60), which is 4 percent higher than the previous dividend of $90. In this situation, both economic earnings and dividends will grow at 4 percent per year.

But does this alter the present value of the dividend stream and hence the price of the common stock relative to a no-growth case? The answer is no. Although the initial dividend is lower ($.90 per share rather than $1.50 per share), it will grow at 4 percent per year, while there will be zero growth in the 100 percent payout. It can be easily shown that, *as of the beginning of the year*, the present values of these two streams are both equal to $15. It is implied by the constant dividend growth model of Williams (1938), among others.[12] The formula states:

$$P_0 = \frac{D_1}{r - g}$$

where P_0 = price per share at the *beginning* of the year (e.g., $t = 0$);
     D_1 = dividend paid at the end of the year (e.g., $t = 1$);
     r = interest rate (assumed constant); and
     g = growth in dividends (assumed constant).

For the no-growth case,

$$P_0 = \frac{\$1.50}{.10 - 0} = \frac{\$1.50}{.10} = \$15$$

For the growth case,

$$P_0 = \frac{\$.90}{.10 - .04} = \frac{\$.90}{.06} = \$15$$

Of course, subsequently a growth in price per share will occur to reflect the retention policy. In the no-growth case, not surprisingly, the price per share remains constant. In the growth case, the price (per share) will grow at the same rate as dividends (per share) and economic earnings (per share). In the example this growth rate was 4 percent. In particular, with 100 shares outstanding, the market value (per share) of the equity will increase from $1500 ($15) at the beginning of the year

[12] The formula follows directly from the equation for the sum of an infinite geo-metric progression and is discussed further in Sharpe (1978). More generally, the term *discount rate* is used rather than the interest rate. However, under certainty, the discount rate is the interest rate, which has been assumed to be constant over time.

($t = 0$) to \$1560 (\$15.60) at the end of the year ($t = 1$). However, since price (per share) and economic earnings per share are growing at the same rate, the price-earnings ratio will be constant and will be the same regardless of the growth assumption. In the example the ratio of price to economic earnings is 10 times in both the no-growth and growth cases.[13] Given the assumptions of this example, the growth rate in dividends and earnings bears a direct relationship to the payout policy of the firm. In particular, the growth will equal the product of the earnings rate on additional investment (here, the interest rate) times the retention ratio, where the retention ratio is defined as that percentage of earnings not paid out in dividends (e.g., one minus the payout ratio).[14] In the numerical example the growth rate of 4 percent is the product of the interest rate of 10 percent times the retention ratio of .40. More elaborate forms of financing (e.g., debt financing and external equity financing) could be introduced, and price per share would still be characterized by the simple dividend growth formula.[15]

---

[13] In the constant dividend growth model the price-earnings ratio P_0/E_1^* is

$$\frac{P_0}{E_1^*} = \frac{K^*}{r - g}$$

For the no-growth case,

$$\frac{P_0}{E_1^*} = \frac{1}{.10 - 0} = \frac{1}{.10} = 10$$

For the growth case,

$$\frac{P_0}{E_1^*} = \frac{.6}{10 - .06} = \frac{.6}{.06} = 10$$

This formula follows from the one introduced above by noting that the payout ratio (K^*) is defined here as the ratio of dividends to *economic* earnings. Divide both sides of the expression by E_1^* (economic earnings) and

$$P_0 = \frac{D_1}{r - g}$$

becomes

$$\frac{P_0}{E_1^*} = \frac{K^*}{r - g}$$

[14] There are no abnormal earnings opportunities (i.e., because the earnings rate equals the interest rate). Both growth and no-growth cases have the same price-earnings ratios. There are no "growth premiums" here, and the price-earnings ratio equals $1/r$ regardless of the growth rate.

[15] Obviously, this statement is being made in the context of the economy-wide assumptions of certainty as well as perfect and complete markets. In this context, the distinction between debt and equity as well as the distinction between external and internal equity financing is trivial. Hence, the emphasis on an all-equity firm is not restrictive in this setting.

3-3. PERMANENT EARNINGS

In the multi-asset example, economic earnings in a certainty setting have two properties that have not been explicitly discussed. (1) The first property is the permanent earnings property. Permanent earnings are equal to that constant (i.e., no growth) dividend, which if received in perpetuity would have the same value as that of the dividend stream that will actually be paid out.[16] Economic earnings equal permanent earnings and are $1.50 per share in both the no-growth and growth examples. Of course, this is obvious for the no-growth case. However, economic earnings have the same property in the growth case as well. As indicated earlier, the investor would be indifferent between receiving a constant dividend of $1.50 in perpetuity or receiving a dividend stream that started at $.90 and grew by 4 percent per year. Hence, the concept applies to growth situations. Permanent earnings can be computed by multiplying the beginning price per share times the interest rate (i.e., $15 times .10 = $1.50).[17]

(2) Economic earnings also have another property, known as a *distributable income* property. It measures the amount of dividends that could be paid out without reducing the present value (i.e., market price) of the remaining cash flows below the beginning-of-period present value.[18] For example, in the no-growth case, the dividend amount ($1.50) is equal to the amount of economic earnings ($1.50), and the result is a constant price per share over time. In the growth case, the payout is less than economic earnings and as a result price per share grows. Alternatively

---

[16] More formally, at $t = 0$,

$$\frac{\text{permanent earnings}}{r} \equiv \sum_{t=1}^{\infty} \frac{D_t}{(1 + r)^t} = P_0$$

$$\text{permanent earnings} \equiv r \cdot \left[\sum_{t=1}^{\infty} \frac{D_t}{(1 + r)^t} \right]$$

$$\equiv r P_0$$

where r = interest rate;

P_0 = price per share;

D_t = dividend in period t.

[17] Specifically, in the growth case,

$$\frac{\$1.50}{.10} \equiv \frac{.90}{(1 + .10)} + \frac{.90(1 + .04)}{(1.10)^2} + \cdots = \$15$$

or

$$\$1.50 \equiv .10 \cdot \$15 = .10 \left[\sum_{t=1}^{\infty} \frac{.90(1 + .04)^{t-1}}{(1 + .10)^t} \right]$$

[18] This concept is also known as distributable income flow [Revsine (1973)], or sustainable income [Davidson, Skelton, and Weil (1979)]. Extensions of the distributable income concept arise when inflation is explicitly introduced.

stated, cash flow less permanent earnings measures the amount of additional investment required in order to keep constant (i.e., to avoid reducing) the present value of the remaining cash flows and hence the price of the share.

The concept of permanent earnings is central to security analysis and security valuation [Cottle, Murray, and Block (1988)]. In security analysis, accounting earnings are used to form assessments of the *permanent earnings* of the firm and its common stock. However, as defined here, the concept of permanent earnings, as well as the concept of economic earnings, is essentially a valuation concept. Permanent earnings are equal to the present value of the remaining cash flows times the interest rate; neither component is an accounting concept.

While permanent earnings are illustrated above in the context of a constant dividend growth model, the concept is general and can be applied to any arbitrary cash flow stream. For example, although often applied only to a multi-asset, infinite-life context, the concept of permanent earnings applies equally to a single, finite-life asset. In the single-asset example the permanent earnings is $100 ($1000 times 10 percent) for year 1 and is $50 ($500 times 10 percent) for year 2. Note that at the beginning of year 1 the investor is indifferent between receiving a constant dividend of $100 in perpetuity or receiving cash flows of $600 and $550 at the end of years 1 and 2, respectively. Both streams have present values of $1000 as of the beginning of year 1. The permanent earnings of the firm and its equity decline over time because the dividend paid ($600 in year 1) exceeds permanent earnings ($100 in year 1) by $500. If the firm had paid out only $100 and invested the additional amount retained, the present value of the remaining cash flows and hence the price per share of common stock would not have declined. Hence, economic earnings, in a single-asset, negative-growth case, also have both the permanent earnings and distributable income properties.

These earnings properties are summarized in Table 3-5. The key feature is that *value and earnings are two sides of the same coin.*

3-4. EARNINGS VERSUS CASH FLOWS AS AN INDICATOR OF FUTURE DIVIDEND-PAYING ABILITY

In this context, the FASB's emphasis on earnings as the primary focus of financial reporting can be examined. The FASB's contention is that dividend-paying ability is better measured by accounting earnings than by current cash flows. The FASB's point is difficult to understand in the no-growth case because cash flows from operations less investment equal earnings. However, consider the single-asset example. The FASB's

TABLE 3-5

Summary of Concepts of Earnings[a]

I. Economic Earnings

Cash flows received plus change in present value of remaining cash flows

II. Permanent Earnings

That constant cash flow which if received in perpetuity would have the same present value as that of the remaining cash flows and computed as the present value at the beginning of the period times the interest rate

III. Distributable Earnings

The amount that could be paid out in dividends without reducing the present value of the remaining cash flows relative to the beginning-of-period value

---

[a] Note that, under the assumptions of this chapter, the market value of an asset or a claim is equal to the present value of the future cash flows. Hence, the term *market value* can be substituted for the term *present value* in the definitions. Obviously, consideration must be made for deposits and withdrawals in defining the earnings of the firm.

contention can be interpreted as saying that the *economic* earnings in year 1 of $100 is a better measure of the dividend-paying capacity of the firm than is the cash flow of $600 that was paid out in dividends. The reason is that a dividend of $600 could not be paid out in perpetuity and as a result reduces the present value of the remaining cash flows.

Also consider the growth case in the multi-asset example. The dividends paid out are only $90, but the economic earnings are $150. The dividend of $90 "understates" the future dividend-paying ability of the firm, because the $90-dividend permits a growth of 4 percent in future dividends. This is reflected in an increase in the present value of the dividend stream from $1500 (at the beginning of the period) to $1560 (at the end of the period). The $60 reflects the present value of the increased dividend-paying ability. The sum of $90 plus $60 (i.e., $150) reflects the total dividend-paying ability and is equal to the economic earnings.

In the security analysis literature a motivation for using accounting earnings as parameters of the security valuation model stems from the belief that accounting earnings ("properly" interpreted and adjusted) provide a measure of the "dividend-paying capacity" of the firm. In this sense, the security analysis literature is interested in the permanent earnings property of economic earnings. Permanent earnings reflect the dividend stream that could be paid out in perpetuity. *Hence, the vector of actual future dividends, regardless of their pattern or length of life, is reduced to a scalar, a single number, called permanent earnings.* It is clear from the definition of permanent earnings how an "earnings" concept can measure the "dividend-paying" capacity (cash flow concept). However, the relationship between accounting earnings and permanent earnings (i.e., economic earnings) is less clear.

3-5. ACCOUNTING EARNINGS AND ECONOMIC EARNINGS

It is common in security analysis to use accounting earnings as an input to a valuation formula, such as the constant dividend growth model. For example, growth in earnings per share is often used rather than growth in dividends per share. Moreover, the ratio of stock price per share to accounting earnings per share (hereafter P/E ratios) can be characterized by the following formula, which is a direct extension of the formula cited earlier.

$$\frac{P_0}{E_1} = \frac{K}{r - g}$$

where P_0, r, and g are defined as before: E_1 equals the *accounting* earnings per share reported for the year; and K equals the ratio of dividends per share for the year (D_1) to *accounting* earnings per share for the year (E_1).

What definitions of accounting earnings are consistent with such an expression for price-earnings ratios? Initially, one would speculate that if accounting earnings equal economic (or permanent) earnings, the expression would be correct. However, as the equation now stands, *any* definition of accounting earnings is consistent because the equation was derived from the constant dividend growth model by merely dividing both sides of the equation by accounting earnings per share (E_1). The result is a P/E ratio on the left-hand side and a payout ratio (K) on the right-hand side. It provides one characterization of the determinants of price-earnings ratios, and it will hold for *any* definition of accounting earnings because it is tautological. If the constant dividend growth model is "valid," then the derived expression for the P/E ratio must follow. In fact, if the constant dividend growth model is valid, then we can divide both sides of the equation by *any arbitrary constant* and the resulting equation will still hold. If accounting earnings measure economic earnings with error, this will be merely reflected in the payout ratio. Although such a characterization is logically valid, it is devoid of any substance or additional insight.

Note, however, that growth in dividends is still used in the denominator of the right-hand side. Suppose that the growth in accounting earnings is used in place of the growth in dividends. This implicitly assumes that the payout ratio will be constant over time. If the payout ratio is not constant over time, the growth in earnings will not equal the growth in dividends, and hence the former cannot be used to measure the latter. If the payout ratio is constant over time, the growth in earnings equals the growth in dividends, and hence the growth in earnings can be used to measure the growth in dividends.

If the payout ratio is a constant, then the definition of accounting earnings used must have certain properties. Intuitively, it would be suspected that if accounting earnings equal economic earnings, this would be a sufficient condition. This intuition is correct. But requiring equality of the two earnings measures is too strong. As long as accounting earnings are proportional to economic earnings by a factor that is constant over time, accounting earnings can be used in the manner described above. Alternatively stated, accounting earnings can be used as if they were a measure of economic earnings. If the constant of proportionality is not one (i.e., if the two earnings are not the same), the price-earnings ratio and the payout ratio will reflect the constant of proportionality to compensate for the inequality. Different measures of accounting earnings are equally "correct" as long as both ratios are appropriately defined. For example, suppose that accounting earnings have the property that they are always exactly twice economic earnings. The price-earnings ratio and the payout ratio, defined in terms of accounting earnings, will be one-half the value of the ratios defined in terms of economic earnings. However, they are equivalent characterizations. For example, suppose that in the earlier growth example, *accounting* earnings are $3.00:

$$\frac{P_0}{E_1} = \frac{\$15}{\$3} = 5 = \frac{\$90/\$3.00}{.10 - .04} = \frac{.30}{.06}$$

$$\frac{D_1}{E_1} = \frac{\$.90}{\$3.00} = 30\%$$

For economic earnings E_1^*);

$$\frac{P_0}{E_1^*} = \frac{\$15}{\$1.50} = 10 = \frac{\$.90/\$1.50}{.10 - .04} = \frac{.60}{.06}$$

$$\frac{D_1}{E_1^*} = \frac{\$.90}{\$1.50} = 60\%$$

Obviously, the growth in accounting earnings per share will equal the growth economic earnings per share and the growth in dividends per share. Note, however, that the P/E ratio cannot be interpreted as the reciprocal of the interest rate, except in the special case in which accounting earnings equal economic earnings.

3-6. ANALYSIS OF ALTERNATIVE ACCOUNTING METHODS

The impact of alternative accounting methods can be analyzed in two respects. (1) An analysis can be conducted of the relationship between economic income and accounting net income under various alternatives. The difference between economic income and accounting income can be thought of as the extent to which accounting income measures economic income with error. Obviously, this requires a setting in which economic income is well defined. The context of this chapter (perfect and complete markets and certainty) provides one such setting. Alternative accounting methods can be analyzed in terms of the *measurement error* that occurs under specified conditions. (2) An analysis also can be conducted of the *descriptive differences* induced by alternative methods under specified conditions. This requires no notion of economic income. Both types of analyses will be illustrated here in the context of alternative depreciation methods.

Measurement Error in Accounting Earnings

Accounting earnings may not be equal to the economic (permanent) earnings of the firm. The difference between accounting earnings and economic permanent earnings can be called the measurement error in accounting earnings. One reason for an error is that a firm can use different accounting methods (e.g., straight-line or accelerated depreciation methods) that can affect the level of accounting earnings. This can induce a difference in the level of earnings that is unrelated to the future dividend-paying ability of the firm. Price-earnings ratios of firms that use different depreciation methods would also differ.

For example, consider a firm that grows by 4 percent per year. If the asset acquisition cost was $1000 in the previous year, this year's asset acquisition cost is $1040. At the beginning of the year the firm holds a one-year-old asset (with one year remaining) and a new two-year asset. The assets purchased are identical to the one illustrated in Tables 3-2, 3-3, and 3-4 *per dollar of acquisition cost*. However, the dollar amount of the asset purchased is assumed to grow by 4 percent per year (i.e., from $1000 to $1040). The financial results, assuming straight-line (SL) and sum-of-the-years-digits (SYD) depreciation, are reported in Table 3-6.

Note that the economic depreciation on this asset is equal to straight-line depreciation. As a result, accounting net income under straight-line depreciation is equal to *economic income*. The book value of the asset, firm, and equity under straight-line is equal to the present value of the remaining cash flows and is equal to the market value of the asset, firm,

TABLE 3-6

Differences in Financial Statement Results
Due to Depreciation Differences

	Depreciation SL	Method[a] SYD
Cash Flows (550 + 624)[b]	$1174	$1174
Depreciation	$1020	1027
Net Income	$ 154	$ 147
Beginning Book Value of Asset, Firm, and Equity		
Original Cost (1000 + 1040)	$2040	$2040
Less: Accumulated Depreciation	500	667
	$1540	$1373
Market Value and Present Value of Assets, Firm, and Equity	$1540	$1540
Market Value of Equity[c] / Net Income	$\dfrac{\$1540}{\$154} = 10X$	$\dfrac{\$1540}{\$147} = 10.48X$
Return on Equity: Net Income / Beginning Book Value	$\dfrac{\$154}{\$1540} = 10\%$	$\dfrac{\$147}{\$1373} = 10.71\%$

[a]SL = straight-line depreciation
SYD = sum-of-the-years-digits depreciation
[b]Cash flows = $550 + (1 + g)$600 = $1150 + g$600$
Depreciation (SL) = $500 + (1 + g)$500 = $1000 + g$500$
Net income (SL) = $150 + g$100$
Depreciation (SYD) = $333 + (1 + g)$667 = $1000 + g$667$
Net income (SYD) = $150 - g$67$
Original cost = $1000 + (1 + g)$1000 = $2000 + g$1000$
Accumulated depreciation (SL) = $500
Accumulated depreciation (SYD) = $667
Market value = present value = book value under SL
Growth Rate = $g = .04$
[c]This is also the price-earning ratio (i.e., market value per share divided by earnings per share).

and the equity. The price-earnings ratio is 10 times, which is the reciprocal of the interest rate. The accounting rate of return is 10 percent, which is the earnings rate (here, the interest rate).[19] This is hardly surprising and would be expected to occur in this growth case as it did in the single-asset (i.e., negative-growth) and no-growth case.

However, the net income under SYD is lower ($147 versus $154). As a result, the price-earnings ratio is higher (10.48 versus 10 times). Moreover, the accounting return (10.71 percent) does not equal the

---

[19] The term *earnings rate* is defined in footnote 8.

earnings rate (10 percent). The difference in depreciation methods can be called the measurement error in depreciation under SYD, and the net income under SYD can be said to measure economic income with error. Obviously, the absolute difference in earnings will change over time as the firm grows. However, the proportional difference in net income, the price-earnings ratio, and the accounting rate of return are a constant for a given level of (constant) growth.

As a result, it is possible to specify the values of the ratio of net income, the price-earnings ratio, and the accounting rate of return as a function of the growth rate. These variables are reported in Table 3-7 for growth rates ranging from 0 percent to 20 percent.[20]

Several inferences can be drawn from the illustration:

(1) Accounting income under straight-line equals economic income, and hence the measurement error is zero.

(2) As a result, the price-earnings ratio under straight-line depreciation remains a constant with respect to the assumed growth rate and is equal to the reciprocal of the interest rate (10 times).

(3) As a result, the accounting rate of return under straight-line depreciation remains a constant regardless of the assumed growth rate and is equal to the earnings rate (10 percent).

TABLE 3-7

Effect of Growth on
Financial Statement Results[a]

Growth Rate	Ratio of Net Income Under SL vs. SYD	Ratio of Market Value of Equity to Net Income		Return on Equity	
		SL	SYD	SL	SYD
0%	1.00	10X	10X	10%	11.25%
4%	1.048	10X	10.48X	10%	10.71%
6%	1.068	10X	10.68X	10%	10.48%
10%	1.119	10X	11.19X	10%	10%
20%	1.241	10X	12.41X	10%	8.94%

[a] Firm assumed to be purchasing an asset with a two-year life and in which straight-line is economic depreciation. The earnings rate and the interest rate are assumed to be 10%. These cases assume that the firms are in "steady state" (i.e., the firms are "mature"). In general, for an asset with a useful life of N years, the firm must be at least N years old. Here, $N = 2$.

[20] Throughout, the firm is assumed to be purchasing a two-year asset whose cash flows are identical to the one illustrated in Tables 3-2 and 3-4 *per dollar of acquisition cost.* The amount (in dollars) of the asset purchased is assumed to grow at the indicated rate.

(4)   Accounting income under SYD depreciation is less than income under straight-line depreciation and, as a result, understates economic income for all positive growth rates, and the proportional difference is greater the higher the assumed growth rate. For the special case of zero growth, accounting income under both depreciation methods and economic income is equal.

(5)   The price-earnings ratio under SYD depreciation exceeds the price-earnings ratio under straight-line depreciation and, as a result, exceeds the reciprocal of the interest rate for all positive rates of growth. The price-earnings ratio is greater the higher the assumed growth rate.

(6)   The accounting rate of return in general does not measure the earnings rate. For the special case in which the growth rate equals the earnings rate, the accounting rate of return will also equal the earnings rate. At growth rates below the earnings rate, the accounting return will overstate the earnings rate; the reverse is true for growth rates below the earnings rate.

It is important to sort out the features that are particular to the illustration from inferences that are applicable in more general settings. In this illustration the economic depreciation is equal to straight-line depreciation. As a result, SYD measures economic depreciation with error and is "too accelerated" for this asset. However, it would be possible to construct other assets whose cash flow pattern implied different patterns of economic depreciation. For example, constant cash flows imply an economic depreciation equal to the annuity or sinking fund method, some forms of linearly declining cash flows are consistent with straight-line depreciation, and some forms of quadratically declining cash flows are associated with SYD depreciation.[21] These are summarized in Figure 3-1.

Therefore, the properties exhibited by straight-line depreciation in Tables 3-2 through 3-7 arise out of the assumption on the pattern of the asset's cash flows. For other types of assets, straight-line depreciation can lead to either an overstatement or understatement of economic income. Hence, the major point of the illustration is *not* the "superiority" of straight-line depreciation. However, two generalizations do emerge.[22]

(1)   When economic income is well-defined, it is possible to examine the "measurement error" associated with alternative accounting methods, such as alternative depreciation methods.

---

[21] This approach is discussed in greater detail in Beaver and Dukes (1974) which examines a comprehensive class of depreciation methods. A bibliography of earlier research is also summarized there.

[22] Obviously, these "generalizations" are made within the context of a setting in which economic income is well-defined (e.g., perfect and complete markets and certainty).

CASH FLOW PATTERN   ECONOMIC DEPRECIATION PATTERN

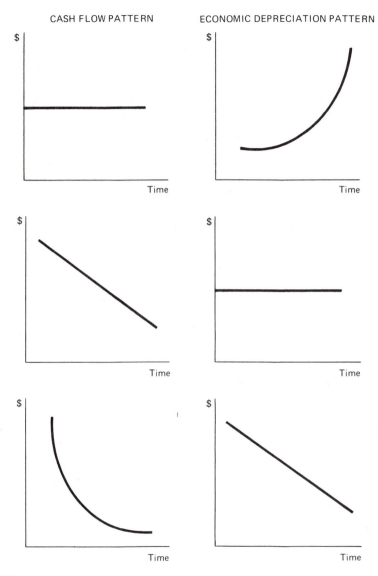

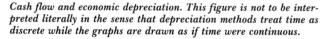

FIGURE 3-1

Cash flow and economic depreciation. This figure is not to be interpreted literally in the sense that depreciation methods treat time as discrete while the graphs are drawn as if time were continuous.

    (2) The nature of the measurement error in general will be a function of (a) the cash flow pattern of the assets (including useful life), (b) the acquisition cost of the assets, (c) the accounting alternative chosen, (d) the growth rate, and (e) the earnings rate.[23]

Extensions of Analysis of Measurement Error

The illustration thus far has focused on alternative depreciation methods. The same type of analysis can be applied to other accounting alternatives. For example, Beaver (1979) examines the properties of historical cost accounting, price level accounting, and replacement cost accounting in a setting of perfect and complete markets and certainty. In principle, any set of alternatives would be amenable to such an analysis.

The discussion this far has also focused on the impact of alternative accounting methods applied to the *same* firm. However, measurement errors can also be induced by applying uniform methods to "different" firms. For example, applying the same depreciation methods (e.g., straight-line) to firms with differing patterns of cash flows can induce measurement errors in one or both firms.

In this context, measurement errors in accounting income can occur under (1) the application of different methods to the same set of events (e.g., the same firm) or (2) the application of the same method to different events (e.g., firms with different types of assets). These constitute two major reasons why accounting earnings may not equal economic earnings and may not reflect the dividend-paying ability of the firm.

Analysis of Descriptive Differences

An analysis can also be conducted of the descriptive differences induced in various financial results by the use of alternative accounting methods. Such an analysis is less ambitious in the sense that it does not require any notion of economic income. With factors (a) and (b) cited at the end of the subsection on measurement error in accounting earnings, the effect of factors (c) and (d) on accounting net income and accounting rate of return can be examined. Moreover, if the market value of the firm, asset, and equity is invariant to the accounting method used, it is also possible to examine the effects of accounting alternatives on price-earnings ratios.[24] Alternatively stated, the analysis of descriptive differences can be viewed as examining the extent to which alternative

---

[23] Note that the cash flows, together with the acquisition cost, jointly determine the earnings rate, which because of the assumptions abut the economy also equals the interest rate.

[24] Clearly, this invariance is an assumption about the valuation process. Perfect and complete markets are sufficient conditions to induce an invariance property.

accounting methods affect financial measures *when they are applied to the same firm*.

Several conclusions emerge from an analysis.[25]

(1) In general, accounting net income, price-earnings ratios, and accounting rates of return systematically vary as a function of the accounting method used. Moreover, the impact on these variables of different accounting methods in general is a function of the growth rate. In other words, in general, for a given firm (i.e., for *given* cash flows and acquisition cost), accounting net income, price-earnings ratios, and accounting rate of return will not only depend upon the accounting method used but also the growth rate.

(2) For a given firm, the difference in accounting net income and in price-earnings ratios under alternative accounting methods is *zero* when the growth rate is *zero* for a "mature" firm, where the age of the firm is at least as great as the useful life of the assets. In general, the difference will vary directly with the growth rate. The difference in net income will be of opposite sign when the growth rate is positive versus negative.[26]

(3) For a given firm, the difference in the accounting rate of return will also be a function of the growth rate. There will be no difference when the growth rate equals the earnings rate. The absolute value of the difference will become proportionately larger as the absolute value of the difference between the growth rate and the earnings rate becomes larger. The difference in accounting rate of return will be of opposite sign when the growth rate is above versus below the earnings rate.

Empirical Evidence
on the Invariance Property

The empirical evidence [Beaver and Dukes (1973)] indicates that price-earnings ratios systematically differ as a function of the depreciation method used for annual report purposes. In particular, firms using accelerated depreciation for annual report purposes, on the average, do in fact have higher price-earnings ratios than firms using straight-line depreciation for annual report purposes (all firms in the sample used accelerated depreciation for tax purposes). Moreover, an analysis of other factors indicated that differences in risk, growth, or payout do not

---

[25] A bibliography of analyses which produce these conclusions appears in Beaver and Dukes (1974).

[26] The negative growth case is not illustrated in Table 3-7. Moreover, these generalizations also apply to finite-lived situations. However, for convenience, the discussion has used the illustration of the constant (infinite) growth firm.

explain this difference. In fact, on the average, the firms using accelerated depreciation have essentially the same risk, growth, and payout as firms using straight-line depreciation. Moreover, when the earnings of the firms using accelerated depreciation are converted to the earnings that would have been reported had straight-line depreciation been used, the differences in price-earnings ratios disappear. In other words, when the earnings of the firms using accelerated depreciation are converted to an accounting basis equivalent to that of the firms using straight-line depreciation, the price-earnings ratios of the two groups of firms are essentially the same. This is consistent with security prices that reflect adjustment for differences in the level of earnings induced by accounting method differences. If prices are not dependent upon the method of accounting used but accounting earnings are, the ratio of price to earnings will be dependent upon the method of accounting used. In other words, even if the prices are the same regardless of which accounting method is used, accounting earnings will be affected by the method chosen. Hence, price-earnings ratios computed under differing accounting methods will differ, even though price-earnings ratios computed under a consistent, uniform method of accounting would show no difference in price-earnings ratios. The evidence supports the invariance property used earlier.[27]

3-7. CONCLUDING REMARKS

In the perfect and complete markets and certainty setting, the concept of economic earnings is well-defined. Moreover, it has several properties. (1) More earnings are better than less in any given year, holding earnings constant in other years. (2) Earnings reflect the stewardship of management and multiperiod effects of management's decisions. (3) Unanimity exists among investors regarding shareholder wealth maximization, which can be characterized in terms of a unanimous preference for projects with greater earnings.

However, in this setting, economic earnings fall out of the analysis as a byproduct of the valuation process. Earnings and valuation are two

---

[27] Note that the evidence does not imply any relationship between earnings under straight-line and economic earnings. An adjustment of the sample firms' earnings to a uniform basis based on an accelerated depreciation method could also have produced the same result (i.e., an equality of price-earnings ratios). The evidence is offered here with respect to the invariance property (i.e., the invariance of prices to the accounting method used for annual report purposes). The context is one of the descriptive differences, not measurement error. Neither the existence of economic earnings nor its relationship to any particular form of accounting earnings is assumed or inferred in the discussion of the empirical evidence.

sides of the same coin. This is readily apparent in the permanent earnings property of economic earnings, where earnings are computed as the present value (or market value) times the interest rate. Value and earnings are linked via the interest rate. One is a stock concept, the other is a flow, and the interest rate is used to make the transition from one to the other. Both are scalars representing a vector of intertemporal future cash flows. The assumptions about the markets ensure that nothing is lost in representing a vector of cash flows in terms of a single member.

In this setting, earnings are redundant and can be derived only after valuation of the firm and its equity has been determined. In other words, the notion of earnings is a valuation concept. To derive economic earnings requires a modicum of knowledge of the present value model. However, no knowledge of financial accounting is required. In particular, the role of the accrual process is unclear. Value and hence economic earnings can be derived directly from an observation of the market values of assets and claims. To be sure, alternative accrual methods can be evaluated in terms of their ability to produce accounting earnings numbers that approximate economic earnings. Also analyses of the descriptive differences in earnings induced by alternative accounting methods can be examined. However, the insight gained from an earnings characterization is not clear. Once value is determined, an earnings concept is redundant. Moreover, the accrual process is unnecessary since observing prices is sufficient.

Of course, these conclusions have been drawn in a special setting. It is possible that in a different setting the accounting earnings take on additional roles. For example, the assumptions of perfect and complete markets would probably be regarded as "unrealistic." However, dropping these assumptions raises questions as to the validity of the present value model and hence the meaning of economic earnings. Earnings based on market values of assets traded in existing markets may not have the desirable properties generally attributed to the "ideal" measure of earnings. Moreover, accounting earnings are typically viewed as one of the determinants of value, not vice versa.

This naturally leads to the next topic—earnings under uncertainty in imperfect, incomplete markets.

BIBLIOGRAPHY

BEAVER, W. "Accounting for Inflation in an Efficient Market." *International Journal of Accounting* (1979), 21–42.

———— AND J. DEMSKI. "The Nature of Income Measurement." *Accounting Review* (January 1979), 38–46.

———— AND R. DUKES. "Interperiod Tax Allocation and Delta Depreciation Methods: Some Empirical Results." *Accounting Review* (July 1973), 549–559.

――― AND R. DUKES. "Delta-Depreciation Methods: Some Analytical Results." *Journal of Accounting Research* (August 1974), 205–215.

――― AND D. MORSE. "What Determines Price-Earnings Ratios?" *Financial Analysts Journal* (July–August 1978), 65–76.

COTTLE, S., R. MURRAY, AND F. BLOCK. *Security Analysis*. New York: McGraw-Hill, 1988.

DAVIDSON, S., L. SKELTON, AND R. WEIL. "Financial Reporting and Changing Prices." *Financial Analysts Journal* (May–June 1979), 41–54.

HIRSHLEIFER, J. *Investment, Interest, and Capital*. Englewood Cliffs, N.J.: Prentice-Hall, 1970.

REVSINE, L. *Replacement Cost Accounting*. Englewood Cliffs, N.J.: Prentice-Hall, 1973.

SHARPE, W. *Investments*. Englewood Cliffs, N.J.: Prentice-Hall, 1978.

TREYNOR, J. "The Trouble with Earnings." *Financial Analysts Journal* (September–October 1972), 41–43.

WILLIAMS, J. *The Theory of Investment Value*. Cambridge: Harvard University Press, 1938.

chapter four

Earnings
Under
Uncertainty

Chapter 3 examined income theory under assumptions of perfect and complete markets and certainty. These assumptions are unrealistic, and the purpose of this chapter is to extend the concept of earnings to a more general setting. The chapter will begin in the setting of perfect and complete markets under uncertainty and then move to imperfect and incomplete markets. An informational perspective to earnings will be introduced, and the chapter will close with a discussion of the role of accrual accounting in such a context.

4-1. PERFECT AND COMPLETE MARKETS
UNDER UNCERTAINTY

With perfect and complete markets, the introduction of uncertainty involves a simple extension of the analysis of the previous chapter. The notion of a perfect market is the same as it was in the certainty setting. The meaning of a complete market in an uncertain setting requires some elaboration. In the multi-period, certainty setting the claims of interest are the future cash flows, and complete markets imply that a rich set of markets exists with respect to the trading of claims to future cash flows. These markets potentially include futures markets and *spot* markets that could open in the future. In an uncertain setting the claims of interest are future, state-contingent cash flows.

As indicated in Chapter 2, uncertainty is characterized by a set of states that could occur in the future. The return from holding a security is uncertain because the cash flow it yields will depend upon which state occurs. For example, a common stock represents a complex claim to a bundle of future, state-contingent dividends. The price of the common stock will be some function of those dividends. The dividends that common stock will actually pay will depend upon which state occurs.

Under certainty, the present value of a claim is characterized by the following expression:

$$_0PV_t = {_0P_t}C_t$$

where $_0PV_t$ is the present value or price as of now ($t = 0$) for a claim to receive future cash flows at time t. $_0P_t$ is the price or present value of a claim to \$1 at time t valued as of now, and C_t is the cash flow to be received at time t. Under uncertainty but retaining perfect and complete markets, a similar characterization of the present value of a claim is possible:

$$_0PV_t = \sum_{s=1}^{S} {_0P_{st}}C_{st}$$

where $_0PV_t$ is the present value or price as of now for a claim to receive future uncertain cash flows at time t. $_0P_{st}$ is the price of a primitive claim to \$1 at time t *if state s occurs*. Each of the prices, $_0P_{st}$, reflects a combination of (1) investors' preferences for cash flows if state s occurs, derived from the underlying preference for state-contingent consumption, and (2) investors' beliefs about the probability that state s will occur. The price of the simple claim, $_0P_{st}$, jointly represents investors' beliefs about the probability that state s will occur *and* their preferences for an additional \$1 of cash flow *if state occurs*. C_{st} is the cash flow to be received from the complex security at time t *if state s occurs*. Hence a complex security is merely a collection of primitive claims.

Valuation under uncertainty is a simple extension of a similar expression under certainty and merely requires an additional indexing of claims to reflect the states as well as the time periods.[1]

---

[1] Remember that the concept of a state involves conditional certainty. If state s occurs, then there is no remaining uncertainty about what will happen. Therefore, the dividends a stock will pay in state s is certain. Moreover, this assessment does not change over time for this reason. While the arrival of information may lead investors to alter their probability that state s will occur, the amount paid at time t if state s occurs remains unchanged. Costless arbitrage, as described in Chapter 3, guarantees that value additivity is preserved (i.e., the price of a complex claim is equal to the sum of the prices of the primitive claims it represents).

Discounting under Uncertainty

A common approach to valuation of complex claims under uncertainty is to take a valuation model derived from certainty, such as the discounted cash flow model, and to replace each variable in that formula with the expected value of that variable to reflect the uncertainty. For example, consider the valuation of a common stock. In the numerator of each term the dividend in period t would be replaced by the expected value of dividends in period t. In the denominator the interest rate would be replaced by a "risky" discount rate. Typically, this is viewed as the expected value of the rate of return on other investments of identical risk.[2]

In a multi-period setting, characterizing the present value or price of a complex claim in terms of discounting expected cash flows at expected rates of return is not possible in general.[3] However, special cases can be derived. A key assumption is independence between the *ex post* past rates of return and the future expected rates of return at any point in time.[4]

A case of discounting at expected values will be illustrated by an extension of the single-asset, all-equity firm discussed in the previous chapter. The possible cash flows are described in Figure 4-1. At $t = 1$, a cash flow of either \$660 or \$540 will be received. Hereafter, the state in which \$660 is received will be called state A, and the receipt of \$540 will occur in state B. Note that the expected cash flows for $t = 1$, assessed as of $t = 0$, is \$600 because each state has an equal chance of occurring. Conditional upon state A occurring, the *expected* cash flow for $t = 2$, assessed as of $t = 1$, is \$605, while the conditional *expected* cash flow for $t = 2$ for state B is \$495.[5] As of $t = 0$, the expected cash flow for

---

[2] One model of equilibrium prices that derives expected returns is the familiar capital asset pricing model (hereafter CAPM). See Sharpe (1978) for further discussion. The "risky" discount rate is also often referred to as the *cost of capital* (or *cost of equity capital* in the case of common stock).

[3] A further discussion of this issue appears in Christie (1987), among others.

[4] Equilibrium rates of return are influenced by the investors' preferences for future wealth (e.g., cash flows), such as the degree of risk aversion [Pratt (1964)]. Also preferences for cash flows may be state-dependent, either because prices of consumption goods are state-dependent or because the preferences for consumption goods are state-dependent. State-dependent preferences for consumption goods are commonly assumed in analyses of perfect and complete markets [Hirshleifer (1970)]. Moreover, they do not violate the Savage (1972) axioms of rational choice. Furthermore, perfect and complete markets do not require expected utility maximization (implied by the Savage axioms), although it is commonly assumed. Perfect and complete markets refer to the structure of the markets, while expected utility maximization refers to individual behavior. It is possible to have either one without the other.

[5] $\$600 = (.5 \times \$660) + (.5 \times \$540)$
$\$605 = (.5 \times \$655) + (.5 \times \$555)$
$\$495 = (.5 \times \$545) + (.5 \times \$445)$

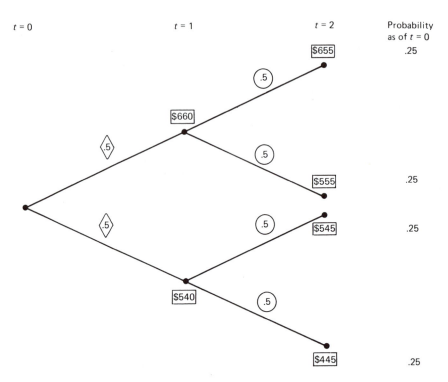

FIGURE 4-1

Cash flows of single-asset firm.

$t = 2$ is $550, which can be computed either as the expected value of $605 and $495 or by weighting each of the four possible outcomes, $655 through $445, by the probability of their occurrence (i.e., .25 in each case). Note that $600 and $550 were the *known* cash flows for the firm in the certainty illustration of Table 3-2. Hence, this illustration extends the asset of the previous chapter to an uncertain setting in which the *expected* cash flows are $600 and $550, respectively.[6] As of $t = 0$, the *expected* rate of return is assumed to be 10 percent for both the first and second period. Moreover, as of $t = 1$, the expected rate of return for the second period is still 10 percent regardless of whether state A or B has occurred.

The independence of the rate of return distributions permits the present value of the firm's assets and the firm's equity to be characterized as if it involved discounting the expected value of future cash flows at the expected value of the rate of return. This is illustrated in Table 4-1. This table begins with the "correct" computation which involves computing the value of the firm and its equity at $t = 1$ for states A and B and then computing the value as of $t = 0$. The computed market value as of $t = 0$ is $1000. However, the alternative computation in Table 4-1 demonstrates that the market value could also have been computed by simply discounting the expected cash flows at $t = 1$ and $t = 2$ at the expected rate of return. This characterization will now be used to illustrate concepts of earnings under uncertainty.

Economic Earnings in Perfect and Complete Markets Under Uncertainty

Under certainty, there is no difference between what is expected and what actually occurs. As a result, there are a number of ways to define economic earnings, all of which are equivalent under certainty. Such definitions were summarized in Table 3-5. Under uncertainty, it is critical to distinguish between *ex ante* or expected economic earnings and *ex post* economic earnings. The hypothetical, all-equity firm is used as an illustration. From the perspective of the firm, the *ex ante (ex post)* earnings can be defined as the expected (actual) cash flows received during the period plus the expected (actual) change in the market prices (i.e., present value) of the assets held by the firm. As in the certainty case, appropriate adjustments would be made for deposits and withdrawals by suppliers of capital. From the perspective of the shareholders, *ex post* earnings are the cash received (i.e., dividends) plus the change in the market price of the common stock. *Ex ante* or expected earnings for the shareholders are equal to the *expected* dividends received during the period plus the *expected* change in the market price of the common stock.

Alternatively, expected earnings can be computed in a manner analogous to the computation of permanent earnings in the certainty case. In an uncertain setting, expected or permanent earnings can be defined as the current market price at the beginning of the period times

---

[6] Note that, in contrast to the illustration of the previous section, cash flows occur at both $t = 1$ and $t = 2$.

TABLE 4-1

Computation of Market Value of Firm and Its Equity

If State A Occurs:		
Cash flow received at $t = 1$		$660
Value of remaining cash flows		
Expected cash flow at $t = 2$		$605
Market value of remaining cash flow at $t = 1$[a]		$550
If State B Occurs:		
Cash flow received at $t = 1$		$540
Value of remaining cash flows		
Expected cash flow at $t = 2$		$495
Market value of remaining cash flow at $t = 1$[a]		$450
Market Value at t $= 0$:		
Value at $t = 1$ if state A occurs		
Cash flow	$660	
Market value	550	$1210
Value at $t = 1$ if state B occurs		
Cash flow	540	
Market value	450	$ 990
Expected value at $t = 1$[b]		$1100
Market value at $t = 0$[a]		$1000
Alternative Computation:		
Expected cash flows as of $t = 0$		
At $t = 1$		$600
At $t = 2$		$550
Present value		
$600 ÷ 1.1		$ 545
$550 ÷ 1.21		$ 455
Total		$1000

[a] $550 = \dfrac{\$605}{(1 + .10)}$; $450 = \dfrac{\$495}{(1 ÷ .10)}$; $1000 = \dfrac{\$1100}{(1 + .10)}$

[b] $1100 = (.5 × \$1210) + (.5 × \$990)$

the expected rate of return for the period. The concepts of *ex post* and *ex ante* earnings are illustrated in Table 4-2. (A single-asset, all-equity firm is assumed, as in Chapter 3. But, in this case, the risky asset illustrated in Figure 4-2 and Table 4-1 is held. Also, state A is assumed to have occurred in the computation of *ex post* earnings. *Ex post* earnings for year 1 are $210. Assessed as of $t = 0$, *ex ante* earnings for years 1 and 2 are $100 and $50, respectively. Assessed as of $t = 1$, *ex ante* earnings are $55 for year 2, given that state A has occurred.[7]

---

[7] Relative to the earnings concepts summarized in Table 3-5, *ex ante* economic earnings have the permanent earnings property, while *ex post* economic earnings have the

TABLE 4-2

Economic Earnings for Single-Asset Firm
(Assuming State A Occurs)

	Year[a]	
	1	2
Expected cash flows as of $t = 0$	$ 600	$ 550
Cash flows as of $t = 1$		
Actual	660	
Expected		605
Market price of asset at *beginning* of year:		
Actual	1000	
Expected as of $t = 0$		500
Actual as of $t = 1$		550
Ex Post Earnings		
From the perspective of the firm:		
Cash flow	660	
Depreciation[b]	(500)	
	160	
Holding gain[c]	50	
Ex post economic earnings	$ 210	
From the perspective of the stockholders:		
Dividend paid[d]	660	
Change in present value of equity[e]	(450)	
Ex post economic earnings	$ 210	
Ex Ante or Expected Earnings		
From the perspective of the firm:[f]		
As of $t = 0$		
Expected cash flow	600	550
Expected depreciation[b]	(500)	(500)
Expected earnings	$ 100	$ 50
As of $t = 1$		
Expected cash flow		605
Expected depreciation		(550)
Expected earnings		$ 55
From the definition of permanent earnings:		
As of $t = 0$		
Beginning market price	1000	500
Expected rate of return	.10	.10
Permanent earnings	$ 100	$ 50
As of $t = 1$		
Beginning market price		550
Expected rate of return		.10
Permanent earnings		$ 55

[a] The beginning (end) of year 1 is $t = 0$ ($t = 1$). The beginning (end) of year 2 is $t = 1$ ($t = 2$).
[b] Depreciation based upon expected market value of asset at beginning of year 2 assessed as of $t = 0$ (i.e., $500).
[c] The holding gain could also be included in depreciation, which would equal $450.
[d] As in the certainty case, the firm is assumed to pay out all cash received.
[e] $450 = $1000 − $550 (where $550 is the actual market price as of $t = 1$).
[f] Although not illustrated here, earnings from the perspective of the shareholders would also produce the same number.

There are several aspects of these earnings concepts worth noting.

(1) *Ex post* earnings can be readily measured from observable cash-flow data and from observable market prices of assets and securities. The role of accrual accounting is not obvious. Moreover, the key items of interest are the cash flows and the market values, and it is not obvious what insight is added by measuring net income, either *ex post* or *ex ante*, once valuation is known.

(2) Actual earnings can differ from expected earnings for several reasons. (a) The cash flow in that period may differ from what was expected. In the illustration, a cash flow of $600 was expected in $t = 1$, yet a cash flow of $660 occurred. (b) The occurrence of the state (i.e., state A or B) may lead to a revision in the distribution of future cash flows. This is apparent in the illustration in which originally a cash flow of $550 for $t = 2$ was expected as of $t = 0$, while the expectation as of $t = 1$ is $605, given that state A occurred. (c) There may also be a revision in the expected rate of return for the second period. This source of *ex post* earnings was not illustrated here and the original expectation of 10 percent for the second period, assessed as of $t = 0$, was not revised at $t = 1$.

(3) So far the discussion has treated the expected rate of return as a given. For any individual, expected earnings are equal to the observed market price times the individual's expected rate of return. However, if market behavior is being characterized, the notion of the expected rate of return requires some elaboration. One possibility is to posit some composite or consensus belief among investors. Where heterogeneous beliefs prevail, each individual will have a personal perception of the "expected" or "permanent" earnings of the firm and its securities, and this perception will vary across individuals. *Hence, while market prices and ex post earnings are publicly observable and known by all, expected (or permanent) earnings are generally not observable and differ among individuals.*[8]

(4) By introducing uncertainty, valuation and the earnings concept become less well-defined in at least two respects. (a) The valuation of multi-period, uncertain cash flows may not admit to any simple characterization, such as discounting expected cash flows at the expected (risky) rate of return. (b) Concepts of *ex ante* (i.e., expected or permanent)

---

distributable earnings property. In the special case in which the expected rate of return remains the same as of the beginning of two adjacent periods (e.g., 10 percent in the illustration), the percentage change in market price is equal to the percentage change in permanent earnings. Here, one of the two components of *ex post* earnings (i.e., the change in price) reflects the change in expected earnings.

earnings depend upon the expected rate of return, which is not directly observable and may vary across individuals.

(5)   Nevertheless, valuation and earnings under perfect and complete markets are still well-defined concepts in the sense that individuals will unanimously prefer market value maximization. Prices are "rich" in reflecting the preferences of individuals, and prices are "rich" in reflecting the multi-period implications of managerial decisions (i.e., stewardship).

(6)   Both the *ex post* and *ex ante* concepts of earnings are derived from the valuation process. If the valuation process is ill-defined, then so is the concept of earnings.

Earnings in a Multi-Asset Setting

It is a simple matter to extend the above notions of *ex post* and *ex ante* earnings under uncertainty to a multi-asset setting. The constant payout-constant growth model is used in Chapter 3 to illustrate the multi-asset setting. A common use of this model in an uncertain setting is to merely replace the payout ratio and the growth rate, known in the certainty setting, with their respective expected values. The interest rate is replaced with the "risky" discount rate, the expected rate of return on securities of identical risk (generically called the *cost of capital*). Needless to say, potentially severe independence assumptions are required here. It is unclear that simply inserting expected values of these variables in a multi-asset, multi-period valuation model leads to a valid characterization of the valuation process. At present, it must be viewed as an *ad hoc* approach which enjoys a considerable usage.

Relationship Between Economic Earnings and Accounting Earnings

As indicated earlier, the concepts of *ex post* and *ex ante* earnings are measures of economic earnings. They are byproducts of the valuation process, and accrual accounting plays no obvious role. However, this framework can be used to examine the relationship between economic earnings and accounting earnings in an uncertain setting. For example, if the firm illustrated in Table 4-2 used straight-line depreciation, at $t = 0$ the expected accounting earnings would be equal to the expected economic earnings. At $t = 1$, either state A or B will have occurred, and the actual accounting earnings will not equal the expected accounting earnings. Moreover, assuming that the depreciation figure is not revised (i.e., historical cost is used), the actual accounting earnings will not in general equal the actual economic earnings. For example, if state A occurs, the accounting earnings will be $160 ($660 − $500), while *ex post* economic earnings are $210. The difference of $50 is the holding gain, which reflects *unanticipated* change in the value of the asset as of $t = 1$ (i.e., $550 − $500). In this illustration, historical cost accounting earnings can be viewed as a mixture of *ex post* and *ex ante* earnings. The unanticipated portion of the cash flows (i.e., $60) are reflected in the accounting net income, based on an actual cash flow of $660. However, the depreciation expense here reflects the anticipated, not the actual, market value of the asset at $t = 1$.[9]

As a result, this hybrid nature of accounting earnings has led to criticism of historical cost accounting. In this setting a movement to market value accounting would make accounting earnings equal to economic earnings. Remember, perfect and complete markets ensure that the asset's entry price equals its exist price equals its value in use. Moreover, the market value of the asset will equal the market value of claims against the assets. This perspective provides a rationale for those who advocate the introduction of market value accounting systems. In a setting of perfect and complete markets such arguments have obvious appeal because economic earnings have the "desirable" properties usually associated with "ideal" income. For example, with respect to the stewardship motivation for financial reporting, earnings under a market value accounting system will reflect the impact of managerial decisions on the future multi-period state-contingent cash flows of the firm. In this vein, consider the proposals of Edwards and Bell (1961), Chambers (1966), and Sterling (1970).

Because economic earnings are well defined, it is possible to examine the "measurement error" associated with alternative accounting methods. Historical cost versus market value accounting provides a ready example. For example, Beaver (1979) uses the setting of perfect and complete markets to examine the properties of historical cost, price level, and replacement cost accounting under various inflationary conditions. It is also possible to extend the depreciation analyses discussed in Chapter 3 to an uncertain setting (e.g., the use of straight-line versus accelerated depreciation methods). However, such an analysis would specify (1) whether *ex post* or *ex ante* earnings are the object of interest, (2) the valuation model assumed, and (3) the nature of the multivariate cash flows and expected rate of return distributions, among other factors.

However, in a setting of perfect and complete markets, market prices are readily available on all assets and securities; hence, the insights gained by such earnings analyses are not clear. The discussion now turns to the case of incomplete markets. In this setting the role of accounting data, such as earnings, is an informational one in which earnings are

---

[9] The ability of historical cost accounting to reflect anticipated future events but not unanticipated events is demonstrated in the context of accounting for inflation in Beaver (1979).

used as an *input* into the valuation process rather than as some output derived as a byproduct of the valuation process. This setting helps to explain how accounting earnings are used in security analysis. Moreover, it helps to explain the shift in emphasis by the FASB and others to an informational perspective and away from an economic income measurement perspective.

4-2. VALUATION IN IMPERFECT OR INCOMPLETE MARKETS

The concept of imperfect markets and its implications is familiar from elementary economics. However, the concept of incomplete markets may be less familiar. A complete market is one in which *primitive* claims can be traded. A primitive claim is a claim to receive $1 if state *s* occurs and receive nothing otherwise. A complex or compound claim is simply a collection of primitive claims. In a complete market it is possible to directly observe the prices of primitive claims or to infer them from the prices of complex claims. In an incomplete market some primitive claims are not tradable. Therefore, prices may exist on complex or compound claims, such as a common stock, but it is impossible to infer the implied prices for primitive claims from the prices of complex claims.

Consider one-period complex securities A and B illustrated in Table 4-3. Which security will sell for the higher price? It might be intuitively appealing to say security A because it has a higher expected value and because the variance of outcomes is smaller. However, in general, the answer will depend upon how much investors value receiving $1 in state 1 versus state 2, as well as the assessed probability of each state occurring. For example, if the price of a primitive claim to $1 in state 2 is greater

TABLE 4-3

Illustration of Primitive Versus Complex Claims

	Security	
	A	B
State 1 (probability of .5)	$100	$40
State 2 (probability of .5)	$50	$100
Price of security[a]	$_0P_{11}100 + {}_0P_{21}50$	$_0P_{11}40 + {}_0P_{21}100$

[a] $_0P_{11}$ = price at $t = 0$ of primitive security to a claim
to receive $1 at $t = 1$ if state 1 occurs.

$_0P_{21}$ = price at $t = 0$ or primitive security to a claim
to receive $1 at $t = 1$ if state 2 occurs.

$$_0P_{11}100 + {}_0P_{21}50 < {}_0P_{11}40 + {}_0P_{21}100 <=> \frac{{}_0P_{21}}{{}_0P_{11}} > 1.2$$

than 120 percent of the price of a primitive claim to $1 in state 1, security B will sell for a higher price than security A.[10] In a complete market, prices of complex securities can be determined from the prices of the primitive securities they represent. Alternatively, it would be possible to infer the prices of primitive securities from the prices of complex securities. In an incomplete market it is impossible to infer the prices of at least some of the primitive securities from the complex securities. This follows from the meaning of an incomplete market. Moreover, in an incomplete market setting it may be impossible to value some complex claims to future cash flow because no market exists in which that claim or claims identical to it are traded and because it may be impossible to infer the value of such a claim from observing the value of other complex claims.

The market for many assets of a firm may be incomplete. A market for the results of research and development expenditures may be incomplete because revealing the results of the research and development project may destroy its value (i.e., a potential buyer need no longer pay in order to obtain the information), although patent rights may partially alleviate this concern. The market for intangible assets (commonly referred to as *goodwill*) is another example. Such incompleteness would make it difficult to value those assets.[11]

Another reason why valuation of a firm's assets may be difficult is imperfection in the markets. Under such imperfections, such as transactions costs, the entry price of the asset (i.e., its replacement costs), the exit price (e.g., its liquidation value), and its value in use (i.e., the present value of the future cash flows) may not be the same.

In a setting of imperfect or incomplete markets, market values no longer necessarily have the properties they did under perfect and complete markets. For example, market value maximization may not be unanimously preferred by shareholders. In general, there will be a lack of consensus because the markets are no longer rich enough to sort out the individual heterogeneity of preferences and beliefs. In some cases, there may be shareholder consensus, but it may be a unanimous decision not to maximize market value. Market value no longer is rich enough to capture the value of all the attributes of a particular project or asset. There can be nonmarketable aspects to a project that override those aspects reflected in market prices. In this sense, valuation is no longer a well-defined process. In other words, it is no longer clear what properties prices possess. *An important implication is that any concept of earnings that is valuation based is no longer a well-defined concept.* Hence, the prop-

---

[10] The computation is provided in the footnote in Table 4-3.

[11] Limited observability of events and costs of opening markets are two other generic reasons for incompleteness, even in an exchange setting.

erties of earnings are no longer clear. Consider the stewardship notion in financial reporting, which provides one motivation for an emphasis upon economic income measurement. In this setting, management's choice function (e.g., market value maximization) is no longer well-defined. Also, it is no longer clear by what criterion management's stewardship function should be evaluated. In particular, economic earnings are no longer an obvious criterion because they do not necessarily fully reflect the multi-period effects of managerial decisions on future cash flows.

It is important to make clear what is meant by saying valuation is ill-defined in an incomplete or imperfect market setting. Prices of complex claims, such as common stocks, can still be observed. Moreover, the valuation process giving rise to those prices may very well be capable of a simple characterization. For example, prices of common stocks may admit to a characterization in terms of expected values of future cash flows discounted at an expected rate of return. Whether or not they do depend in part upon the independence of rates of return. In this sense, the valuation process may be well-defined. Moreover, *ex post* earnings may be measured by dividends and market price changes for a security that is traded. Similarly, permanent earnings can be defined for any asset or claim (e.g., common stock) as the price times the expected rate of return. However, in an incomplete market the prices of some of the firm's claims cannot be valued because of the incompleteness, and the observed market prices of claims for which markets do exist may no longer have the same "optimality" properties because of imperfection or incompleteness.[12]

This leads to a different perspective within which to view financial statement data, such as accounting earnings. This perspective is called an *informational perspective*, which was discussed in an earlier chapter. The next subsection explores accounting earnings under uncertainty in an incomplete market setting.

Earnings from an Information Perspective

Securities such as common stocks possess value because they possess certain attributes that are valued by investors, such as claims to future dividends. Prices can be characterized in general as dependent upon investors' expectations regarding these attributes. The role of information is to alter investors' beliefs about the attributes, and hence information can alter stock prices. In particular, a role of earnings is to alter beliefs about the firm's ability to pay future dividends, and it is

---

[12] As a result, the rationale for market value accounting discussed above can no longer be invoked and may *partially* explain opposition to market value accounting proposals.

consistent with the FASB statement that earnings are an indicator of future dividend-paying ability.

A conceptual relationship can be developed between accounting earnings and the price of common stocks by introducing three critical links: (1) a link between security price and future dividends, (2) a link between future dividends and future earnings, and (3) a link between future earnings and current earnings.[13]

Prices and Future Dividends

Future dividends and price are linked via a valuation model. In general, the valuation model will depend upon the amount of the dividend to be received in each state in each time period, the beliefs of the investors regarding the probability of each state, and the value of receiving $1 in state s in period t. As indicated earlier, a typical approach to valuation under uncertainty is simply to extend the model under certainty by replacing each of the valuation parameters, which were known with certainty, with the expected value of the analogous variables under uncertainty. In this special case, price can be characterized as if it were a function of the expected value of future dividends.

In general, prices may be a function of nonearnings information (i.e., information about future dividends that are not conveyed by accounting earnings). However, if the earnings and dividends are assumed to be dependent, prices can also be viewed as a function of the expected value of future earnings. For example, any level of expected dividends is associated with a level of expected earnings, and the two are linked by a payout ratio.[14] This link between dividends and earnings is the second component in the price-earnings relationship.

Future Dividends and Future Accounting Earnings

In order for earnings to have informational content, there must be a perceived relationship between earnings and the attributes that are assumed to give rise to a security's value. In this context, a perceived relationship between future earnings and future dividends (the attribute that causes a security to have value) is assumed.

Future earnings are relevant to the extent that they are perceived

---

[13] A formal treatment of the set of relationships appears in Ohlson (1979).

[14] Alternatively stated, associated with each state is a known level of dividends and earnings, and hence associated with the expected value of dividends in period t is an expected value of earnings in period t. A payout ratio in period t can be defined as the ratio of the two expected values.

to be statistically dependent with future dividends. This is one interpretation of the assertion that earnings are an indicator of future dividend-paying ability. Although it enjoys widespread usage, the concept of "future dividend-paying ability" is not well-defined. In perfect and complete markets the price of the security would be a measure of the security's perceived future dividend-paying ability, and an earnings measure derived from price presumably would also be an indicator of dividend-paying ability.

In a setting of imperfect or incomplete markets the concept of dividend-paying ability is not necessarily reflected in a readily available market price statistic. The concept of dividend-paying ability and the perceived relationship between earnings and dividends are primitive assumptions in this setting. At one level, empirical evidence [Fama and Babiak (1968) and Watts (1973), among others] indicates that earnings changes are correlated with dividend changes. Hence, the assumption of a statistical dependence between future earnings and future dividends appears to be a reasonable one. One of the most common and simplest assumptions is that future earnings and future dividends are linked via a payout ratio which is constant over time.

However, sole reliance on the empirical findings is tenuous without a deeper conceptual basis for this relationship. It may be intuitively appealing to conclude that the observed dependency arises because of management's perceptions of the ability of earnings to reflect dividend-paying ability. However, this begs the deeper questions and leaves a weak foundation for the relevancy of earnings. The fundamental problem is, of course, that there is no general theory of managerial choice (e.g., market value maximization) under imperfect or incomplete markets. A better conceptual foundation would exist if a theory were available that explained why managers held such a perception in the context of their choice behavior.

Future Accounting Earnings and Current Accounting Earnings

The relationship between past earnings and future earnings is expressed in terms of the stochastic process that is perceived to be describing earnings over time. From this perspective, events occurring within a particular period may be atypical (i.e., transitory) and not expected to have the same impact on earnings in subsequent periods. Strikes and catastrophic events are two examples of this type of event. Accounting earnings can be viewed as two components: permanent earnings and transitory earnings. Permanent accounting earnings can be thought of as the expected value of future accounting earnings, and as of any point in time, is a vector rather than a single number.[15] Moreover, as time passes, the expected or permanent earnings for a given year may change.

Accounting earnings are relevant because they reflect events that lead to an alteration of beliefs about the future dividend-paying ability of the firm. The prediction of earnings is part of a larger analytical process in which the ultimate concern is the prediction and valuation of the dividend stream. Earnings are an important informational source about future dividend-paying ability. Accounting earnings are *not* a valuation concept as are economic earnings. Nor are accounting earnings necessarily viewed as even a surrogate for such valuation concepts. Its major relevance arises out of its perceived relationship to future dividend-paying ability.

An analysis of earnings involves two issues. (1) What is the relationship between earnings and future dividend-paying ability under various accounting methods? (2) What is the relationship between currently observable data and future earnings?

With respect to the first issue, there are certain factors which may permanently affect the level of accounting earnings but not in a way that implies different dividend-paying power. The nature of the financial reporting system is a major contributor of such factors. Consider the effects of unanticipated inflation. The revenues and many of the expenses will increase with inflation, but some expenses such as depreciation under historical cost will not. The result will be an increase in net income that is greater than the rate of inflation, even if nothing has changed in real terms. Hence, there will be a portion of the change in accounting earnings that may not be associated with a change in dividend-paying ability.

With respect to the second issue, future earnings can be described in terms of the revenue and expense components that comprise earnings. Earnings forecasting can involve forecasting those income statement items on an item by item basis.[16] The earnings forecast would then be an aggregation of the forecasts of the individual components. Moreover, each income statement item can be further decomposed. For example, each item could be described as the product of a future price times a future quantity. For example, future sales are the product of future

---

[15] More formally, permanent earnings are a vector $\{E(X_{t+1}), E(X_{t+2}) \ldots \ldots E(X_{t+k})\}$ where $k > 0$ and where $E(X_{t+k})$ is the expected earnings for time $t + k$ assessed as of time t. Either an individual or market-wide perspective can be taken here, as long as a given perspective is consistently maintained throughout. In the former case, the beliefs are those of a particular individual; in the latter case, the beliefs are a composite or consensus across investors.

[16] Obviously, the earnings forecasting issue can be viewed as an information choice problem, discussed in detail in Chapter 2. Demski and Feltham (1972) explore the forecasting issue in such a setting.

selling price times future quantities (of output) sold; future cost of goods sold is the product of future prices of inputs times the quantity of inputs required to produce the quantity of output sold. Of course, each of these variables is uncertain and must be forecasted as well. Future depreciation expense is a function of the future price of the depreciable assets to be purchased and the quantity of such assets. From this perspective, the forecasting of future accounting earnings includes (1) an assessment of the distribution of (a) future quantities of outputs, (b) future prices of output, (c) future quantities of inputs, and (d) future prices of inputs and (2) the accounting methods used to transform these raw data into earnings numbers.

Forecasting Future Earnings from Current Earnings

Needless to say, the above forecasting approach is extremely ambitious. Typically, the problem of forecasting earnings is viewed somewhat more modestly. In a more limited setting the question becomes one of how to use past and current earnings so as to best forecast future earnings. This section provides a simple example and it illustrates permanent versus transitory components of accounting earnings.

The information content of current and past earnings for future expected earnings will depend upon how much of the current and past earnings is expected to persist. For example, suppose that current earnings are larger or smaller than expected because of certain events that originated in the current year. These events will be called the *unexpected component* of this year's earnings or *shocks* to the earnings series. The implications of these shocks for the permanent (i.e., expected) accounting earnings depend upon the process perceived to govern the time series behavior of accounting earnings. Alternatively stated, the importance of these shocks depends upon the extent to which they are expected to impact upon the level of future earnings.

A numerical example is provided in Table 4-4. Earnings per share changed from $1.50 for the year ending at $t = 0$ to $2.00 for the year ending at $t = 1$. As of $t = 0$, the expected future earnings are also assumed to be $1.50.[17] In other words, for simplicity, the change in earnings is equal to the unexpected portion of earnings. What is the expected future earnings as of this year, given that this year's earnings were $.50 above the expected? The importance of this short-run change

---

[17] In order to simplify the discussion, it is assumed that expected earnings are the same for all future periods as of any given point in time (i.e., *no growth in earnings per share is expected*). More formally, $E(X_{t+k}) = E(X_{t+1})$ for all $k > 1$, where $E(X_{t+k})$ is defined in footnote 19.

TABLE 4-4

*Relationship Between Current Earnings
and Permanent Earnings*

Actual Earnings:	
For the year ending at $t = 0$	$1.50
For the year ending at $t = 1$	$2.00
Permanent (or Expected) Earnings:	
As of $t = 0$	$1.50
As of $t = 1$	
Case 1 (100% sensitivity)	$2.00
Case 2 (0% sensitivity)	$1.50
Case 3 (intermediate case)	$1.50 to $2.00
Case 4 (greater than 100% sensitivity)	More than $2.00

in earnings depends in a large part upon the nature of the earnings process. For some earnings processes, it is relatively unimportant. For other processes, it is critical because changes in near-term earnings (e.g., changes in current earnings) can have implications for *permanent* earnings, *future* dividends, and hence *current* stock price. Four cases are illustrated in Table 4-4.[18]

In the first case, if the events that caused this year's change in earnings are expected to persist (i.e., have a permanent effect on the level of future expected earnings), all of the earnings change can be regarded as "permanent" in the sense that it is a measure of the change (i.e. $.50) in expected earnings. All of current earnings are permanent (i.e., expected earnings are $2.00 for all future periods). The transitory component is zero. This is the so-called *random walk* case and there is a one-to-one relationship between percentage changes in current earnings and percentage changes in expected earnings. A 33 percentage change in earnings ($2.00 − $1.50/$1.50) implies a 33 percentage change in expected earnings.

By contrast, consider the second case in which the events that caused

---

[18] In general, expectations regarding future earnings will be conditional on both past and current earnings, as well as nonearnings information. However, in order to simplify the discussion, the role of current earnings is illustrated. The more general setting is described in Box and Jenkins (1976) and Nelson (1973). From this perspective, the illustration assumes that earnings are generated by an IMA (1,1) process. For this class of processes,

$$X_t - X_{t-1} = a_t - \theta a_{t-1}$$

where X_t is the earnings for period t, a_t is the unexpected "shock" in period t, and θ is a coefficient that reflects the effect of a_{t-1} on X_t. $E(X_{t+k}|X_t) = X_t - \theta a_t$ for $k > 0$. In the illustration, $a_0 = 0$, $a_1 = \$.50$, $X_0 = \$1.50$, and $X_1 = \$2.00$. This implies that $E(X_1|X_0) = \$1.50$. The four cases illustrated assume that θ equals 0, 1, between 0 and 1, and less than 0, respectively. $E(X_{t+k}|X_1) - E(X_{t+k}|X_0) = (1 - \theta)a_1 = (1 - \theta)\$.50$ for $k > 0$.

this year's earnings change are expected not to persist (i.e., to have no effect on the level of future expected earnings). All of the earnings change can be regarded as "transitory" and will lead to no revisions in expectations regarding future earnings. Here there is a zero relationship between percentage changes in current earnings and percentage changes in expected earnings. A 33 percentage change in current earnings would lead to *no* change in expected earnings (i.e. \$1.50 − \$1.50/\$1.50). Of the current earnings of \$2.00, the permanent earnings are \$1.50 and the transitory component is \$.50.

There is a third, intermediate case in which the nature of the current period events is such that only a portion of the earnings changes the level of future expected earnings. In this case, the change in earnings contains both a "permanent" and a "transitory" component. Here there would be less than a one-to-one relationship between percentage changes in current earnings and percentage changes in future expected earnings. In other words, the 33 percentage change in current earnings implies a change in permanent earnings of less than 33 percent but greater than 0 percent.

Finally, in the fourth case, the nature of the current period events is such that the events are expected to have an even greater impact on future years' earnings than they did on this year's earnings. This could happen when events have permanent effects on the level of expected earnings but occur randomly throughout the year. Therefore, on the average, an event impacts on this year's earnings for only six months of the fiscal year, but it will impact on future earnings for all twelve months of the future fiscal years. In this case, the change in this year's earnings understates the impact on the level of expected earnings. As a result, there is more than a one-to-one relationship between percentage changes in the current year's earnings and percentage changes in the future year's expected earnings. A 33-percentage change in this year's earnings leads to a percentage change in expected earnings of more than 33 percent. In fact, in the example just cited, there would be about a two-to-one relationship (i.e., a 33 percent change implies a 66 percent change in expected earnings). The relationships in these four cases can be expressed as sensitivity coefficients. The sensitivity coefficient is the proportion of the earnings change that is permanent and would be 100 percent, 0 percent, less than 100 percent but greater than 0 percent, and greater than 100 percent for cases one through four, as summarized in Table 4-4.

Prices and Earnings: An Illustration

With the three links described, a relationship between current earnings and the current price of the security can be derived. The relationship depends upon the nature of each of the three links. This relationship can be illustrated by making some simple assumptions about each of the three links.

With respect to the first link (between current price and future dividends), an extremely simple valuation relationship is adopted. No growth in dividends is assumed (i.e., as of time t, $E(D_{t+1}) = E(D_{t+k})$ for all $k > 1$). It is further assumed that current price is proportional to future expected dividends, and the factor of proportionality (ρ) is constant over time [i.e., $P_t = \rho E_t(D)$].[19]

For the second link (between future dividends and future earnings), a constant payout ratio (K) over time is assumed. The implication is that revisions of expected earnings can be easily translated into revisions of expected dividends. Revisions in future expected earnings lead into identical proportional revisions in expected future dividends.[20]

Since expected earnings are assumed to differ from expected dividends by a constant payout ratio, current price can also be expressed in terms of future expected earnings (i.e., $P_t = \rho K E_t(X)$). In the spirit of the no growth in dividends assumption, the assumed payout ratio is 100 percent. Assume further that $\rho = 10$. In this setting the perpetual stream of "constant" (i.e., no-growth) dividends will have a market price equal to 10 times the expected future dividend and the ratio of price to permanent accounting earnings is also 10 [or $P_t = 10E_t(X)$]. From Table 4-4, the expected earnings at $t = 0$ are $1.50, the expected dividends are also $1.50, and the price of the share is $15.00 ($10 \times $1.50). The ratio of price to expected earnings is 10 times (alternatively, price is equal to 10 times expected earnings).

The third and final link is the relationship between current and future earnings. Four cases were discussed earlier and are used here.

With these specific assumptions about the links, it is possible to examine the sensitivity of stock price changes to earnings changes. By

---

[19] $E_t(D) = E(D_{t+1}) = E(D_{t+k})$, which are the expected future dividends assessed as of time t. Intuitively, it may be tempting to think of ρ as the reciprocal of the risky discount rate (i.e., cost of equity capital). However, this interpretation is unnecessary and assumes discounting using expected values.

[20] $E(D_{t+k}) = KE(X_{t+k})$ for all $k > 0$ as of time t. $E(D_{t+k})$ is the expected dividend at time $t + k$ assessed as of time t, and K is the payout ratio. In the no-growth case, $E(D_{t+1}) = E(D_{t+k})$ for all $k > 1$ assessed as of t. Let $E_t(D) = E(D_{t+1}) = E(D_{t+k})$ assessed as of t; then

$$\frac{E_{t+1}(D) - E_t(D)}{E_t(D)} = \frac{E_{t+1}(X) - E_t(X)}{E_t(X)}$$

where $E_t(X) = E(X_{t+1}) = E(X_{t+k})$ assessed as of t. More compactly stated ($\Delta \equiv$ change from t to $t + 1$):

$$\frac{\Delta E(D)}{E_t(D)} = \frac{\Delta E(X)}{E_t(X)}$$

the first two links introduced above, *the percentage changes in price, the percentage change in expected dividends, and the percentage change in expected earnings are equal.*[21] In other words, the sensitivity of percentage changes in price to percentage changes in *expected* earnings (i.e., permanent accounting earnings) is one to one. For example, a change in expected earnings (e.g., of 33 percent) will lead to an equal change in price (e.g., 33 percent).

However, the sensitivity of a stock price change to change in *current* earnings depends upon what process is perceived to be governing earnings. Under case one, percentage changes in current earnings are equal to percentage changes in *expected* earnings. Here the sensitivity of price changes to *current* earnings changes is also expected to be one to one. For example, from Table 4-4, a 33 percent change in current earnings would lead to a 33 percent change in stock price (e.g., a price change from $15 to $20). In case two there is zero sensitivity between current earnings changes and price changes because all shocks are transitory and have no information content with respect to future earnings or future dividends. In this case, the stock price would be expected to remain the same (e.g., $15). If the process of earnings is described by case three, the sensitivity between stock price changes and earnings changes would be less than one. A 33 percent change in current earnings will imply a percentage change in price of less than 33 percent (e.g., price would be less than $20 but more than $15). In case four the price change sensitivity would be greater than one to one. A 33 percent change in current earnings would lead to a percentage change in price of greater than 33 percent (e.g., price would be greater than $20).[22]

The purpose of the preceding discussion was to provide a conceptual framework for linking earnings and prices, not to illustrate the precise procedure by which the analysis would be conducted in all situations. The general analysis would involve an identification of the events that led to the earnings change and an assessment of their permanent versus transitory components. This is obviously a highly judgmental process, and the appropriate case may vary across firms and vary for a given firm over time.

---

[21] More formally, $E_t(D) = K \cdot E_t(X)$ and $P_t = \rho E_t(D)$. Hence, with k and ρ constant,

$$\frac{\Delta P}{P_t} = \frac{\Delta E(D)}{E_t(D)} = \frac{\Delta E(X)}{E_t(X)}$$

where $\Delta \equiv$ the change from t to $t + 1$.

[22] In all four cases, the new price can be computed by multiplying expected earnings (as reported in Table 4-4) by 10 (the ratio of price to *expected* earnings). Note that the ratio of price to *current* earnings would be 10, 7.5, between 7.5 and 10, and above 10 for each of the four cases, respectively.

Relationship Between Permanent Accounting Earnings and Permanent Earnings as a Valuation Concept

In this illustration a link can be drawn between permanent earnings as a valuation concept and permanent accounting earnings. Even in imperfect or incomplete markets, permanent earnings can be defined as the current price times the expected rate of return.[23] If the expected value of the rate of return is assumed to be constant, percentage changes in *permanent earnings* will be equal to percentage changes in *price*. However, the previous section provided an illustration in which percentage changes in price were equal to percentage changes in permanent accounting earnings. In this case, percentage changes in permanent earnings as a valuation concept are equal to percentage changes in accounting earnings.[24] Of course, in general, no such simple relationship will exist.

A Role of Accrual Accounting: An Illustration

From an informational perspective, a function of a financial accounting reporting system is to provide information that potentially will alter investors' beliefs about the future dividend-paying ability of the firm. As such, accrual accounting can be viewed as a cost-effective compromise between merely reporting cash flows and an ambitious policy of "full" disclosure. The choice then involves selecting that accrual system that provides the most valuable information, subject to cost considerations. The issues that arise in choosing the "best" information system in a multiperson setting were discussed in Chapter 2 and are relevant to the choice among accrual systems.

An accrual can be viewed as a form of forecast about the future, and as such accrual accounting can be viewed as a cost-effective way of conveying forecasts or expectational data. This is illustrated in a simple

---

[23] This is directly analogous to the definition of permanent earnings under certainty, where the price was multiplied by the interest rate. More formally, as of time t, permanent earnings $\equiv E_t(R) \cdot P_t$, where $E_t(R)$ is the expected rate of return assessed at time t and P_t is the market price at time t. Note that this concept can be defined where *some* markets are imperfect or incomplete, as long as price is observable. For example, consider a common stock which is actively traded but represents claims to assets for which the markets are imperfect or incomplete. If it is assumed that discounting at expected values is a valid characterization of valuation, permanent earnings are open to the further interpretation that they are equal to that level of constant, *expected* dividends, which if received in perpetuity would have a discounted present value equal to the present value of the dividend stream currently expected.

[24] With $E_t(R) = E(R)$ for t and $t + 1$,

$$\frac{E(R)P_{t+1} - E(R)P_t}{E(R)P_t} = \frac{\Delta P}{P_t} = \frac{\Delta E(X)}{E_t(X)}$$

setting. Consider the financial results reported in Table 4-5. What are the earnings for the year? One possible answer is $50,000 ($1,200,000 − $800,000 − $350,000). However, since this makes no allowance for uncollectable accounts, such a number would be considered optimistic. The aging of the receivables provides one source of information upon which to base an estimate or *forecast* of the amount of uncollectable accounts. The bottom panel of Table 4-5 indicates the possible amounts that actually will be collected and the credit manager's assessment of the probability of each state. For simplicity, only four states have been assumed. A second possible measure of net income would be to take a "pessimistic" forecast based on the assumption that nothing will be collected until the cash is actually received. In this case, the estimated uncollectables would be $310,000 with a loss of $260,000.[25] However, neither optimism nor pessimism need be adopted, and some attempt could

TABLE 4-5

Accrual Accounting as a Forecast

The company began operations this year. On December 31 the following selected financial statement items were reported:

Accounts receivable	$ 310,000
Sales (gross)	$1200,000
Cost of goods sold	$ 800,000
Other operating expenses	$ 350,000

The credit terms to customers are the amounts due within 30 days after billing. An aging of the accounts receivable account reveals the following:

Current	$200,000
30–60 days	$ 50,000
60–90 days	$ 30,000
90–120 days	$ 20,000
Over 120 days	$ 10,000
	$310,000

The credit manager indicates the following:

State of the World	Probability
Will collect $310,000	.25
Will collect $300,000	.30
Will collect $280,000	.40
Will collect $250,000	.05

---

[25] A less extreme variation of this approach is provided by installment sales accounting which recognizes no gross margin until the receivable is collected. The realized gross margin would be $296,667 [i.e., $400,000 × ($890,000 ÷ $1,200,000)] and the corresponding loss is $53,333.

be made to represent an intermediate situation by choosing some measure of central tendency. If the expected value is chosen, the expected collectables are $292,000, the implied estimated uncollectables are $18,000, and the implied earnings are $32,000. However, the expected value is only one measure of central tendency. The median amount of collectables is $300,000 and the implied estimated uncollectables are $10,000 for a reported earnings of $40,000. If the modal (i.e., most likely) value is chosen, the average amount of collectables is $280,000 for an estimated uncollectables of $30,000 for a reported earnings of $20,000.

Thus far, six measures of earnings have been derived depending upon how the information on collectability is treated. A multitude of earnings numbers arise in part because there is an attempt to capture an entire probability distribution over several states in a single number. Obviously, there are a variety of ways to do this, and these are only a few of the possibilities. For example, perhaps some information should be incorporated on the variability as well as the central tendency of the possible outcomes (e.g., a certainty equivalent approach that "risk adjusts" the central tendency measures by some variability measure). Moreover, there has been no allowance made for the fact that these amounts will not be received immediately but at some time in the future. There are present value considerations to be considered here.

If perfect and complete markets are assumed, all of these considerations would be fully reflected in the "price" at which the firm could sell those receivables. The market price reflects these judgmental factors. In this sense, the accrual could be viewed as an attempt to surrogate the valuation process. In perfect and complete markets the market price of the asset could be used to measure earnings and no reliance on accrual accounting is required.

The premise here is, of course, that accrual accounting plays a role precisely because markets are imperfect or incomplete. For example, in some cases receivables can be sold (e.g., receivables can be factored). However, the firm may choose not to sell its receivables because of some perceived imperfection or incompleteness in the market (e.g., its "value in use" exceeds its "exit price"). Similarly, the accounting system may not incorporate such information for the same reasons. However, the issue of how to aggregate the underlying data arises. There typically will be a number of alternatives.

There can be some loss of information via aggregation (e.g., the entire probability distribution of the credit manager will not be reported). However, the premise is that the aggregation can be more informative than merely reporting cash flows. Given that the price of a security is a function of what is expected in the future, it is not unreasonable to suppose that accrual accounting, if it provides data on management's expectations about the future, may in fact convey information over and above the cash flows.

However, much of the information arising out of the accruals is of a short-term nature (e.g., accruals with respect to current assets such as receivables and inventories). A major long-term accrual is depreciable plant and equipment. However, here the accrual process relies upon "boilerplate" allocation rules, such as straight-line depreciation, and estimates of useful lives based on guidelines motivated in part by income tax considerations. Moreover, depreciation under historical cost has been particularly subject to considerable criticism because of inflation. Hence, the area for the greatest potential for accrual accounting is also the area that has been the target of severe criticism. As a result, it is not immediately obvious that accrual accounting accomplishes its purpose, as stated by the FASB. As such, the merits of accrual accounting are still largely an open issue. The next chapter provides some empirical evidence on this issue.

4-3. CONCLUDING REMARKS

This chapter has explored the nature of earnings under conditions of uncertainty. The initial setting was perfect and complete markets in which earnings and valuation are still well-defined, and conceptually this setting constitutes a modest extension of the certainty case. However, there were some aspects of introducing uncertainty worth noting. (1) Economic earnings can still be defined but a distinction must be drawn between *ex post* and *ex ante* (or expected) earnings. The latter concept is analogous to the concept of permanent earnings under certainty. (2) Either earnings measure is a byproduct of the valuation process. They cannot be defined until the valuation process has been specified. (3) The merits of measuring earnings, given valuation is known, is not obvious. (4) Neither *ex post* nor *ex ante* earnings involve any obvious reliance upon accrual accounting. (5) Valuation under uncertainty may not admit to any simple characterization, such as discounting the expected value of future cash flows at the expected value of the (risky) rate of return. (6) Permanent earnings are no longer directly observable if expectations of investors are not directly observable. Moreover, permanent earnings are personalistic and differ across individuals if beliefs are heterogeneous.

Under imperfect or incomplete markets, valuation is no longer a well-defined process in the sense that market prices may no longer fully reflect the preferences of individuals. In some cases, market prices may not simply exist, and in other cases, observed market prices may not fully capture the value of the claim because of some imperfection. In this setting there may be no unanimity among shareholders, and, if there is, that unanimity may not be the maximization of market value. As a result, the properties of prices are unknown, as are the properties of any earnings number derived from price. Hence, a price-oriented approach no longer has the obvious appeal it does in a perfect and complete markets setting.

In this setting, accounting earnings can be viewed from an "informational" perspective. Earnings are a source of information used by investors in the process of assessing the value of securities. However, earnings do not necessarily bear any simple, direct relationship to the valuation process as economic earnings did in the perfect and complete markets case. In particular, the price-earnings process can be viewed as consisting of three elements: (1) a link between current price and future dividends, (2) a link between future dividends and the future earnings, and (3) a link between future earnings and current earnings. With these three elements, it is possible to link conceptually prices and accounting earnings. A simple illustration was provided in which the percentage change in expected (i.e., permanent) accounting earnings was equal to the percentage change in price.

In this setting a role of accrual accounting is to provide an information system that is a cost-effective compromise between merely reporting cash flows and a more ambitious disclosure policy. A simple illustration was provided in the context of estimating uncollectable receivables. An accrual can be viewed as a forecast about the future. Given that the price and the value of a security is a function of expected future cash flows, it may not be unreasonable to assert that accrual accounting conveys information that cannot be extracted from an analysis of past cash flows. However, an inspection of the nature of the accruals makes this superiority less than clear-cut. The efficacy of accrual accounting still remains essentially an open issue. However, this chapter has attempted to present some of the conceptual aspects of this issue and to provide a framework for interpreting accounting earnings in a setting of uncertainty and incomplete markets. Ultimately, the nature of the choice among accrual systems is essentially that of choosing among information systems in a multi-person setting, as discussed in Chapter 2.

BIBLIOGRAPHY

BEAVER, W. "Accounting for Inflation in an Efficient Market." *International Journal of Accounting* (1979), 21–42.

_____"Market Efficiency." *Accounting Review* (January 1981).

BOX, G., AND G. JENKINS. *Time Series Analysis: Forecasting and Control.* San Francisco: Holden-Day, 1976.

CHAMBERS, R. *Accounting Evaluation and Economic Behavior* (Englewood Cliffs, N.J.: Prentice-Hall, 1966.

CHRISTIE, A. "On Cross-Sectional Analysis in Accounting Research." *Journal of Accounting and Economics* (December 1987), 231–258.

DEMSKI, J., AND G. FELTHAM. "Forecast Evaluation." *Accounting Review* (July 1972), 533–548.

EDWARDS, E., AND P. BELL. *The Theory and Measurement of Business Income*. Berkeley: University of California Press, 1961.

FAMA, E., AND H. BABIAK. "Dividend Policy: An Empirical Analysis." *Journal of the American Statistical Association* (December 1968), 1132–1161.

HIRSHLEIFER, J. *Investment, Interest, and Capital*. Englewood Cliffs, N.J.: Prentice-Hall, 1970.

NELSON, C. *Applied Time Series Analysis*. San Francisco: Holden-Day, 1973.

OHLSON, J. "Risk, Return, Security-Valuation and the Stochastic Behavior of Accounting Numbers." *Journal of Financial and Quantitative Analysis* (June 1979), 317–336.

PRATT, J. "Risk Aversion in the Small and in the Large." *Econometrica* (January–April 1964), 112–136.

SAVAGE, L. *The Foundations of Statistics*. 2d rev. ed. New York: Dover Publications, 1972.

SHARPE, W. *Investments*. Englewood Cliffs, N.J.: Prentice-Hall, 1978.

STERLING, R. *Theory of the Measurement of Enterprise Income*. Lawrence, Kan.: University of Kansas Press, 1970.

WATTS, R. "The Information Content of Dividends." *Journal of Business* (April 1973), 191–211.

chapter five

The
Evidence

Prices can be viewed as arising from an equilibrium process in which the price depends upon the individuals' endowments, tastes, beliefs, and the state that occurs. Similarly, from an informational perspective, earnings can be viewed as a signal from an information system in which the signal depends upon the state that occurs. If prices and earnings depend upon common aspects of the state, it is reasonable to expect to observe a relationship (i.e., a statistical dependency) between prices and earnings. In particular, if earnings alter investors' beliefs about the attributes that cause securities to be of value, a statistical dependency between earnings and prices can arise. Security price research refers to this statistical dependency as *information content*. The motivation for doing so is the premise that such a dependency is consistent with the ability of earnings to alter investors' beliefs and hence to possess information content.[1]

---

[1] More generally, the statistical dependency between price and any informational variable is referred to as the *information content* of that variable, and prices are said to *reflect* that variable. The term information content is somewhat of a misnomer in the sense that statistical dependency could arise merely because of a reliance of prices and earnings upon a common set of events. The *marginal* information content of earnings may be zero, once

The nature of the relationship between prices and earnings depends upon the nature of the equilibrium process producing prices and the information system producing earnings. In the context of the previous chapter, prices are viewed as dependent upon expectations regarding future dividend-paying ability. The three-element framework developed was used to illustrate a specific relationship by adding additional assumptions about each of the three links. This framework provides a basis for interpreting price-earnings relationships and will be used here to interpret some empirical research on the observed relationship between prices and earnings.

There are few areas in finance or accounting that have received as much attention as the relationship between stock prices and accounting earnings. This chapter will provide a brief nontechnical summary of some of the evidence on that relationship and will discuss its implications. A more detailed discussion of this research appears in Foster (1986) and Griffin (1987).

Based on the empirical research several conclusions appear warranted. (1) There is a significant, positive correlation between price changes and earnings changes. (2) Although significant, it is not a simple one-to-one relationship.[2] (3) One reason is that prices behave as if earnings are perceived to possess a transitory component. (4) Security prices act as though investors "see through" accounting method differences among firms, at least with respect to depreciation method differences. (5) Price changes appear to be more highly correlated with earnings changes than with changes in "cash flow."[3] (6) Prices act as if accounting earnings are an important source of information, but only one of many sources. (7) Prices can be used to forecast earnings. (8) Measures of systematic risk in security prices are significantly positively correlated with measures of systematic volatility in accounting earnings.

5-1. PRICE CHANGES AND EARNINGS CHANGES

Early research by Benston (1966) and Ball and Brown (1968) explored the relationship between security price changes and earnings changes.[4] Ball and Brown found a significant association between the

---

the effect of these correlated (omitted) variables are considered. This distinction will be discussed later.

[2] There are two aspects here. (1) The correlation coefficient is less than one. (2) The sensitivity (or elasticity) of price changes to earnings changes is less than one.

[3] More precisely, "cash flow" is operationally defined in these studies as earnings plus depreciation expense (primarily). Hence, it is similar to funds provided by operations and is not literally cash flows.

[4] Throughout this chapter the term *security prices* will refer to the prices of common stock securities and the term *earnings* will refer to accounting earnings.

sign of the price changes and the sign of the earnings changes. For the years in which a firm experiences positive residual earnings change, there tends to be positive residual price change and, conversely, for the years in which there is a negative residual earnings change.[5] Beaver, Clarke, and Wright (1979) subsequently extended the Ball and Brown study by incorporating the magnitude of the earnings change, as well as its sign. Table 5-1 reports some of the results of that study, which is based on annual earnings changes for the years 1965 through 1974. Table 5-1 reports the average residual percentage change in earnings and the residual percentage change in price for six of twenty-five portfolios. The twenty-five portfolios were constructed based upon their residual percentage change in earnings. Portfolio 1 consists of those securities that experienced the greatest residual decline in earnings (a

TABLE 5-1

Relationship Between Residual Percentage Changes in Price and Percentage Changes in Earnings

Portfolio	Residual Percentage Change in EPS	Residual Percentage Change in Price	Beta[a]
1	− 154.8	− 17.5	1.23
2	− 12.7	− 9.0	.98
3	0.4	− 2.1	.88
4	9.0	2.0	.98
5	23.4	10.4	1.01
6	185.1	29.2	1.15

[a]The beta is based on a return on a "market" portfolio, with equal weights assigned to securities. The betas originally reported were based on a "market" portfolio return with market value weights. The relative behavior is identical under either definition of beta. The market portfolio consists of all New York Stock Exchange securities, and the beta of the market portfolio is one, by construction.
Source: Beaver, Clarke, and Wright (1979), Table 3.

[5] The security price variable is unsystematic return (i.e., μ_t as defined in footnote 12 of Chapter 2). This variable is the *residual* percentage change in price (adjusted for dividends) after taking out the effects of market-wide price movements, measured by the percentage change in price (adjusted for dividends) of a market portfolio. Similarly, the changes in accounting earnings were measured relative to previous changes in earnings or relative to market-wide changes in earnings. Hence, Ball and Brown called the *residual* change in earnings the *forecast error*. Positive forecast errors are called favorable earnings changes, and negative forecast errors are called *unfavorable* earnings changes. The forecast errors have also been interpreted as a measure of unexpected changes in earnings. Hereafter, the unsystematic return will be referred to simply as the *residual* percentage change in price, and the earnings forecast error will be referred to as the *residual* percentage change in earnings.

mean decline of 154.8 percent), while Portfolio 6 consists of those securities that experienced the greatest residual increase in earnings (a mean increase of 185.1 percent). Portfolios 2 through 5 represent securities that experienced intermediate residual changes in earnings. The mean residual percentage change in earnings is reported in Table 5-1. Portfolios were reformed each year and results reported here refer to pooled results over the 1965 through 1974 period. The mean residual percentage change in price for the portfolios is also reported in Table 5-1.

There is a significant, positive correlation between the residual percentage change in earnings and the residual percentage change in price. Over the years studied, the average rank correlation is .74 and is statistically different from zero.[6] Moreover, not only is the relationship positive and significant, but the magnitude of the differences in security price changes is sizable. The residual percentage change in price ranges from −17.5 percent for Portfolio 1 to 29.2 percent for Portfolio 6.

To better understand the magnitude of this difference, consider two hypothetical portfolios, each of which starts with $10,000 at the beginning of the year. By the end of the year the average terminal value of Portfolio 1 would be only $8250, while the average terminal value of Portfolio 6 would be $12,920. The terminal value of Portfolio 1 is $1750 less than expected, while the terminal value of Portfolio 25 is $2920 more than expected.[7] The terminal value of Portfolio 6 (the most favorable earnings group) is 157 percent of the terminal value of Portfolio 1 (the least favorable earnings group). Hence, the magnitude of the differences in price changes indicates that not only is the relationship statistically significant, but it is also large enough to be economically important.

What are the implications of these findings? At a minimum, the findings imply that there is a correlation between the events that affect accounting earnings changes and changes in security prices. The evidence is also consistent with the contention that prices behave as if investors perceive that accounting earnings convey information about the value of a security. In the context of the framework developed in Chapter 4, security prices behave as if investors perceive that current earnings are statistically dependent with future earnings and the future dividend-paying ability of the firm. Hence, prices act as if current earnings changes

---

[6] The correlation is based on all twenty-five portfolios.

[7] Because the residual percentage change in price subtracts out an adjustment for market-wide conditions, the expected value of the residual is zero, and, as of the beginning of the year, the expected value of each hypothetical portfolio is $10,000. In other words, before knowledge of earnings, the expected change in the terminal value of each portfolio is zero.

possess a *permanent* component. In other words, a portion of the change in earnings is associated with a permanent alteration in the level of expected paying ability. In this context, the evidence is also consistent with the contention that prices behave as if investors perceive that earnings convey information (i.e., altering their beliefs) about future earnings and future dividend-paying ability.

5-2. RELATIONSHIP IS NOT ONE-TO-ONE

Given the results reported in Table 5-1, it might be tempting to conclude that earnings consist entirely of a permanent component and that there is a simple one-to-one relationship between percentage changes in earnings and percentage changes in security prices. However, two aspects of the evidence also indicate that such a conclusion would be incorrect.

(1) Although the correlation is high at the portfolio level, it is considerably weaker at the individual security level. However, it is still positive and statistically significant. The average correlation is only .38, instead of the .74, reported for the portfolio results.

This difference in correlation is to be expected, since grouping the data into portfolios has the effect of diversifying away a portion of the transitory components in earnings. As a result, the correlation would be expected to increase as data are grouped into portfolios. Beaver, Clarke, and Wright (1979) grouped data into twenty-five portfolios in each year based on earnings changes (six of which were reported in Table 5-1). Had the study grouped the data into fewer portfolios (e.g., ten portfolios or five portfolios), subsequent evidence by Beaver, Lambert, and Morse (1980) indicates that the correlation would be close to one.

(2) A less than one-to-one relationship is also evident from Table 5-1. The percentage change in price is smaller than the percentage change in earnings for the extreme portfolios. While the earnings of Portfolio 1 decline by 154.8 percent, the price declines by only 17.5 percent. While the earnings of securities in Portfolio 6 increase by an average of 185.1 percent, the price increases by only 29.2 percent. A similar behavior is observed for the other portfolios. Based on data from 1958 through 1976, Beaver, Lambert, and Ryan (1987) report a sensitivity (i.e., the slope of the regression of percentage change in price on percentage in earnings) averaged only .31, which was significantly different from both zero and one. In other words, prices generally move in the same direction as earnings but appear not to move as far. Prices, of course, may be changing for other uncorelated factors, which affects

the correlation. However, the sensitivity of price changes with respect to earnings changes is less than one, which cannot be explained merely by the presence of other uncorrelated factors. The lack of perfect correlation and a sensitivity of less than one is consistent with prices acting as if a portion of earnings is perceived to possess a transitory component.

5-3. PERMANENT VERSUS TRANSITORY COMPONENTS OF EARNINGS

There are several possible reasons why the relationship exhibits less than perfect correlation or why the sensitivity of price changes with respect to earnings changes is less than one. (1) There are other sources of information about future dividends and future earnings besides current earnings. Even though current earnings is one important source of information, it is not the only source of information. Announcements of litigation, contract awards, petroleum discoveries, future capital expenditures, anticipated strikes, and the awarding of charters for casinos in New Jersey are examples of events that may affect future earnings but may not be reflected in current earnings. (2) There are other sources of changes in stock prices that are not related to changes in future earnings or future dividends. For example, consider economy-wide events such as changes in interest rates or risk premiums. (3) Earnings changes reflect transitory factors that affect the current year's earnings that are expected not to alter (or at least only partially alter) the level of future expected earnings. (4) There are changes in earnings per share, which are not expected to alter the dividend-paying ability of the firm. Changes in depreciation methods and reliance on historical cost basis of accounting are two among many possible examples.

The price-earnings ratios of securities behave as if investors perceive that a portion of earnings consists of a transitory component. Table 5-2 reports some of the findings from a study of price-earnings ratios by Beaver and Morse (1978). The study finds that stocks which have high price-earnings ratios at the end of a year have experienced low earnings growth in that year and high earnings growth in the subsequent year. Similarly, low price-earnings ratios stocks experience high growth in the year just ended and low growth in the subsequent year. This is exactly the behavior that would be expected if (1) earnings are perceived by investors to contain a transitory component and (2) earnings behave as if they contain a transitory component.

The Beaver and Morse study constructed portfolios based upon year-end price-earnings ratios for a sample of firms with a December 31 fiscal year-end. The price-earnings ratio was computed as the ratio of price on December 31 divided by earnings per share (before extraordinary items). The study then examined the behavior of one-year earnings growth in the year just ended and the one-year growth in the subsequent year. This relationship was examined for portfolios constructed in each of the years 1956 through 1974. Table 5-2 reports the pooled results for the nineteen years, 1956 through 1974. Portfolio 1 consists of those securities with the highest price-earnings ratios (a median of 50 times earnings), while Portfolio 6 consists of those securities with the lowest price-earnings ratios (a median of 5.8). Portfolios 2 through 5 represent intermediate portfolios with respect to price-earnings ratios, and the median values of the price-earnings ratios of these portfolios are also reported in Table 5-2. For Portfolio 1, the median earnings growth in earnings in the year just ended relative to the earnings of the previous year was −4.1 percent, while for Portfolio 6, the median earnings growth in the year just ended was 26.4 percent. It may seem anomalous that high price-earnings stocks would have poor earnings growth and conversely for low price-earnings stocks. However, as will be shown shortly, this is exactly what would be expected if earnings are perceived to contain a transitory component. In the next year the median earnings growth of Portfolio 1 was 95.3 percent, while the median earnings growth for Portfolio 6 was −3.3 percent. Again, this is consistent with earnings actually behaving as if they contained a transitory component.

Effect of Transitory Component: An Illustration

The effect of a transitory component in earnings on price-earnings ratios and earnings growth can be demonstrated by the simple illustration shown in Table 5-3. Suppose that *expected* earnings per share is $1.00 for all years. Also assume that *actual* earnings per share in years 1 and 3 was $1.00 and in year 2 is $.75. Assume that price per share is

TABLE 5-2

Relationship Between Price-Earnings Ratios and Earnings Growth

Portfolio	Median Price Earnings	Median Earnings Growth in Same Year	Median Earnings Growth Next Year
1	50.0	−4.1%	95.3%
2	20.8	10.7%	14.9%
3	14.3	9.6%	12.9%
4	11.1	10.0%	8.8%
5	8.9	10.8%	5.2%
6	5.8	26.4%	−3.3%

Source: Beaver and Morse (1978), Tables 3 and 5.

TABLE 5-3

Effect of Transitory Component in Earnings

	Year 1	Year 2	Year 3
Expected earnings per share (EPS)	$1.00	$1.00	$1.00
Price per share	$10	$10	$10
I Negative Transitory Component			
Actual earnings per share	$1.00	$ .75	$1.00
Price-earnings ratio	10	13.3	10
Growth in EPS	—	−25%	+33%
II Positive Transitory Component			
Actual earnings per share	$1.00	$1.25	$1.00
Price-earnings ratio	10	8.3	10
Growth in EPS	—	+25%	−20%

$10 and remains $10 throughout because expected earnings have not changed. In year 2 the price-earnings ratio is 13.3 times ($10/$.75), while the growth in earnings is a *minus* 25 percent [($.75 − $1.00)/$1.00)]. As of the end of year 2, the growth in earnings in year 3 is 33 percent [($1.00 − $.75)/$.75)]. In this case, there was a negative transitory component to earnings of $.25. Conversely, assume the same facts as before except that there is a *positive* transitory component to earnings in year 2 of $.25 (i.e., the earnings per share in year 2 is $1.25). The price-earnings ratio at the end of year 2 would be 8.3 times ($10/$1.25), and the growth in earnings is a positive 25 percent [$1.25 − $1.00)/$1.00)]. However, as of the end of year 2, the growth in earnings per share is a *minus* 20 percent [$1.00 − $1.25)/$1.25)]. A high price-earnings ratio (13.3 times) is associated with low contemporaneous growth (−25 percent). A low price-earnings ratio (8.3 times) is associated with high contemporaneous growth (+25 percent). In other words, there is *negative* correlation between price-earnings ratios and earnings growth in that year, as was reported in Table 5-2.

Similarly, a high price-earnings ratio (13.3 times) is associated with high expected growth in the next year (+33 percent), and low price-earnings ratios (8.3 times) associated with low expected growth in the next year (−20 percent), as reported in Table 5-2. In other words, the transitory component in earnings is expected to induce a positive correlation between price-earnings ratios in the current year and growth in earnings in the subsequent year. This can be explained by observing that both the price-earnings ratio and the next year's subsequent growth in earnings contain the same denominator ($.75 in the first case and $1.25 in the second case). Therefore, when earnings per share is transitorily low, both price-earnings and next year's growth will be transitorily

high. Conversely, when earnings contain a positive transitory component, both price-earnings ratios and next year's expected growth will be
transitorily low. Hence, price earnings and subsequent growth will be
positively correlated.

In sum then, market prices act as if earnings are perceived to
contain a transitory component. Moreover, the actual behavior of earnings confirms this perception. In other words, earnings per share behaves as if there is a transitory component to earnings, which is caused
by events that impact on current earnings but affect expected future
earnings only partially or not at all.[8]

5-4. SECURITY PRICES AND DIFFERENCES IN ACCOUNTING METHODS

Certain events may permanently affect the level of accounting earnings but not in a way that implies a change in the value of the security.
The nature of the financial accounting system is a major contributor to
such events. For example, a firm may change its method of accounting
for depreciation. This can produce a change in earnings that is "permanent" in the sense that the level of earnings is expected to be permanently affected, but it may not be an event that alters the firm's
dividend-paying ability. Also, there are more subtle effects of the financial accounting system on earnings. Consider the effects of unanticipated
inflation. Revenues and many expenses increase with inflation, but some
expenses such as depreciation (under historical cost) do not. The result
is an increase in net income that is greater than the rate of inflation,
even if nothing has changed in real terms. Hence, there can be a portion
of the change in accounting earnings that is not associated with a change
in dividend-paying ability.

Firms are permitted to use different accounting methods (e.g.,
straight-line or accelerated depreciation methods) that affect the level
of accounting earnings. For example, firms with net growth in asset
acquisitions will report higher net income under straight-line depreciation than under accelerated depreciation. This induces a difference in
the level of earnings across firms that is unrelated to the future dividend-
paying ability of the firm. Price-earnings ratios of firms that use different
depreciation methods would be expected to differ, after taking into
account other reasons for differing price-earnings ratios. Empirical evi-

---

[8] Events that affect future earnings and hence current price but not current earnings
(i.e., factor (1) cited above) would also induce a positive correlation between price-earnings
ratios and future growth, but there are no obvious reasons why negative correlation
between current growth and price-earnings ratios would result.

dence by Beaver and Dukes (1973) suggests that price-earnings ratios systematically differ as a function of the depreciation method used for annual report purposes. The results are summarized in Table 5-4. The method used for tax purposes is accelerated depreciation and the difference refers to the depreciation method used for annual reports purposes only. In particular, firms that use accelerated depreciation would be expected to have lower earnings and hence higher price-earnings ratios than firms that use straight-line depreciation, assuming risk, growth, and other things are equal. The evidence indicates that firms using accelerated depreciation, on the average, do in fact have higher price-earnings ratios (16.61 versus 15.08). Moreover, an analysis of other factors indicates that there were no differences between the two groups with respect to risk or earnings growth. In fact, on the average, the firms using accelerated depreciation had essentially the same risk and growth as firms using straight-line depreciation. Moreover, when the earnings of the firms using straight-line depreciation were converted to the earnings that would have been reported had accelerated depreciation been used, the differences in price-earnings ratios essentially disappeared. The average price-earnings ratio increased to 16.2 when the earnings of the straight-line group were computed under accelerated depreciation. In other words, when the earnings of the firms using straight-line depreciation were converted to an accounting basis equivalent to that of the firms using accelerated depreciation, the price-earnings ratios of the two groups of firms were essentially the same. This is consistent with a

TABLE 5-4

Differences in Price-Earnings Ratios, Risk, and Earnings Growth for Firms Using Accelerated Versus Straight-Line Depreciation

| | Depreciation Group | | | |
| | Accelerated | | Straight-Line | |
Variable	Mean	Standard Deviation	Mean	Standard Deviation
Market beta[a]	1.003	0.25	1.009	0.33
Average price-earnings ratio[b]	16.61	6.72	15.08	3.82
Earnings growth[c]	0.043	0.11	0.045	0.10

[a]Computed from a time series regression of monthly security return data from January, 1950, through December, 1967.

[b]Computed as the median of the ratio of price per share divided by earnings per share at fiscal year end based upon annual data from 1950 through 1967.

[c]Computed as annual rate of growth in earnings available for common assuming continuous compounding over the eighteen-year interval 1950 through 1967.

Source: Beaver and Dukes (1973), Table 2. Reprinted with permission.

security price formation process that adjusts for differences in the level of earnings induced by accounting method differences. Even if prices are not dependent upon the method of accounting used but accounting earnings are, the ratio of price to earnings will be dependent upon the method of accounting used. In other words, the prices are independent of which accounting method is used, but accounting earnings are affected by the method chosen. Hence, price-earnings ratios computed under differing accounting methods will also differ, even though price-earnings ratios computed under a consistent, uniform method of accounting would show no difference in price-earnings ratios.

Archibald (1972) has examined the security price behavior at times when firms changed their method of depreciation for annual report purposes from accelerated to straight-line. He finds that prices behave as if the change in methods has no favorable impact on security prices, even though earnings are greater under the new method than they otherwise would have been. Similarly, Cassidy (1976) finds that there is no impact on security prices of firms that switched from normalization (or deferral) of the investment tax credit to flow-through, even though the effect of the change would be to make earnings greater than they otherwise would have been if they had been computed under the old method. Hong, Kaplan, and Mandelker (1978) conclude that the use of the pooling treatment of accounting for business combination produced no apparent superior stock price performance relative to that of firms that used the purchase treatment of accounting for their business combinations, even though pooling will lead to higher reported earnings than the purchase treatment. Duke (1976) finds that security price behaves as if investors implicitly regard research and development expenditures as assets, even though the firm entirely expensed these expenditures in the year of incurrence for annual report purposes. Foster (1977b) finds that the security prices of property-liability insurance companies behave as if unrealized gains and losses on marketable securities are part of earnings, even though such items are not reported as such by the insurance firms. Moreover, Foster (1975) finds that "pro forma" earnings of life insurance companies that attempt to adjust for the conservative accounting treatment of assets and liabilities under reported earnings show a higher association with security prices than reported earnings do. Beaver and Dukes (1973) find that price changes are more highly associated with a hypothetical class of earnings numbers using more accelerated depreciation than reported earnings. This evidence is consistent with the contention that prices behave as if investors "look beyond" reported accounting earnings and attempt to make adjustments for the effects of events on earnings that do not imply altered dividend-paying ability. The adjustment process appears to include adjusting for differences in earnings among firms induced by using *different* accounting methods (e.g., depreciation method differences and purchase versus pooling), for differences in earnings among firms induced by using the *same* accounting method (e.g., research and development and the insurance industry practices), and for changes in earnings among firms induced by changing methods of accounting (e.g., depreciation method and investment credit method changes). As a result, prices act as if they are not a function of the method of accounting used, while the ratio of price to earnings does. Such changes are another reason for a less than one-to-one relationship between price changes and earnings changes.[9]

Choice of Accounting Method: A Contracting Perspective

The changes in accounting methods discussed previously were treated as if they had no effect on the dividend-paying ability of the firm and hence no effect on the price of common equity. Clearly not all accounting changes would have that property. For example, changes in accounting methods for financial reporting purposes that were accompanied by similar changes for tax purposes could well be expected to affect the after-tax cash flow of the firm and hence future dividend-paying ability. The switch of inventory valuation methods from FIFO to LIFO is often cited as an example of such an accounting change. More generally, a change in accounting methods can affect stock price if it is perceived to alter the production or financing activities of the firm in such a way as to alter the expected after-tax future cash flows.

The contracting hypothesis focuses on particular ways in which changes in accounting methods can alter the production and financing activities. The contracting hypothesis argues that the firm is affected by a number of "contracts" which are defined in terms of accounting numbers. As a result, a change in accounting method can be expected to alter the numbers in such a way that the economic impact of that contract is affected. Compensation plans, debt covenants, and tax laws are frequently cited as illustrations. More subtle, yet potentially important, effects can be induced by implicit, social contracts which in turn permit changes in accounting methods to induce changes in "political costs" borne by the firm.

Watts and Zimmerman (1986) offer an excellent statement of the contracting hypothesis and summary of the existing empirical evidence with respect to stock price effects. They review several studies of man-

---

[9] These findings are open to alternative interpretations because of a number of factors such as self-selection on the part of firms that choose a particular method or that choose to change methods. These factors are discussed in detail in Gonedes and Dopuch (1974) and Foster (1980).

datory changes in accounting methods—changes required because of a change in an accounting standard by some regulatory body such as the FASB. For example, Watts and Zimmerman conclude that Leftwich (1981) and Collins, Roseff, and Dhaliwal (1981) provide partial support for the proposition that accounting standard changes affect firms' share values via their debt contracts.

In contrast to evidence cited previously, this research focuses on mandatory accounting changes rather than voluntary ones (e.g., changes in depreciation method). Watts and Zimmerman claim that tests of mandatory changes are more powerful tests of the contracting hypothesis. In fact, they suggest that Holthausen's study (1981) of voluntary changes, which finds no stock price effects, as consistent with their claim.

5-5. EARNINGS VERSUS "CASH FLOW"

Several studies have examined whether earnings changes or changes in "cash flow" are more highly associated with changes in security prices. In this context, "cash flow" is defined as essentially funds provided by operations and is typically measured as earnings plus expenses that do not drain working capital (e.g., depreciation, depletion, and amortization of various noncurrent balance sheet items).[10]

Beaver and Dukes (1972) find that residual changes in prices are generally more highly associated with residual changes in earnings than with changes in "cash flow." Ball and Brown (1968) also analyzed residual "cash flow" changes and found that they were not as successful as residual earnings changes in "predicting" the sign of residual price changes. Both of these studies treat earnings and "cash flow" as mutually exclusive variables. Patell and Kaplan (1977) formulate the issue differently and ask the question whether or not cash flow data possess information content over and above that of annual earnings. Patell and Kaplan are unable to reject the hypothesis that no additional information content exists.

One difficulty in interpreting these results is that earnings and cash flow variables tend to be very highly correlated and treated as if they were released simultaneously. As a result, it is difficult to distinguish differences in information content. Wilson (1986, 1987) examines a sample of firms where cash flow and funds flow data were announced subsequently to earnings. Wilson finds that these data do have an incremental impact over and above that provided by earnings as reflected in price movements on that subsequent announcement date.

---

[10] "Cash flow" studied here is not literally cash flow. In this sense, the evidence does not directly address the earnings versus cash flow issue.

5-6. OTHER SOURCES OF INFORMATION

The studies by Benston (1966) and Ball and Brown (1968), among others, indicate that much of the price reaction associated with earnings occurs prior to the announcement of annual earnings. This "anticipatory" effect is consistent with the notion that prices reflect earnings expectations and is illustrated in Figure 5-1. The Ball and Brown study is based upon 261 New York Stock Exchange firms and their annual earnings announcements for the years 1957 through 1965. The set of lines in the upper half of Figure 5-1 shows the cumulative, residual price change in the months surrounding the announcement of positive residual earnings changes (month 0). The positive slope indicates that residual price changes are positive for several months prior to the announcement. In fact, only a small proportion of total price movement occurs in the month of the announcement. The announcements of negative residual earnings change as shown in the bottom half of Figure 5-1. Of course, here the slope is negative. Again, much of the downward draft has occurred by the month of the announcement. Overall, only 10 percent of the cumulative price movement occurs in the month of the announcement.

This effect is not surprising because there is other information being publicly released during the year that permits investors to revise their predictions of annual earnings. Quarterly earnings, quarterly dividends, and earnings forecasts by analysts and management are examples. For example, Brown and Kennelly (1972) find that residual price changes in the months prior to the announcement of annual earnings are associated with residual changes in quarterly earnings. This evidence, among others, has led to the interpretation [Benston (1976)] that annual earnings are not timely information and are preempted by alternative, more timely sources.

By contrast, studies indicate that there is a significant price reaction in the week of the announcement of annual earnings [Beaver (1968)]. The study focuses on price movements without attempting to specify the direction of the price changes, as the Benston and the Ball and Brown studies do. The study is based upon 143 New York Stock Exchange firms for the years 1961 through 1965. Figure 5-2 reports the magnitude of the residual price change, ignoring its sign, in the week of the announcement relative to other weeks during the year. There is an obviously large "spike" at week 0 (the week of the announcement). This finding means that "large" price changes (ignoring direction) are more likely to occur during the week of the annual earnings than at other times during the year. Roughly speaking, the average price change (squared) during the announcement week is approximately 167 percent

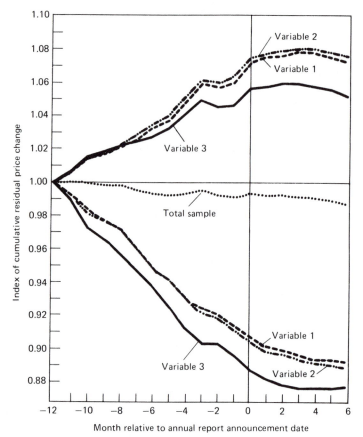

FIGURE 5-1

Monthly residual price change for positive and negative residual earnings changes. The top set of lines represents the cumulative residual price change associated with **positive** *residual earnings changes measured three ways (i.e., variables 1 through 3). The bottom set of lines represents the cumulative residual price changes associated with* **negative** *residual earnings changes measured three ways. The cumulative residual price changes start with a hypothetical portfolio of 1.00 (e.g., $1) twelve months prior to the announcement. The graph shows the value of that portfolio over time.*
Source: Ball and Brown (1968), Figure 1, p. 169.

of a "normal" or average price change (squared) during other weeks in the year.

Later studies have examined these relationships using daily data. Applying the Ball and Brown research design to the days surrounding the annual (and quarterly) earnings announcements, Foster (1977a) finds a small, but statistically significant residual price change the day before

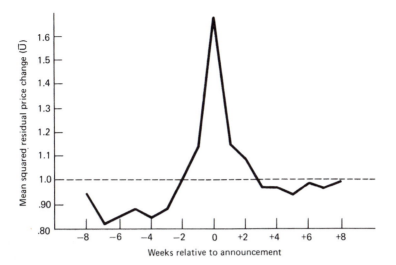

FIGURE 5-2

Residual price changes (ignoring sign) in weeks surrounding earnings announcements. For each week, the unsystematic return was squared (to abstract from the sign of the price change) and divided by the average weekly squared unsystematic return for that firm during a "nonreport" period. This ratio was then averaged across 506 announcements. The average is $\overline{U}$. The dotted line represents the value of $\overline{U}$ in nonreport periods during the rest of the year.
Source: **Beaver (1968), Figure 6, p. 91.**

and day of the earnings announcement. This price movement is illustrated in Figure 5-3. Applying an approach similar to Beaver, Morse (1978) also finds a statistically significant price reaction the day before and day of the earnings announcement. This is illustrated in Figure 5-4.

The price reaction the day before can be due to a variety of reasons. In particular, Morse and prior studies used the day the earnings announcement appeared in the *Wall Street Journal* as the announcement day. Many earnings announcements are released over the Dow-Jones newswire (often called the broad tape) the day before the article appears in the *Wall Street Journal*. Patell and Wolfson (1984) have examined stock price reactions to earnings on an intraday (i.e., transaction-by-transaction) data. They found that a significant reaction to the earnings announcement as it is released over the broad tape. A major portion of the reaction occurred within two hours of the announcement, but with detectable traces into the next day. Spillover into the next day is more likely on announcements made late in the trading day. These findings suggest that stock prices react very quickly to earnings announcements, once they are released.

Prices act *as if* earnings announcements alter investors' beliefs in

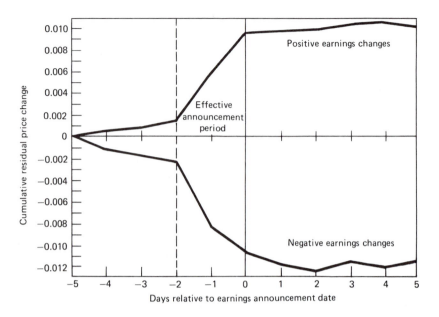

FIGURE 5-3

Daily residual price change for positive and negative residual earnings changes. The graph represents a composite across all four quarters. The results for the annual earnings and for each of the other three quarterly announcements are similar to the composite. The graph uses zero as the initial value and sums the residual percentage price changes.
Source: **Foster (1978), p. 350.**

such a way as to alter the price of the security. Some have found these results paradoxical when compared to the Benston and the Ball and Brown conclusions. However, the resolution of the paradox is relatively simple. The anticipatory price movements indicate that earnings expectations are being revised as quarterly and other data are being released. Hence, the earnings expectations models used in Benston and in Ball and Brown are potentially badly misspecified because they fail to reflect the most up-to-date information upon which earnings expectations are based. For example, to predict the direction of the price change in the month of an earnings announcement involves an inclusion of information available up to the beginning of the month of announcement. To predict the direction of the change in price in the week of an earnings announcement involves a consideration of information upon which earnings expectations were based as of the beginning of the week of the announcement.

In other words, the earnings expectations models were not updated

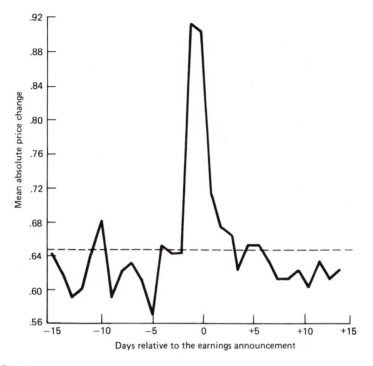

FIGURE 5-4

Residual price changes (ignoring sign) in days surrounding earnings announcements. Mean absolute price change is similar to U as described in Figure 5-2, except the absolute value, rather than squaring, is used to abstract from the sign. The dotted line represents the sample average.
Source: **Morse (1978), Figure 2.**

for information coming onto the market during the year. Hence, the earnings expectations models are becoming increasingly misspecified as the announcement month approaches. In order to predict the *direction* of the price change in a month close to, or including, the announcement month, the earnings expectation model must include the information released and reflected in prices up to that month. At a minimum, this involves an incorporation of quarterly earnings, as well as dividends, earnings forecasts by management and analysts, announcements of litigation, contracts awarded, and in principle all information reflected in prices. Hence, it is hardly surprising that a residual earnings change, defined relative to a benchmark where the most recent firm-specific information is last year's earnings, has limited ability to predict the direction of the price change in the final month of the announcement.

Initially (e.g., twelve months prior to the announcement), the Ball and Brown earnings models are not as badly misspecified because they rely upon data available at the beginning of the fiscal year. However, as the year progresses and other information arrives, the earnings expectations model is increasingly out-of-date, and, in this sense, increasingly misspecified. Hence, it is not surprising that residual earnings changes defined relative to such a benchmark provide a limited basis for predicting the direction of the price change in the final months before the announcement. Similarly, it is not surprising that a method of detecting price changes that does not require a specification of the direction of the impact upon price is able to identify a significant price reaction.

In sum, then, earnings appear to be one source of information that alters security prices, although they are only one of many such sources. How "important" are earnings? The answer depends upon the perspective taken. One way to view the relative importance of earnings is to consider a pie chart such as that in Figure 5-5. The pie represents all the sources of information that alter or affect security prices. Earnings represent one small slice of the pie. However, the pie consists of many small slices (indicated by dashed lines), and no one slice is very large. In one sense, earnings are not important because they represent only a small portion of the total. But in another sense, earnings are very important, in that their slice may be at least as large as any other slice in the pie, particularly if the price reaction to a type of announcement is considered in terms of the frequency of occurrence of that type. Moreover, the other data may be sources of information about earnings. If earnings are viewed as important information, it is natural that investors would attempt to obtain other information that would permit them to

FIGURE 5-5

Earnings relative to all other information.

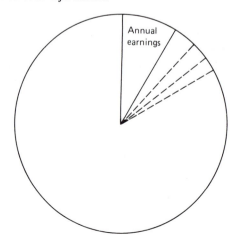

Annual
earnings

predict earnings. It would be somewhat anomalous if earnings were deemed to be unimportant merely because investors were obtaining other data that permitted them to successfully predict earnings.

However, it is important to emphasize again that the empirical evidence has not shown that prices are responding directly to earnings. For example, other data often accompany an earnings announcement by a firm. Moreover, over the course of a year (e.g., as in the Ball and Brown study) earnings changes may be highly correlated with other information released during the year. Earnings changes may exhibit a significant contemporaneous association with price changes because they are correlated with other data to which prices are reacting. Currently, research has not yet sorted out this issue. In this sense, the importance of earnings is still an open issue.

5-7. SECURITY PRICES AS PREDICTORS OF ACCOUNTING EARNINGS

Thus far, the empirical evidence regarding the relationship between security prices and earnings has treated earnings as a predictor (i.e., an explanatory variable) for prices. This is a natural way to view the relationship since earnings are typically viewed as one of the sources of information used in assessing dividend-paying ability which in part determines security price. However, recent research has turned around the familiar price and earnings relationship and has used price as a predictor (i.e., forecaster) of accounting earnings.

As stated in Chapter 4, prices at any given point in time can be viewed as if they are a function of future, expected earnings. Prices reflect investors' expectations regarding future earnings. The potential richness of price with respect to expectations is described in Muth's (1961) seminal essay on rational expectations. If prices are based upon an information system with many signals other than earnings, prices can potentially reflect information about future earnings that is not reflected in current and past earnings. For example, prices may respond before earnings to certain events or information. A mineral discovery, news about an anticipated strike next year, or the awarding of gambling casino franchises in New Jersey are but a few examples.

If prices are viewed as "reflecting" other information, then prices can be used as a surrogate or proxy for that information. Recent work by Beaver, Lambert, and Morse (1980) indicates that price-based forecasting models of earnings can predict future earnings "better" (i.e., with a lower mean error) than forecasting models based upon a statistical extrapolation of past and current earnings. In particular, previous evidence by Ball and Watts (1972), Albrecht, Lookabill, and McKeown

(1977), and by Watts and Leftwich (1977) indicates that the "best" statistical model for forecasting earnings using current and past earnings data is called the *random walk with a drift model*. Under this model, next year's earnings are forecasted to be equal to this year's earnings plus a drift term equal to the average change in earnings over some past period. This model has been extremely robust against challenges since its use by Ball and Brown (1968). Beaver, Lambert, and Morse (1980) use a price-based forecasting model which results in lower forecasting errors than the random walk with a drift model. These results are reported in Table 5-5. The price-based model produces a lower error in 55 percent of the cases. In the higher price-earnings portfolios the margin of superiority tends to be more pronounced. This superiority is possible because the information upon which earnings forecasts are based is ex-

TABLE 5-5

Analysis of Earnings Forecast Errors from Two Forecasting Models[a]

	Price-Based Model[b]	Random Walk With Drift[c]
	Times Lower Error	Times Lower Error
Portfolio 1[d]	374	312
Portfolio 2	340	348
Portfolio 3	337	349
Portfolio 4	336	350
Portfolio 5	393	292
Portfolio 6	364	319
Portfolio 7	389	294
Portfolio 8	399	283
Portfolio 9	414	267
Portfolio 10	408	272
TOTAL[e]	3754	3086

[a] The forecast error is actual earnings per share less forecasted earnings per share divided by actual earnings per share.
[b] $f(X_{t+1}) = F(g_{t+1}|P_t/X_t)X_t + X_t$ where $F(X_{t+1})$ is the forecasted earnings per share. $F(g_{t+1}|P_t/X_t)$ is the forecasted earnings growth conditional on the price-earnings ratio, and X_t is earnings per share in year t.
[c] $F(X_{t+1}) = X_t + d_t$, where $F(X_{t+1})$ is the forecasted earnings per share in year t, and d_t is the security-specific drift term.
[d] Portfolio 1 is the lowest price-earnings ratio portfolio and Portfolio 10 is the highest price-earnings ratio portfolio.
[e] Computation of t-value:

$$\frac{\text{actual} - \text{expected}}{.5\sqrt{N}} = \frac{3754 - 3420}{.5\sqrt{6840}} = \frac{334}{41.35} = 8.08$$

Source: Beaver, Lambert, and Morse (1980), Table 4.

panded to include price in addition to past earnings. Price is used as a surrogate for other data that convey information about future earnings.

Beaver, Lambert, and Morse also examine the relationship between percentage changes in price and concurrent percentage changes in earnings. Based on sensitivity of price changes to earnings changes, prices act as if investors perceive the earnings process to be dramatically different from a random walk with a drift. In particular, prices act as if earnings are perceived to be a compound process (i.e., mixture of two processes). The first process reflects the effects of events on earnings that have no impact on security prices. This first process is called a *garbling process*. The second process reflects the impact on earnings of events that also have an impact on security prices. The second process appears to behave in a lagged manner with respect to price changes. The earnings process, which is a mixture of these two processes, can be viewed as a garbling of the second process. If earnings are a mixture of two processes, security prices can be used to extract information about the behavior of compound processes that cannot be obtained from the earnings series alone.

5-8. EARNINGS VOLATILITY AND SYSTEMATIC RISK

The discussion thus far has focused on prices as a function of expected earnings, among other factors. Mean-variance portfolio theory suggests that price is also a function of the perceived systematic risk (i.e., beta) of the security, among other factors.

Empirical evidence by Beaver, Kettler, and Scholes (1970) and Beaver and Manegold (1975), among others, has shown that measures of systematic earnings volatility (i.e., accounting earnings betas) show significantly positive correlation with a security's beta defined in terms of security returns. For example, the correlation at the portfolio level ranges between .7 to 8.[11] Beaver, Clarke, and Wright (1979) have shown that securities with the greatest percentage changes in earnings also have the highest betas. This is illustrated in Table 5-1 in which the extreme Portfolios 1 and 6 have higher betas than the intermediate portfolios do.

In sum, prices act as if earnings volatility are associated with systematic risk. Moreover, the evidence is consistent with the more ambitious interpretation that earnings convey information about the systematic risk of the common stock.

---

[11] This is based upon an average of the correlations for the net inome to net worth accounting beta with the market beta, using total period data to compute the betas. See Table 7 of Beaver and Manegold (1975).

5-9. CONCLUDING REMARKS

The chapter summarizes the results of some of the empirical research on the relationship between earnings and security prices. Several conclusions are offered. (1) Earnings changes and price changes show a significant, positive correlation. (2) Although significant, the relationship is not simply one-to-one. (3) This occurs in part because prices act as if earnings are perceived to contain a transitory component. In simple terms, a portion of earnings is not expected to persist, and hence the "permanent" level (i.e., the expected value) of future earnings is not equal to the current level. (4) Security prices act as if investors "see through" the effect on earnings of accounting method differences, both across firms and over time. (5) Price changes appear to be more highly associated with earnings changes than with cash flow changes. This constitutes one source of evidence bearing on the FASB contention that earnings are a better indicator of future cash flow generating ability than current cash flows are. (6) Prices act as if earnings are a potentially important source of information, but only one of many sources. (7) Security prices can be used to infer expectations regarding future earnings, and prices imply a forecast of earnings that has a lower forecast error than the "best" statistical forecasting model, based upon past and current earnings. (8) Measures of systematic risk have a significant positive correlation with measures of earnings volatility.

There are a number of open or unresolved issues. The issue of the relative efficacy of earnings versus cash flow data has not been resolved. Moreover, virtually all of the studies have found a statistical dependency between earnings and prices, which is consistent with the hypothesis that earnings convey information. However, for the most part, careful attention has not been given to other sources of information available to investors at the same time. As a result, it is difficult to say whether the observed significant relationships are due to reliance by investors upon earnings or whether earnings are correlated with the information that does affect security prices. Studies using daily or intraday data come the closest to resolving this issue. Subject to this ambiguity, stock prices act as if earnings convey important information or, at the very least, are correlated with important information.

BIBLIOGRAPHY

ALBRECHT, W., L. LOOKABILL, AND J. MCKEOWN. "The Time Series Properties of Annual Earnings." *Journal of Accounting Research* (Autumn 1977), 226–244.

ARCHIBALD, T. R. "Stock Market Reaction to Depreciation Switch-Back." *Accounting Review* (January 1972), 22–30.

BALL, R. "Changes in Accounting Techniques and Stock Prices."

Empirical Research in Accounting: Selected Studies. Supplement to the *Journal of Accounting Research* (1972), 1–38.

———— AND P. BROWN. "An Empirical Evaluation of Accounting Income Numbers." *Journal of Accounting Research* (Autumn 1968), 159–178.

———— AND R. WATTS. "Some Time Series Properties of Accounting Income." *Journal of Finance* (June 1972), 663–681.

BEAVER, W. "The Information Content of Annual Earnings Announcements." *Empirical Research in Accounting: Selected Studies.* Supplement to the *Journal of Accounting Research* (1968), 67–92.

BEAVER, W., R. CLARKE, AND W. WRIGHT. "The Association Between Unsystematic Security Returns and the Magnitude of the Earnings Forecast Error." *Journal of Accounting Research* (Autumn 1979), 316–340.

———— AND R. DUKES. "Interperiod Tax Allocation, Earnings Expectations, and the Behavior of Security Prices." *Accounting Review* (April 1972), 320–332.

———— AND R. DUKES. "Interperiod Tax Allocation and Delta Depreciation Methods: Some Empirical Results." *Accounting Review* (July 1973), 549–559.

———— S. KETTLER, AND M. SCHOLES. "The Association Between Market-Determined and Accounting-Determined Risk Measures." *Accounting Review* (October 1970), 654–682.

———— R. LAMBERT, AND D. MORSE. "The Information Content of Security Prices." *Journal of Accounting and Economics* (March 1980), 3–28.

———— R. LAMBERT AND S. RYAN. "The Information Content of Security Prices: A Second Look." *Journal of Accounting and Economics* (July 1987), 139–157.

———— AND J. MANEGOLD. "The Association Between Market-Determined and Accounting-Determined Measures of Systematic Risk." *Journal of Financial and Quantitative Analysis* (June 1975), 231–284.

———— AND D. MORSE. "What Determines Price-Earnings Ratios?" *Financial Analysts Journal* (July–August, 1978), 65–76.

BENSTON, G. "Published Corporate Accounting Data and Stock Prices." *Empirical Research in Accounting: Selected Studies 1966.* Supplement to the *Journal of Accounting Research* (1966), 1–14.

———— "There's No Real News in Earnings Reports." *Fortune* (April 1976), 73–75.

BROWN, P., AND J. KENNELLY. "The Informational Content of Quarterly Earnings." *Journal of Business* (July 1972), 403–421.

CASSIDY, D. "Investor Evaluation of Accounting Information: Some Additional Evidence." *Journal of Accounting Research* (Autumn 1976), 212–229.

COLLINS, D., M. ROSEFF, AND D. DHALIWAL. "The Economic Determinants of the Market Reaction to Proposed Mandatory Accounting Changes in the Oil and Gas Industry: A Cross Sectional Analysis." *Journal of Accounting and Economics* (March 1981), 37–71.

COMISKEY, E. "Market Response to Changes in Depreciation Accounting." *Accounting Review* (April 1971), 279–285.

DUKES, R. "An Investigation of the Effects of Expensing Research and Development Costs on Security Prices." *Proceedings of the Conference on Topical Research in Accounting.* Edited by M. Schiff and G. Sorter. New York University, 1976.

FOSTER, G. "Accounting Earnings and Stock Prices of Insurance Companies." *Accounting Review* (October 1975), 686–698.

———— "Quarterly Earnings Data: Time Series Properties and Predictive Ability Results." *Accounting Review* (January 1977a), 1–21.

———— "Valuation Parameters of Property-Liability Companies." *Journal of Finance* (June 1977b), 823–836.

———— "Accounting Policy Decisions and Capital Market Research." *Journal of Accounting and Economics* (March 1980), 29–62.

———— *Financial Statement Analysis.* 2d ed. Englewood Cliffs, N.J.: Prentice-Hall, 1986.

GONEDES, N. AND N. DOPUCH. "Capital Market Equilibrium, Information Production, and Selecting Accounting Techniques: Theoretical Framework and Review of Empirical Work." *Studies on Financial Accounting Objectives: 1974.* Supplement to the *Journal of Accounting Research* (1974), 48–129.

GRIFFIN, P. *Usefulness of Investors and Creditors of Information Provided by Financial Reporting.* 2d ed. Stamford, Conn.: Financial Accounting Standards Board, 1987.

HOLTHAUSEN, R. "Evidence on the Effect of Bond Covenants and Management Compensation Contracts on the Choice of Accounting Techniques: The Case of the Depreciation Switchback." *Journal of Accounting and Economics* (March 1981), 73–109.

HONG, H., R. KAPLAN, AND G. MANDELKER. "Pooling vs. Purchase: The Effects of Accounting for Mergers on Stock Prices." *Accounting Review* (January 1978), 31–47.

LEFTWICH, R. "Evidence of the Impact of Mandatory Changes in Accounting Principles on Corporate Loan Agreements." *Journal of Accounting and Economics* (March 1981), 3–36.

MAY, R. "The Influence of Quarterly Earnings Announcements in Investors' Decisions." *Empirical Research in Accounting: Selected Studies.* Supplement to *Journal of Accounting Research* (1971), 119–163.

MORSE, D. "Asymmetrically Distributed Information in a Market Setting: Theoretical and Empirical Approaches." Unpublished doctoral thesis, Stanford University, 1978.

MUTH, J. "Rational Expectations and the Theory of Price Movements." *Econometrica* (July 1961), 315–335.

PATELL, J., AND R. KAPLAN. "The Information Content of Cash Flow Data Relative to Annual Earnings." Unpublished working paper, Stanford University, August, 1977.

———— AND M. WOLFSON. "The Intraday Speed of Adjustment of Stock Prices to Earnings and Dividend Announcements." *Journal of Accounting and Economics* (June 1984), 223–252.

WATTS, R. AND R. LEFTWICH. "The Time Series of Annual Accounting Earnings." *Journal of Accounting Research* (Autumn 1977), 253–271.

———— AND J. ZIMMERMAN. *Positive Accounting Theory*. Englewood Cliffs, N.J.: Prentice-Hall, 1986.

WILSON, G. P. "The Relative Information Content of Accrual and Cash Flows: Combined Evidence at the Earnings Announcement and Annual Release Date." *Studies on Alternative Measures of Accounting Income.* Supplement to *Journal of Accounting Research* (1986), 165–200.

WILSON, G. P. "The Incremental Information Content of the Accrual and Funds Components of Earnings after Controlling for Earnings." *Accounting Review* (April 1987), 293–322.

chapter six

Market Efficiency

Chapter 2 viewed financial statement data as information to investors, among others. Chapters 4 and 5 developed this perspective further and explored the conceptual and empirical relationship between accounting earnings and security prices. This emphasis on earnings and prices is appropriate given the prominent role they play in the financial reporting environment. However, a related aspect of the environment is the relationship between security prices and information generally, including accounting earnings, other financial statement data, and information appearing outside the financial statements. The relationship between prices and information is called *market efficiency*. As defined here, a securities market is said to be efficient with respect to an information system if and only if the prices act *as if* everyone observes the signals from that information system. In other words, prices act *as if* there is universal knowledge of that information. If prices have this property, they "fully reflect" the information system.[1]

---

[1] This chapter is structured around four earlier articles [Beaver (1973a, 1976, 1980a, and 1981)], in which many of these issues are discussed in greater detail. Other treatments of this subject appear in Dyckman and Morse (1986) and Foster (1986).

6-1. PRICES AND INFORMATION

What information is fully reflected in prices is of potential importance to policy makers, such as the SEC and the FASB, to management as preparers of financial statements, to auditors as certifiers of those statements, to information intermediaries as consumers of and competitors to those statements, and to investors.

Each of these major constituencies, for diverse reasons, has a vital interest in the prices of a firm's securities and the effect of information on prices. The interest in security prices arises because of the economic consequences associated with security prices. For example, changes in prices of a security alter the market value of the investor's wealth. This change in wealth can affect the opportunity set of the investor. Hence, in general, price changes will be associated with alterations in the investor's consumption-investment behavior, although the nature of the alteration will depend upon many factors, such as the nature of the investor's preferences. The price of the security also affects the terms on which the firm obtains additional financing. This in turn can affect management's perceived cost of capital and alter the nature of the projects undertaken. At an economy-wide level, capital formation and resource allocation can be affected.

While prices may be of immediate interest, the ultimate concern is with the attendant consequences. The economic consequences of market efficiency are essentially those of information in a multi-person setting. The economic consequences of financial reporting, as discussed in Chapter 2, provide a basis for an analysis of the implications and importance of market efficiency.

A few words are in order at the outset regarding the purposes of this chapter. The purpose of the chapter is *not* to take a position in favor of or against market efficiency with respect to a particular information system. Further the purpose of the chapter is *not* to provide a detailed, in-depth technical evaluation of the research. The summary of the research will be very brief and clearly nontechnical. The reasons for not adopting either of these purposes will become apparent as the discussion progresses. Instead, the chapter will focus upon several aspects of market efficiency, including its origins, definitions, various forms, evidence, research design issues, counterevidence, theories, implications, and importance to and acceptance by the financial reporting constituencies.

6-2. ORIGIN OF THE MARKET EFFICIENCY
CONCEPT

The issue of market efficiency with respect to financial statement information originated in the practice of security analysis, which was defined as the process of finding mispriced securities.[2] In this context, market inefficiency was expressed as a departure of a security's price from its "intrinsic value." The process of using financial statement data to find mispriced securities is exemplified by the seminal work of Graham and Dodd (1934), which represents an attempt to formalize the art of security analysis as it is practiced by the professional investment community. Hence, the professional investment community introduced this concept, and much of the professional investment industry sells services to clients based on the contention that they can successfully find mispriced securities.

The concept of the "intrinsic value" of a security is intriguing and is distinctive to security analysis. A security, such as a common stock, can be thought of as a commodity, much like other goods and services. As with other commodities, securities possess value because they are perceived to possess attributes desired by individuals. Common stocks are thought to possess value because they represent claims to future, uncertain cash flows in the form of future dividends. In elementary discussions of the demand for a commodity, prices are viewed as reflecting individuals' wealth, tastes, and beliefs.[3] These factors are typically viewed as being personal or subjective and different across individuals. Indeed, with respect to most commodities, the influence of endowments, preferences, and beliefs on prices and the subjective nature of the "value" of a commodity are readily acknowledged. Yet security analysis has introduced the notion of the "intrinsic value" of a security. The role that endowments and preferences play in determining "intrinsic value" has not been well-defined. The use of the term *intrinsic* appears to connote an objective concept, independent of subjective influences. For example, Graham and Dodd (1934, p. 17) defined *intrinsic value* as:

> In general terms, it is understood to be that value which is justified by the facts, ...

In many respects, securities are unlikely candidates for a notion of intrinsic value. Consider a relatively simple commodity, such as oranges. Although we occasionally hear statements that "oranges are a good buy," rarely do we speak of the "intrinsic value" of an orange and rarely do we characterize the market for oranges as inefficient in the sense that the price of oranges differs from their intrinsic value. Typically, the

---

[2] Two major forms of investment analysis are technical analysis and fundamental analysis; the latter is concerned with the use of financial statement data. Studies of market efficiency using technical analysis have a history of their own but are not the concern of this chapter.

[3] Throughout the analysis, belief differences across individuals will be characterized as if they arise solely because of informational differences. With information sufficiently broadly defined, this is not a restrictive assumption, and it facilitates the exposition.

value placed on an orange is readily acknowledged to be subjective. Yet, given that intrinsic value notions do not intrude into the discussion of market for relatively simple commodities, it is paradoxical that such a concept is attributed to a complex commodity such as a common stock. It is complex in the sense that its valuable attributes are complex claims to future, state-contingent dividends. Individuals will differ in their beliefs about the future and in their preferences for cash flows conditional upon a particular future state occurring. The value of such a claim will reflect this subjectivity and diversity. For example, if probabilistic assessments are treated from a subjectivist, personalistic viewpoint, the meaning of intrinsic value is ambiguous in a world of heterogeneous beliefs, even if individuals were identical in their endowments and preferences. In this sense, a common stock is an unlikely candidate for the notion of "intrinsic value."

Notwithstanding its ambiguity, notions of intrinsic value continue to play a role in discussions of the price formation process. For example, the FASB's *Tentative Conclusions* (1976a, p. 32) defines fundamental security analysis as the search for mispriced securities, which are defined in terms of intrinsic value. The FASB relies upon a definition provided by Lorie and Hamilton (1973, p. 114), who define intrinsic value as

> . . . the value that the security *ought* to have and will have when other investors have the same insight and knowledge as the analyst.

This definition is presumably still personalistic because insight and knowledge can vary across individuals (including analysts). There are a number of interpretations of an individual's meaning when using the term *intrinsic value*. Although the notion of intrinsic value is unnecessary to the development of a concept of market efficiency, it may be helpful to have an understanding of what might be meant by such a term, given its frequent use.

One interpretation of the intrinsic value of a security to an individual is the price of the security that would prevail if everyone else possessed the same *endowments, preferences*, and *beliefs* as that individual. A somewhat more subtle form would permit the heterogeneity of endowments and preferences to affect price. In this context, an individual would assess the intrinsic value of a security as the price that would prevail if everyone else possessed the same beliefs and information as that individual but would retain their own endowments and preferences. Either version involves an assessment of what prices would prevail under these hypothetical conditions. Alternatively, the belief component of the definition could be depersonalized by positing universal access to some fine information system, such as the union of everyone's information system or the finest information system conceivable. Clairvoyance is still another option. However, the definition must still address the endowment and preference component, and in this sense, *intrinsic value* remains an "intrinsically" subjective concept.

6-3. DEFINITIONS OF MARKET EFFICIENCY

Subsequent notions of market efficiency did not explicitly rely on intrinsic value and are illustrated by the following definition, which appears in Fama (1970):

> A securities market is efficient if security prices "fully reflect" the information available.

As Fama, among others, points out, the terms *fully reflect* and *information available* are vague and nonoperational. In fact, definitions can be contrived that make the definition of market efficiency circular. For example, define the information available as that which is fully reflected in prices. In this case, all securities markets are efficient by definition. However, the definition was intended more as an intuitive description of the concept rather than a rigorous definition. An attempt was made to clarify the concept by focusing on a major implication of market efficiency known as the *fair game* property. If the market is efficient with respect to some information, the investor is playing a fair game with respect to that information. The fair game property of market efficiency provided a helpful analogy to a "fair coin" in intuitively explaining price behavior. Alternatively stated, if the market is efficient with respect to some information, the abnormal expected returns from trading strategies based on that information are zero. The "inability to earn abnormal returns" was a particularly important implication of market efficiency to the professional investment community. Their interest in market inefficiency stems from the perceived ability to find securities with abnormal expected returns. Any market inefficiency that is not associated with abnormal expected returns is academic from their perspective because their services are often based on arguments that such abnormal returns will accrue to purchasers of their services.

The fair game and *abnormal expected returns* approach to market efficiency suffers from a number of ambiguities. For example, abnormal returns must be defined relative to some benchmark of *normal expected returns*. In many early empirical studies the returns on a market portfolio were used as the benchmark against which to compare the return performance of portfolios arising from a trading strategy based on information. However, it was felt that such a benchmark might be inappropriate, if the strategy tended to result in portfolios whose "risk" was different from that of the market portfolio. Portfolio theory and the capital asset pricing model permitted the specification of a *risk-adjusted* return benchmark and was perceived to be a contribution to empirically testing market efficiency. However, there are other ambiguities associated with such notions, which are similar to those related to the meaning of intrinsic value. For example, how is the concept of abnormal expected returns to be viewed when investors hold heterogeneous beliefs? These issues are discussed in greater detail in Beaver (1981).

Market Efficiency and Universal Access to Information

Market efficiency is defined here in terms of universal access to the information system of interest. Specifically,

> The market is efficient with respect to some specified information system, if and only if security prices act *as if* everyone observes the information system[4]

If prices have this property, they are said to *fully reflect* that information. This definition can be illustrated by early empirical studies of market efficiency. This research [Archibald (1972), Ball (1972), and Comiskey (1971), among others] examines the security price behavior of firms that switched from an accelerated method of depreciation to straight-line depreciation in reporting to shareholders in the annual report. However, both before and after the change the firms used an accelerated depreciation method for tax purposes.

In this context, market efficiency means that prices act as if every investor knows that the firms changed depreciation methods, knows what those methods are and what impact they have on reported earnings, knows that there was no change in depreciation method for tax purposes, and knows the potential implications for managements' motivation to make such a change. Obviously, such universal knowledge does not literally exist. However, the definition of market efficiency states only that prices act *as if* such a condition holds. In other words, the prices that prevail with limited knowledge of such information among investors are the same as prices that would prevail if everyone literally knew such information. This may explain in part why many find the concept of

---

[4] A more formal statement of this definition is: The market is efficient with respect to some information system (η) if and only if the prices of the securities are the same as they would be in an otherwise identical economy (with the same configuration of preferences and endowments and information systems) except that every individual has access to η as well. See Beaver (1981) for a further discussion of this definition.

market efficiency difficult to accept. Other reasons are discussed later in the section on acceptance by the various constituencies.

The choice of a definition is a function of the purpose it is intended to serve. One purpose is simply to describe and classify a set of security price studies. However, Rubinstein (1975) has criticized price-oriented market efficiency definitions on the grounds that they ignore the effects on portfolio holdings. Rubinstein argues in favor of a volume or trading-oriented definition of market efficiency. He argues that the market might be efficient by the price definition because aggregate demand could be the same under either information setting (i.e., limited versus universal access to the information of interest). Yet portfolio positions might be different, and each individual would not be in the same economic position under either setting. Hence, the release of the information to everyone could induce effects on each individual, even though prices remain unchanged. For example, suppose that some market participants regard the signal as "favorable" and others regard it as "unfavorable." They would trade with one another but there would not necessarily be an effect on price. As a result, a particular constituency, such as the financial reporting policy makers, may be interested in more than one definition of market efficiency. A price-oriented definition is emphasized here because the prior allegations of market inefficiency were expressed in terms of prices, and the empirical research was intended to address those allegations. However, adopting this view does not imply that a price-oriented definition is the only one of potential interest.

The definition used here focuses upon the identity of equilibrium security prices under two information configurations. Loosely speaking, the securities market is said to be efficient with respect to some specific information if prices act *as if* everyone knows the information. The definition has several important attributes. (1) It permits a definition of market efficiency in a world of individuals who are heterogeneous with respect to beliefs and information. (2) It permits endowments and preferences to play a natural role in influencing prices. (3) It permits individuals to perceive the market to be inefficient with respect to some information even if it is not.[5] (4) It gives the term *fully reflect* a well-defined meaning. (5) It focuses upon prices as opposed to beliefs or actions. (6) It relates directly to prior allegations of market inefficiency and to the set of empirical research that has been directed at those

---

[5] An individual may perceive the market to be inefficient with respect to some information even though it is not, when prices fully reflect a richer (i.e., finer) information system than the individual's. In this case, the individual myopically perceives the market to be inefficient, yet universal knowledge of that information would not alter prices. See Beaver (1980a) for further discussion.

allegations. (7) It permits the concept to be as finely partitioned with respect to information as may be desired and it avoids severe definitions of market efficiency.[6]

6-4. FORMS OF MARKET EFFICIENCY

In any discussion of market efficiency it is critical to specify the information systems for which market efficiency condition is being defined. This is critical because the market may be efficient with respect to some information systems but not others. In general, statements such as "the market is efficient" or "the market is not efficient" are ambiguous and incomplete.

Fama (1970) delineated three major forms of market efficiency; weak, semi-strong, and strong:

1. The market is efficient in the weak form if prices *fully reflect* information regarding the past sequences of prices. This form of market efficiency has obvious implications for technical analysis, and it includes the *random walk theory* of stock prices. Empirical evidence concerning weak form market efficiency has been collected since 1900 and is summarized in Cootner (1964). The implications for accounting for marketable equity securities are discussed in Beaver (1971, 1973b).

2. The market is efficient in the semi-strong form if prices *fully reflect* all publicly available information, including financial statement data. Trading strategies based upon published financial statement data will not lead to abnormal returns.

3. The market is efficient in the strong form if prices *fully reflect* all information, including inside information. Hence, even having access to non-published inside information will not lead to strategies promising abnormal expected returns.

The three forms described above are best thought of as a coarse partitioning of all information systems into three broad categories in which the boundaries between them are not precisely defined (e.g., what is meant by publicly available information?). However, the distinction was useful for classifying empirical research on market efficiency, which was Fama's (1970) original intent in introducing the distinctions. For many purposes, it may be critical to more finely partition the information systems of interest. For example, market efficiency with respect to the

---

[6] These are discussed in greater detail in Beaver (1981). Other definitional aspects are discussed in LeRoy (1976), Fama (1976), and Rubinstein (1975).

prices of firms that switched accounting methods is a finer partition of semi-strong form efficiency. Market efficiency with respect to the prices of firms' securities that switched accounting methods for reporting purposes but not for tax purposes is a still finer partition. Market efficiency with respect to firms that switched from accelerated depreciation to straightline depreciation for annual reports purposes only is a still finer partition.

It is important to distinguish the relationship among the three types of market efficiency described. The information systems described in weak form efficiency are a proper subset of the information systems described in semi-strong form efficiency, which in turn are a proper subset of the information systems described in strong form efficiency. Hence, a motivation is provided for the terms *weak, semi-strong* and *strong.* As a result, strong form efficiency implies semi-strong form efficiency implies weak form efficiency. However, the implication does not work in the reverse order. Weak form efficiency does not necessarily imply semi-strong form efficiency, and semi-strong form efficiency does not necessarily imply strong form efficiency. This latter distinction is important because most of the empirical evidence relates to semi-strong form efficiency. Evidence on strong form efficiency is scarce and mostly anecdotal. Even if the evidence is interpreted as supporting market efficiency with respect to published financial statement data, such evidence does not imply that the market efficiency exists in the strong form. Moreover, evidence supporting strong form inefficiency would not contradict or conflict with evidence concerning semi-strong efficiency.

6-5. EVIDENCE REGARDING MARKET EFFICIENCY

The chapter does not contain an in-depth discussion of the evidence for several reasons. (1) Some of this research is summarized in Chapter 5. (2) The research on market efficiency with respect to accounting data is voluminous and constantly developing. (3) Excellent, detailed discussions of these studies are available [Foster (1986)]. (4) The nature of the evidence and the strength of the findings either supporting or rejecting market efficiency are constantly changing and are the subject of current controversy and debate. Notwithstanding the current state of the art, the concept, implications, and theory of market efficiency are likely to be of continuing interest and concern. Hence, the chapter focuses on these aspects of market efficiency. This section briefly summarizes a sample of the early work which tended to alter perceptions regarding market efficiency.

Empirical research characterized as efficient market research has been the subject of considerable attention in recent years. Critics of financial accounting standards [e.g., Briloff (1969, 1972)] implied that securities could be mispriced because of accounting practices. The empirical research (e.g., on changes in accounting method) arose in response to these contentions and were offered as tests of these contentions. The research represents an important methodological contribution to financial accounting research because it subjects the allegations to empirical testing. It constitutes a more systematic and more rigorous use of evidence than had occurred previously and was one of the major areas of research that contributed to the introduction of empirical testing in accounting research. As such, it was a considerable departure from the nature of prior financial accounting research.

The empirical evidence has been concerned with two aspects of the relationship between financial statement data and security prices. The first aspect is the speed with which prices reflect financial statement data, and the second is whether prices react in a "proper" manner to financial statement data.

With respect to the first issue, the evidence [e.g., Beaver (1968) and May (1971), among others] indicates that prices respond quickly to announcements of annual and quarterly earnings. Moreover, studies find that security prices *anticipate* earnings prior to the earnings announcement [e.g., Ball and Brown (1968) and Brown and Kennelly (1972)]. This anticipatory effect may occur because of the availability of other information that permits investors to revise expectations about earnings. While this is consistent with investors attempting to predict earnings, it is also consistent with earnings merely being correlated with those events that investors perceive to convey information. However, the timeliness aspect of price behavior is not of major concern to accounting critics, such as Briloff (1972), who are not as much concerned with how fast prices react to reported earnings but rather with the *propriety* of the price reaction.

The propriety of response, of course, is a difficult issue to address because experts in financial accounting may disagree on what a "proper" response would be. The lack of consensus among experts as to the "best" accounting method is a reflection of this heterogeneity of opinion. A prime example is the controversy over interperiod tax allocation. The proper response as viewed by the advocates of tax deferral would presumably differ from the proper response as viewed by the opponents of comprehensive deferral. More generally, posing the "proper" reaction to a signal from an information system is tantamount to assuming an unequivocal way of interpreting the signal in terms of revising beliefs. If a subjectivist, personalistic view of probabilities is adopted, "proper" reactions in any objective sense are not well-defined.

As a result, the early research attempted to focus on special cases in which it was hoped that even experts with generally diverse judgments could reach a consensus on what price reaction would be expected in a market that was efficient with respect to the information under study. The event chosen for study was the switch in depreciation methods from accelerated to straight-line depreciation for reporting purposes [Archibald (1972), Ball (1972), Comiskey (1971)].

Needless to say, the empirical studies cannot directly observe the prices that would prevail in the hypothetical situation in which everyone knows of the change in accounting method and its attendant implications. Instead, the empirical studies infer the security price behavior that would be observed *if such a condition held.* The early studies held that if the market were efficient with respect to this information, the changes in prices, *ceteris paribus,* would be zero. Via residual analysis and other aspects of the research design, an approximation of the *ceteris paribus* condition was attempted. As Gonedes and Dopuch (1974) have pointed out, tests of market efficiency have *assumed* that the information effect would be zero in a market that fully reflected the information. A contextual argument (i.e., no direct impact on cash flows) was typically offered to justify such an assumption. However, if the announcement of the change conveyed information, a nonzero expected price change could be posited in a market efficient with respect to this information.

The evidence was interpreted by the authors to imply that no price increase was associated with changing to a depreciation method that leads to higher reported earnings than would have been reported had no change been made. Alternatively, prices act as if investors look beyond accounting numbers and take into account the fact that earnings are being generated by a different accounting method. Further evidence supporting this contention is provided in the analysis of price-earnings ratios of firms using accelerated versus straight-line depreciation [Beaver and Dukes (1973)]. Also, other studies indicate that prices more closely follow certain nonreported forms of earnings than they do reported earnings [e.g., Dukes (1976), Foster (1975), Beaver and Dukes (1973), among others]. This finding is consistent with a market in which earnings and financial statement data are only part of the information reflected in prices, in contrast to a market in which there is sole, myopic reliance placed upon reported earnings.

In sum, this early evidence is regarded as consistent with the contention that prices react quickly and in a "sophisticated" manner with respect to financial statement data.[7]

---

[7] The term *sophisticated* as used in this context means that prices act as if every one has access to an information system that includes accounting "expertise" (e.g., knowledge of depreciation methods, their impact on earnings, tax implications, etc.).

Role of Anecdotal Evidence

Although much of the early counterevidence to market efficiency was anecdotal in nature, it cannot be summarily dismissed. But one must be careful in interpreting anecdotal evidence. Viewing an anecdotal example as representative of a larger set of observations is considerably different from viewing it as an anomaly. Moreover, even when the anecdotal case is being offered as an anomaly, it is important to ascertain if in fact it is anomalous.

A well-known example illustrates the point. Briloff's "Castles of Sand?" article in *Barron's* (February 2, 1970) harshly criticized the accounting practices of land development companies. Apparently nothing appeared in the article that was not already publicly available. Yet shortly after the appearance of the article, several land development company common stocks experienced a sharp decline in price. Is this evidence consistent with market efficiency with respect to published accounting data? It is difficult to assess such evidence for a variety of reasons. (1) There may be other factors operating at the same time that could account for the drop in price. For example, evidence indicates that, on average, approximately 30 percent of security price changes is explainable on the basis of movements in a market-wide index. Industry factors could also be important. (2) There may be *ex post* sample selection bias. In other words, this incident has received widespread attention precisely because a large price decline occurred after the fact. A more valid test would be to examine all of Briloff's articles.[8] For example, were sharp price declines also associated with articles that preceded and followed "Castles of Sand?" What is the average effect on price of all the articles, not just the ones which *ex post* we know were followed by a large price decline? (3) Even if it were assumed that there is a price effect of the articles, it would not necessarily contradict market efficiency with respect to published data. The market may view the article as information, even if no apparently new data are provided. The market may impute a nonzero probability that Briloff "knows more than he is telling" (e.g., inside information). Alternatively, the market may be imputing an increased probability of regulation of the land development companies because of the criticism.[9] This includes not only changes in regulation of accounting

---

[8] By chance alone, price declines would be associated with *some* of the articles. For example, consider a sample of price changes consisting of a random selection of firms and time periods. Some of the price changes will be negative, and a few of the price declines will be large. Briloff's analysis of McDonald's, *Barron's* ("You Deserve a Break . . .", July 8, 1974), provides another example of the "Castles of Sand?" phenomenon.

[9] Professor J. Zimmerman of Rochester has suggested that Briloff's attacks provided *prima facie* evidence for regulators to justify further action. The effect of Briloff's testimony

for land development companies but regulation of their operating practices as well, since the article extended beyond the accounting practices and made evaluative statements about management practices and motives. Subsequently, the AICPA formed a committee to examine the standards and practices of accounting for land development companies.

The point is not that the example "proves" market efficiency, but rather that the issue of market efficiency does not stand or fall on the basis of an anecdotal example. It highlights the limitations of using anecdotal evidence as an evidentiary base for testing hypotheses. For any one observation, there will always be a number of interpretations or theories that could explain it. Anecdotal evidence is a low power test and tends to be not as informative as that obtained from a more carefully constructed research design.

Foster (1979) examines a sample of Briloff's articles and adjusts for the effects of market-wide events on the stock prices of the firms criticized by Briloff. The Foster study avoids much of the first two criticisms listed above. Foster finds a permanent, negative effect on price associated with the publication of the articles. In other words, the articles are perceived to possess information content.[10] Is this evidence of market inefficiency? Apart from issues of research design, such as those raised by issues 1 and 2 above, an interpretation of these findings depends upon the extent to which the factors mentioned in issue 3 are operating. Since this is currently largely a matter of conjecture, the interpretation of these findings is controversial and ambiguous. Some appear to be willing to interpret the evidence as inconsistent with market efficiency with respect to previously publicly available information, while others interpret the articles as a form of information not previously available [e.g., Foster (1979)]. Also, the price effects can be "self-fulfilling" if the articles are perceived to induce changes in beliefs about future cash flows because of factors such as increased probability of regulation or litigation.

6-6. MARKET EFFICIENCY ANOMALIES

Although much of the earlier anomalous evidence is anecdotal, more recent empirical evidence finds systematic differences in security returns associated with trading strategies based on size, price-earnings ratios, and market-to-book ratios, among others. These variables tend

---

before the Moss Subcommittee on Oversight and Investigations Committee on Interstate and Foreign Commerce (May 20, 1976) is consistent with this hypothesis.

[10] In this security price context, information content means that a statistical dependency exists between the signals of an information system and stock prices. This concept of information content is discussed in Chapter 5.

to be highly correlated over time and may reflect some element of risk or some other factor included in a more complete model of capital asset pricing. If so, these return differences reflect the nature of the capital asset pricing relationship not a market inefficiency with respect to some informational item.

The most relevant research concerns the behavior of security returns after the announcement of earnings. The importance of earnings to the financial reporting process has previously been discussed. The research examines the post-announcement return behavior associated with an earnings forecast error, a measure of unexpected earnings which has been constructed to have minimal correlation over time. Rendlemen, Jones, and Latane (1982) find post-announcement security return differences for as much as 90 days after the earnings announcement, and find that the post-announcement returns vary directly with the sign and magnitude of the earnings forecast error. Foster, Olsen, and Shevlin (1984) report similar results for a 60-day period after the earnings announcement. Taken at face value, the evidence would appear to be inconsistent with a market that fully reflects earnings at the time of the announcement.

However, work by Patell and Wolfson (1984) on intraday day suggests an extremely *rapid* reaction to earnings announcements, where *rapid* is defined in terms of hours after the announcement. It is possible that security prices react significantly yet only partially to the information when it is released. Even if this were the case, there is no reason to see why the slowness to respond is particular to earnings information. Because of the attention given to earnings by the financial press, it is an unlikely candidate to be subject to slowness to respond. However, is slowness to respond to information a general property of security prices?

Beaver and Landsman (1981) examine the subsequent security return behavior of "winner" and "loser" portfolios, where winner portfolios are those where the security prices have reacted favorably to the arrival of information in the months prior to selection and conversely for the loser portfolios. If security prices were slow to react to information in general, the winner (i.e., the favorable information) portfolio would continue to exhibit favorable returns, while the loser portfolio would continue to exhibit unfavorable return performance. Instead, no difference in return performance was found between the two portfolios in the months after portfolio selection.

Foster, Olsen, and Shevlin (1984) conduct a similar test, which constructs portfolios according to past security return performance, but they select portfolios on earnings announcement dates. If there is some incomplete, slow process of responding to earnings announcements, post-announcement return differences would be expected. They found no such differences. In contrast to the earnings forecast errors studied by

Foster, Olsen, and Shevlin, which possessed some degree of correlation over time, the portfolios constructed according to security returns did not. Dyckman and Morse (1986) observe that these findings suggest that the post-announcement differences in return are caused by differences in asset pricing not fully captured in the measure of abnormal return.

In any event, the results taken as a whole are indeed anomalous, and hopefully the paradox will be removed by future research. In the interim Foster (1986, p. 399) observes with respect to the anomalous evidence:

> Notwithstanding this evidence, the efficient market model continues to play an important role in the literature. One reason is that competing models are not well articulated. A second reason is that non-market inefficiency explanations for the anomalous evidence exist.

Another anomaly is raised by Wyatt (1983). Why does management appear to ignore the efficient market hypothesis? Alternatively stated, in an efficient market with respect to publicly available accounting data, why does management care about which accounting method is used to report a transaction? Wyatt documents several transactions where management appears to care about the accounting method and is willing to incur costs in order to structure a transaction in order to have a desired effect on reported results. Following are at least two explanations.

First, in many cases management does not believe security markets are efficient with respect to publicly available financial reporting data. Market efficiency does not necessarily require a majority of corporate management to believe in it. Corporate managements do not tend to be strong advocates of market efficiency. In fact, corporate managements typically contend their stock is underpriced.

Second, management may be motivated to structure a transaction in a particular way for reasons other than perceptions of market inefficiency. As discussed in Chapter 5, many of the firm's contracts, such as management compensation and bond covenants, are defined in terms of accounting numbers. These contracting effects may be of concern to management.

6-7. RESEARCH DESIGN ISSUES

As with empirical research in other disciplines, the efficient market research is the subject of much controversy and is subject to diverse interpretations. Some aspects of its controversial nature will be discussed in the section on acceptance by constituencies. The discussion in this section will focus on five research design issues: (1) the relationship between the definition of market efficiency and the tests of market efficiency, (2) the power of the test and the choice of the null hypothesis, (3) interstudy comparability and the variety of topics and methods choices available to the researcher, (4) self-selection bias, and (5) the markets studied.

With respect to the first issue, it is obvious that the empirical studies do not directly test market efficiency. The security prices that would prevail if there were universal access to the information are not observed. Instead, the empirical studies attempt to infer the security price behavior that would be observed *if such a condition held*. The research on change in depreciation methods cited earlier provides an example.

The empirical evidence is commonly interpreted as showing no price effects associated with the change in method and is further interpreted as evidence consistent with an efficient market. Prior to these studies, it was argued that a change in depreciation methods would induce a price change because of a myopic reliance on the earnings number (i.e., market inefficiency with respect to this information). Although the empirical evidence is generally taken to be supportive of market efficiency, it is possible to argue that the change prevented a price decline that otherwise might have occurred. Moreover, it is interesting to speculate on what interpretation would have been placed on the results had a price effect been found. An argument could have been advanced that the change in method itself conveyed information, and hence a price effect is consistent with an efficient market [Gonedes and Dopuch (1974)].

With respect to the second issue, market efficiency is typically formulated in terms of the null hypothesis of no price change. Market efficiency is then not rejected, unless it can be rejected at "publishable" levels of significance. In this context, the power of the test (i.e., the ability to reject the null when it is false) is critical. Failure to control for other factors influencing price changes (even when they are uncorrelated with the event of interest) can reduce the power of the test. An alternative approach would be to adopt "market inefficiency" as the null. The purpose of the analysis would be to see if extant research methods produce results that are capable of rejecting the null of inefficiency. This, of course, requires a specification of what "inefficiency" means in terms of prices. In many cases this is unclear. However, in the change in depreciation methods illustration, positing a constant price-earnings multiple provides an estimate of the expected price change and constitutes a possible null hypothesis.

The third issue of research design concerns interstudy comparability in general and specification of the security return metric in particular. Since Ball and Brown's (1968) study the literature has extended this early work by expanding the set of signals examined, by expanding the technology for measuring the informational variable (e.g., choice of earnings forecasting model), and by expanding the technology for deriving a security return metric. As a result, we have experienced a contemporaneous expansion of both the topics studied and the methods used to study them. In many cases, a study will alter both topic *and* method simultaneously, making comparison with previous studies difficult. When a difference in results is observed, it is difficult to identify the source of the difference, since more than one dial on the research machine has been turned. Because there has been the tendency to turn more than one dial at a time in each additional study, it is difficult to infer the reason for the different results.[11]

A fourth research design issue is self-selection bias. Evidence suggests that many of the firms studied differ from other firms in a systematic fashion [Foster (1978)]. For example, firms that switch depreciation methods do so for a reason and may differ in systematic ways from firms that do not change. Similarly, firms that switch to LIFO or firms that use the pooling versus purchase treatment may differ from the complement firms. If so, it may be difficult to interpret the security price behavior. As indicated earlier, market efficiency tests constitute an indirect test of the hypothesis. The research is attempting to infer if the price is the same as it would have been if the event had not occurred (e.g., no change in depreciation methods). If firms differ in a systematic way, then there is a confounding effect here which can be viewed as a correlated omitted variable. This may induce ambiguity in the interpretation of the results.

A fifth research design issue is the securities markets studied. For the most part, samples have been drawn from firms listed on the exchanges. Most frequently, the New York Stock Exchange has been the population from which the samples are drawn. Although listed securities represent the bulk of the market value of common stocks traded, they constitute only about 3500 of over 10,000 securities registered with the SEC. It is difficult to determine the extent to which the evidence of listed securities can be generalized to the over-the-counter (OTC) market. For example, those who believe that analysts are the "force" that makes the market efficient often argue that the OTC market may be inefficient with respect to many items of information. Evidence indicates that such companies receive little or no analyst following [SEC (1977)].

Is it then appropriate to infer less market inefficiency for such securities? Such an argument presumes that analysts are the force that has an effect on market efficiency for larger companies. This is a plau-

---

[11] Two aspects of this issue have been explored in Brown and Warner (1980) and Beaver (1980b).

sible story, but it is at present an untested one. Moreover, even if this assumption were accepted, it does not follow that the market in which analysts are not operating will be inefficient. Such an argument not only assumes that analysts are the force but more strongly they are the *only* force that can have an effect on market efficiency. There may be alternative mechanisms. For example, for OTC securities, the broker-dealers who "make" the market in that particular stock may fulfill this role. They stand ready to buy and sell shares at announced bid and ask prices. Such individuals would appear to have natural incentives to ensure that no one "knows" more than they do. As a result, the bid and ask prices may reflect the information in the possession of the broker-dealer, and such an information system may be extensive. Moreover, as will be shown, theories of market efficiency need not rely upon the existence of "experts" such as analysts or broker-dealers.

Additional empirical research directly replicating the earlier market efficiency tests on unlisted securities would appear to be warranted before drawing conclusions about the degree to which unlisted securities markets are or are not efficient. Research by Shores (1987) indicates that in many respects the behavior of over-the-counter stocks with respect to earnings announcements is similar to that of listed securities.

In sum, a number of research design issues may lead to a difficulty in interpreting market efficiency research. Many of these issues are also discussed in Foster (1980). These research design issues induce an ambiguity into the interpretation of the results and are a common basis used by the research community in judging empirical evidence.

6-8. THEORIES OF MARKET EFFICIENCY

It is one matter to define market efficiency, and to have empirical evidence bearing on the issue, but it is another to explain why or how market efficiency with respect to specific information systems is attained. This involves a theory of the process by which information becomes reflected in prices. Unless individuals are characterized as throwing away something of value, information is not used because it is costly. Yet much of the empirical research has examined market efficiency with respect to publicly available information, such as changes in depreciation methods for annual report purposes. Why would one ever expect prices *not* to "fully reflect" publicly available information? Won't market efficiency hold trivially? The answer of course lies in the possibility that such data are not universally available at zero cost to all individuals.

Knowledge of the change in methods may not be universal. Moreover, there may not be universal (costless) access to other information on the implications of the change. In other words, it may be costly to obtain the training (e.g., knowledge of depreciation methods, under-standing that a firm can have a different set of books for tax and for annual report purposes, etc.) and hence such knowledge is not universal. However, interpretation of the change goes beyond this and involves the assessment of management's motivations for changing depreciation methods (e.g., reflecting managements' expectations about future earn-ings, or plans for additional asset acquisitions). Such analysis (i.e., in-formation) is provided by the financial and accounting community, but perhaps not costlessly. Hence, market prices might not reflect this po-tentially costly information. This constitutes a simplified explanation of why a nonzero probability of market inefficiency with respect to "publicly available" information might be assessed. However, despite the cost of the information, security prices might act *as if* the information were costlessly available to all investors. This provides one interpretation of the empirical research on semi-strong form efficiency. In particular, from this perspective the empirical studies of change in accounting meth-ods are viewed as testing market efficiency with respect to more infor-mation than merely the knowledge that a change took place (i.e., "so-phistication" of the use of the data is also an issue).

As indicated earlier, many appear willing to give the analyst com-munity credit for being the mechanism by which market efficiency is attained [Bernstein (1975)]. The role of such information intermediaries has not yet been explicitly modeled. However, Kihlstrom and Mirman (1975), Grossman (1976), and Grossman and Stiglitz (1975) provide anal-yses of conditions under which market efficiency would or would not obtain. In these models, individuals "extract" information from prices. In the Grossman and Stiglitz model, individuals choose to become in-formed or uninformed, and at equilibrium each individual is indifferent, because either action (after deducting information costs) offers the same expected utility. In order for there to be incentives to purchase infor-mation, prices cannot "fully reflect" the information obtained. Hence, the market must be inefficient with respect to that information. In the Grossman model every individual is equally uninformed in that each receives a garbled signal, but prices act as an aggregation of everyone's information, such that the price "reflects" information that is superior to that held by each and every individual. However, individuals extract this superior information from prices and the price "fully reflects" that superior information. In this model there are also issues of private in-centives for information production, since each individual is assumed to costlessly observe price (and extract information from it), which elimi-nates the incentive to privately seek information if it is costly (i.e., a free rider phenomenon occurs).

In a related vein, Verrecchia (1979) has constructed a model in which price acts as an aggregator of beliefs (as distinct from an aggregator of information). As the number of individuals increases, prices behave *as if* everyone observed the ungarbled signal. The major difference is that there is no explicit learning from prices involved. Hence, while prices reflect the ungarbled signal, individual beliefs or portfolios may not reflect this information. Neither Grossman nor Verrecchia requires the existence of a subset of "initially" more informed individuals (e.g., superior analysts). The models are partial equilibrium in which assumptions regarding the contracting opportunities permitted are central. For example, these analyses deal with private information production. Had contracts which permitted collective production (or nonproduction) of information been considered, the information production incentives could be dramatically altered. One such collective choice would be centralized production of signal, thereby avoiding the costs of redundant production. Many of the issues related to the institutional structure of information production are discussed in Gonedes (1976) and in Chapter 7.

Illustration of a Theory

The crux of a theory of market efficiency which does not rely upon the existence of a set of "experts" is that the level of knowledge reflected in prices is greater than merely the "average" level of knowledge among investors in the market. Some simple analogies illustrate this point. Consider each individual containing a "small" amount of knowledge and a considerable amount of idiosyncratic behavior. This can be modeled as each individual receiving a garbled signal from an information system that provides an ungarbled signal disguised by a "noise" component. The garbling is so large that any inspection of that individual's behavior provides little indication that such an individual is contributing to the efficiency of the market with respect to the ungarbled information system. Moreover, assume that this is true for every individual who comprises the market. However, the idiosyncratic behavior, by definition, is essentially uncorrelated among individuals. As a result, security price, which can be viewed as a "consensus" across investors, is effectively able to diversify away the large idiosyncratic component, such that only the knowledge (i.e., the ungarbled signal) persists in terms of explaining the security price. By analogy, the individual investor beliefs can be viewed akin to individual securities and the security price can be viewed as an aggregate akin to a portfolio.

The small amount of knowledge is the systematic component across investors. Although it is dwarfed by the idiosyncratic behavior at the individual investor level, it is the only portion that persists at the security price level. This does not require the existence of any "experts." Moreover, the quality of the knowledge reflected in prices is considerably higher than the average quality of knowledge across the individuals who comprise the market. Analogously, in portfolio theory the variance of return of any portfolio is strictly less than the average variance of the securities' returns that comprise the portfolio, if securities' returns are uncorrelated with one another.[12]

Forecasting Football Games

The fact that a consensus can reflect "greater than average" knowledge or insight is illustrated in a seemingly unrelated context—the prediction of outcomes of football games. On Fridays during the 1966 through 1968 football season the *Chicago Daily News* reported the predictions of each of the members of the sports staff about which team would win the weekend game. In addition to each individual forecast, there was a "consensus" forecast, which was determined by which team was favored by the majority of those forecasting. The forecasting accuracy (i.e., percentage of correct predictions) was also reported for each forecaster on a cumulative basis. The results reported on the last Friday of November (essentially the end of the college season) are summarized in Table 6-1.

TABLE 6-1

Forecasting Outcomes of Football Games[a]

	1966	1967	1968
Total forecasters (including consensus)	15	15	16
Total forecasts made per forecaster	180	220	219
Rank of consensus[b]	1 (tie)	2	2
Median rank of forecasters	8	8	8.5
Rank of best forecasters:			
J. Carmichael (1966)	1 (tie)	8	16
D. Nightingale (1966)	1 (tie)	11	5
A. Biondo (1967)	7	1	6
H. Duck (1968)	8	10	1

[a]Taken from "Here's How Our Staff Picks 'em," *Chicago Daily News*, November 25, 1966 (p. 43), November 24, 1967 (p. 38), and November 29, 1968 (p. 43).
[b]When all three years are combined, the consensus outperforms every one of the forecasters (i.e., ranks first).

[12] In fact, much stronger statements can be made. The variance of return for the portfolio will be strictly less than the average variance, as long as the returns are less than perfectly correlated (i.e., there will be some diversification effect). Moreover, the variance of the return of the portfolio can be strictly less than the variance of *every* one of the securities that comprise it. For example, assuming uncorrelated returns and equal variances across security returns, the variance of the portfolio return will be strictly less than the variance of *every* one of the security returns for any portfolio with two or more securities.

The striking feature of the consensus is that it performs considerably better than average (its rank is considerably above the median rank of 8, 8, and 8.5). In fact, in 1966 it is tied for first, and it is the second best forecaster both in 1967 and 1968. In both of these years it missed being tied for first by one game out of over 200 games predicted.

In principle, the consensus could have forecasted more accurately than every one of the individuals who comprise it, even though it is no more than a simple composite of their respective forecasts. To explore this possibility further, the performance of the "best" forecasters in each of the years was examined in the other years. Their "superior" performance could be due to a mixture of two factors: (1) above average forecasting ability and (2) "luck." The winners who tied with the consensus in 1966 (Carmichael and Nightingale) ranked eighth and eleventh in 1967 and sixteenth and fifth in 1968. Biondo, the 1967 winner, ranked seventh and sixth in 1966 and 1968, while Duck, the 1968 winner, ranked eighth and tenth in 1966 and 1967. Three conclusions appear warranted: (1) Luck accounts for a substantial portion of "superior" performance. (2) Above average skill accounts for part of the performance, at least for three of the four individuals. (3) However, the above average performance is not great enough to be "superior" (i.e., to beat the consensus). *If all three years are combined, the consensus outperforms each of these four forecasters, as well as all of the others, of course.* Based on 619 forecasts pooled over 1966 through 1968, the consensus has the highest percentage of correct predictions.[13]

The purpose of this illustration is not to demonstrate that no superior forecasters of football games exist. Most certainly, the illustration is not introduced to show that no superior analysts exist. However, the example does illustrate the following: (1) The consensus can predict better than the average of the individuals who comprise it. (2) In principle, a consensus can outperform everyone who comprises it. (3) Superior forecasting, defined as outperforming the consensus, requires more than merely being "better than average" and perhaps even more than being the best individual forecaster. (4) This is no quirk. The same principles operating in favor of the diversification in portfolios are operating here. Once these principles are understood, these results are completely expected, reasonable, and logical.[14] However, those not familiar with this principle may find it nonintuitive and surprising. (5)

---

[13] An analogous situation in portfolio theory is described in footnote 12. Libby (1981) discusses a number of other contexts in which a composite judge outperforms the average of those comprising the consensus.

[14] A similar situation was reported in the February 18, 1980, issue of *Business Week*, in which the *consensus* forecast of the 1979 GNP by thirty economists in December, 1978, outperformed twenty-nine of the thirty forecasters and tied for first (p. 10).

Reliance upon "experts," individuals of above average insight, knowledge, and skill, is not required in order to produce a consensus that reflects considerably more knowledge, insight, and skill than the average. This result obtains even if all individuals are of average quality.

In sum, the consensus can forecast better than every one of the individuals who comprise it, even though it was no more than a simple composite of their respective forecasts. *In any event, it is clear that the consensus predicts better than the average of the individuals who comprise the consensus.* This is so because consensus forecasts, like security prices, can "diversify" out of the idiosyncratic behavior (e.g., school loyalties, limited knowledge, etc.) of the individuals.[15]

Summary

In sum, the empirical research arose in response to claims in the financial and accounting community that market inefficiencies existed. As a result, the empirical findings have largely preceded a formal, conceptual development and until recently there existed little or no formal foundation. A variety of theories of market efficiency are being explored. At the present time, they are insufficiently developed to provide a guide to empirical research in the form of empirically testable propositions. However, their further development offers considerable promise for the existence of hypotheses that flow from a theoretical model and precede empirical testing of the hypotheses. This enriched theoretical foundation can also remove at least some of the ambiguity associated with the interpretation and the generalizability of the results.

6-9. IMPLICATIONS OF MARKET EFFICIENCY

This section is devoted to a discussion of the implications of assuming that the market is efficient *with respect to publicly available information* (i.e., semi-strong form efficiency). The reason for doing so is not that the evidence is complete, nonconflicting, or unassailable. Empirical evidence seldom is. This section will explore the implications of market efficiency for two reasons. First, there is at least enough evidence sup-

---

[15] Needless to say, this is an extremely simple model of investor behavior mainly designed to illustrate the diversification effects that may be operating on price. Obviously, if some "errors" in judgment are systematic, this bias will persist at the aggregate level as well and will not be diversified away. As a historical note, I adopted this view of the market while conducting the research reported in Beaver (1968) which dealt with the relationship between prices and volume. Since then, this view has been introduced in my classes as one possible theory of stock price formation. Bagehot (1971) and Treynor (1974) have taken a similar view and question the lack of independence across investors.

porting it to warrant discussing the implications. Second, given that the efficient market has received considerable attention, it is helpful to separate the implications from the nonimplications.[16]

Discussing the implications is important but difficult. The difficulty arises partly because of the reasons discussed previously (e.g., lack of theoretical underpinning). However, a difficulty also arises because the potential implications of market efficiency cannot be discussed in isolation but rather in the context of other judgments of fact and value judgments. To the extent possible, the discussion will be explicit about the other judgments, perceptions, and assumptions being introduced. However, an element of subjectivity and personal opinion inevitably creeps into a discussion such as this. The statements that follow illustrate why many constituencies in the financial reporting environment have shown an interest in and perceive that they are affected by market efficiency. However, as will become apparent, many of the statements made have not been derived rigorously and rely upon intuition. Moreover, empirical evidence is often lacking on critical links, which establish the importance of market efficiency to these various constituencies. With this disclaimer, the following implications are offered.

(1) The efficient market implies that the substance rather than the form of disclosure may be the more important policy issue. A market that is efficient with respect to published data may not be efficient with respect to nonpublished data. Hence, bringing an item of information into the public domain (i.e., disclosure) is an issue of substance. However, once in the public domain, it is unclear whether or not the format used to display the data is a substantive issue, *at least in its impact on security prices.* For example, while it may be important that an item appear somewhere in the annual report, it may not make any difference in terms of the price of the security whether the item is reported in the footnotes or in the body of the statement.[17] Similarly, it would make little difference whether or not the income statement effects of an item are explicitly reported, if they could be inferred from balance sheet disclosure. For example, it is not clear that the IRS restrictions on reporting the income statement effects of LIFO constitute a substantive constraint.

(2) It may be naive to believe that merely because an item does

[16] This section borrows heavily from Beaver (1976).

[17] In principle, the format could convey information regarding management's expectations. However, such an effect remains undocumented empirically. The discussion also assumes that there are no second-order effects that would alter the cash flows of the firm. For example, if the lending opportunities of a firm are influenced by the location of financial leases in the balance sheet, security prices could be altered by format choices. More generally, it assumes no effect that would alter the production or financing decisions of the firm.

not appear in the financial statements it is not reflected in prices. Security prices reflect a rich information system of which the financial statements may be only a part.

Consider this implication in the context of replacement cost disclosures. What was the likely impact on security prices when the SEC replacement cost data [Accounting Series Release (ASR) 190] were first disclosed in early 1977? If we adopt the naive notion of price formation implicit in some articles in the popular financial press (e.g., *Business Week,* September 22, 1975, pp. 106–109), we are asked to believe that the market has been fooled by the "illusory" profits reported under a historical cost system. If so, then are we to expect a massive reduction in stock prices when the replacement cost data are produced? Such an outcome was unlikely, for a number of reasons. For example, a market that relies upon a broad information system already may be attempting to interpret the implications of price increases in the product and factor markets for the firms' future cash flows.[18] This may or may not involve attempts to directly form assessments of the replacement cost of assets. However, once we abandon a perception of a naive market relying only upon reported numbers, there is no obvious reason to predict any systematic adjustment of stock prices across firms. In particular, there is no reason to believe that there will be a downward revision in prices because the replacement cost data will imply lower earnings.[19]

Does this necessarily imply that there would be no impact on security prices? No impact is a possibility if the data are redundant or are perceived to be so fraught with measurement problems that they convey no information beyond what is already available. However, even imprecise data can convey information, so there is the possibility of price revisions at the time of the disclosure. The direction of the price change, however, will be difficult to predict because it will, in part, be determined by the expectations of the market at the time of the announcement. There is no obvious reason why the market has systematically underestimated or overestimated the implications of the data for security prices. Obviously, after-the-fact prices may be revised, but will the revision be systematic across firms? There may be certain systematic revisions within an industry because the prediction errors may be correlated among firms within a given industry. But these will tend to cancel out across industries

---

[18] For example, Falkenstein and Weil (1977) have shown that estimates of replacement cost data can be made from published information.

[19] The discussion has been silent on whether or not the disclosure would affect the cash flows of the firm. While there are no first-order effects, there may be second-order effects in the form of implications for changes in future tax legislation or changes in management's decisions. However, even if these effects are present, they may be discounted prior to the announcement, so that no systematic effect is necessarily expected at the time of announcement.

if the prediction errors are uncorrelated across industries. Of course, there may be a systematic reaction that will not cancel out. However, *ex ante* it is not obvious what the direction of the effect on prices will be (i.e., the expected value is still zero). Research by Beaver, Christie, Griffin (1980), Boatsman (1980), and Ro (1980) supports the contention that there have been no systematic effects on stock prices at the time of the disclosures. Easman et al. (1979) contend that in years prior to ASR 190 disclosures prices act as if they reflect replacement cost adjustments.

(3)   The research, together with the informal evidence cited above, can affect the way in which we view the role of information intermediaries. For example, if information is a perishable commodity and the analyst community is a competitive one, it may be difficult for any one analyst to demonstrate consistently superior performance.[20] However, from a broader perspective, superior performance may not be the appropriate metric by which to measure the contribution of the analyst community. Every analyst may be playing approximately a zero-sum game against the rest of the community. But, this does not necessarily imply that the net effect of the activities is valueless. The process of competing analysts searching for information may in part result in security prices that reflect a richer information system. In this sense, the activities of the analyst community may in part be a public good [Bernstein (1975)]. From this perspective, evaluation of performance in terms of ability to generate abnormal returns may be inappropriate.

Noting the public good aspects of analysts' activities raises the issue of governmental regulation of their activities.[21] The SEC has the legislative authority to alter the nature and level of such activities (e.g., its powers over disclosure). Presumably, reduction of resources spent on private-sector information search and the prevention of wealth redistribution because of information asymmetries would be two of the concerns of the SEC.

The SEC can affect the analyst community not only by altering the nature of mandated disclosure but also by regulating the manner or process by which information flows from corporations to analysts. For example, under what conditions may an analyst receive and act on information not generally available without fear of litigation?[22]

---

[20] These statements could also apply to other information intermediaries.

[21] The public good aspect of analysts' activities also raises questions about the financing of their activities. In the "classic" public good setting there will be a tendency for the underproduction of such information to the extent that nonpurchasers of the information cannot be excluded from its benefits [see Gonedes and Dopuch (1974)]. Tie-in sales are one conventional device for private sector sale of public goods. The defunct fixed commission structure could be viewed in this light. For a related discussion, see Boudreaux (1975).

[22] Currently, the mosaic theory (*SEC* v. *Bausch & Lomb, Inc.*, 1976) has been offered

(4) The role of accrual accounting is unclear. Although it is premature to conclude that the marginal value of income determination is zero, it is an issue that remains essentially unexamined. It is related to the issue of aggregation of financial data. To the extent that data items are processed (e.g., aggregated) by investors in a relatively uniform manner, it may be cost-effective to have the corporation perform the process once, rather than have the process performed several times over by analysts and investors.

The problem is, of course, that there may be no consensus on the method of aggregation, and generally there is a loss of information when aggregating. Hence, when presented with aggregated data, analysts, among others, may incur costs in an attempt to restore the lost information (e.g., interview management). So the cost of processing may not be related to the level of aggregation in any simple fashion. Moreover, in addition to the cost issues, there are consequences of nondisclosure due to aggregated data. Hence, the appropriate level of aggregation is not a trivial issue, and accrual accounting can be viewed as a potentially cost-effective compromise between a more ambitious disclosure policy and merely reporting cash flows.[23]

(5) The issue of disclosure may have to be reconsidered. The SEC has been concerned about differential disclosure between the "average investor" and the professional. This assumes that the "average" investor is actively and literally involved in trying to interpret the implications of disclosure for the price of stock (Kripke, 1973).[24] The average investor who has no expertise in financial or accounting matters may be deferring the analysis to those who have a comparative advantage (e.g., the information intermediaries).[25] Another aspect is selective disclosure among information intermediaries, such as analysts. The interest of the average investor may be protected by ensuring that a given data item is disclosed to a number of analysts so that they (not the average investor) can compete with one another for the implications and interpretations of that item for the cash flows and price of security.

---

as a basis for answering that question. However, the mosaic theory is deficient conceptually and lacks operationality. The mosaic theory states that two types of information exist: items that have meaning standing alone and items that have no meaning standing alone but take on meaning when placed in the grand mosaic of other information. The former is potentially sensitive information, while the latter carries less risk if transmitted. See Beaver (1978) for further discussion.

[23] For an excellent discussion of the aggregation issue in an accounting context, see Ijiri (1967, 1975) and Sorter (1969).

[24] In fact, a major premise of the Securities Acts is reliance on intermediaries (e.g., analysts) to interpret and disseminate the data contained in SEC filings [The Wheat Report (1969, p. 52) and Douglas (1933)].

[25] The term *average investor* refers to the investor who does not have professional skills in processing and interpreting the data. The term *nonprofessional* would be more descriptive.

(6)   Policy makers may wish to reconsider the nature of the concern for the naive investor. If the investor, no matter how naive, is in effect facing a fair game with respect to publicly available information, can the investor still be harmed? If so, how? The naive investor can still be harmed, but the potential harm may not occur because of price effects due to firms reporting accelerated versus straight-line depreciation for annual report purposes. Rather, harm can occur when firms are following policies of less than full disclosure, with insiders potentially earning monopoly returns from access to that inside information.

There may be other consequences as well. Portfolio positions held by investors may differ even though the prices are the same. For example, Beaver (1973a) cites "improperly" diversified portfolios as one of the consequences of "erroneously" perceiving the market to be inefficient.[26] Other consequences include the direct costs of reporting, disseminating, certifying, and processing the information, the costs of privately seeking the information if it is not publicly available, the costs paid to analysts and others to perform that function for the investor, and transactions costs such as brokerage fees.

Nonimplications

There appears to be a number of unwarranted interpretations drawn from the assumption of market efficiency. In some cases, the interpretations cannot be drawn unless additional structure is assumed. In other cases, the interpretations do not fully appreciate the process by which security prices arise and the process by which security prices reflect information. Several specific illustrations are provided in an attempt to document these assertions.

(1)   Market efficiency does not connote social desirability or any other normative connotation. The term *market efficiency* in this respect is an unfortunate choice of words. Market efficiency is concerned with the relationship among information and security prices. No value laden or normative connotations are implied. For example, a society might unanimously choose to have a securities market that is efficient with respect to a coarser information system over one that would be efficient with respect to a finer information system.[27]

---

[26] See footnote 5 of this chapter for an example, as well as nonimplication 3 in the subsection on nonimplications.

[27] Similarly, there is no direct or simple relationship between the "greater" market efficiency and "improved" allocation resources. Hence, a distinction must be made between *allocational* and *informational* efficiency. They are distinct concepts and the relationship between them has not been rigorously derived. The subject of this chapter is *informational* efficiency.

(2) Market efficiency does not imply clairvoyance. The future is uncertain, the prices reflect investors' expectations—expectations which may or may not be realized. Hindsight can often suggest that security prices reflected an expectation that differed greatly from the realization. However, this is not evidence of market inefficiency but rather of the nature of uncertainty. Even an efficient market does not have a crystal ball. A number of large "surprises," causing substantial revisions in security prices, is consistent with an efficient market. It is not valid to evaluate the efficiency of a set of security prices in the light of information that only became available after those prices were formed.

A somewhat more subtle variation is to suggest that the market did have the information available but incorrectly interpreted subsets of the information. For example, certain signals were ignored, which with the benefit of hindsight we "know" should have received much greater attention. At any point in time there will be a number of signals available and it is unlikely that each signal, considered individually, leads to the same prediction of the future. To examine the evidence retrospectively and determine what would have led to the best forecast is not valid and relies upon hindsight just as much as the earlier scheme.

(3) An efficient market does not imply that investors will necessarily perceive the market to be efficient. There may be widespread perceptions of market inefficiencies even though the security prices fully reflect published information. Beaver (1981a) discusses several reasons for this. Here two possible reasons are discussed. First, any one investor may be aware of only a portion of the information that is reflected in prices. As a result, from this myopic perspective, securities may appear to be mispriced because prices reflect information not available to that individual. Second, interpreting price responses to information requires a model of the expectations underlying those prices. We may be tempted to interpret the market's response to prices in light of a simplistic, naive expectations model. For example, annual earnings per share may be 30 percent above the previous year's figure; yet the prices might react adversely to the announcement if an increase of more than 30 percent had been expected. Information has arrived since the publication of last year's earnings, and this information may have led to a substantial revision in earnings expectations since the last year's earning announcements. At a minimum, quarterly earnings and dividend announcements are capable of altering expectations. Forecasts by management and by analysts are also a source of expectations changes. More qualitative information on contract awards, acquisitions, litigation, and product development may also play an important role. In this respect, it is not surprising that the empirical evidence cited in Chapter 5 indicates that expectation models of earnings which use last year's earnings as their most recent input have limited ability to explain price movements in the one or two months prior to the announcement of the subsequent year's earnings.

In sum, it may be difficult to understand prices and price changes without knowledge of the information set reflected in prices and without knowledge of the expectations embedded in prices. This inference process is particularly difficult because prices reflect a composite across investors, who differ with respect to information and expectations as well as other factors such as wealth and attitudes toward risk. It is not surprising to find particular cases in which the price reaction to information seems anomalous. However, one must be careful to avoid labeling our inability to explain such phenomenon as evidence of market inefficiency, market irrationality, or that all-absorbing residual, "market psychology."

The first three nonimplications of the efficient market deal with common misunderstandings about the meaning of an efficient market or the process by which information becomes reflected in prices. There is a second class of nonimplications that deals with using the concept of market efficiency to evaluate adequacies or deficiencies in the current institutional structure. The concept of market efficiency by itself is not sufficiently rich to warrant inferences regarding institutional structure. Two illustrations are provided. For purposes of continuity, these will be numbered consecutively with respect to the previous nonimplications.

(4) The efficient market does not imply that information intermediaries, such as analysts, are useless. The efficient market concept is silent on the value of their services. There is nothing in either the definition or the evidence concerning market efficiency that specifies the process or institutional mechanism by which information becomes reflected in prices. Analysts may play an important role in the process of generating and disseminating information to the investment community. However, although the efficient market evidence, in and of itself, does not indict analysts, it does not support them either.

(5) The efficient market does not imply that no basis can be provided for governmental intervention in the disclosure process. In order to draw inferences regarding the role of governmental intervention in disclosure decisions, additional analysis of the nature of the institutional mechanism by which information becomes reflected in prices is required. Earlier it was suggested that the analyst community may play an important role in such a process. However, quite frankly, little is known in a formal way about the process. Corporations have incentives to provide information voluntarily to the analyst community, and the analyst community has incentives to search for information from corporations and other sources. Given this flow of information in the private sector, the additional information content of the mandated disclosures

of the SEC may be minuscule. The basis for governmental intervention must stem from some aspect of the private-sector incentives that cause them to be imperfectly aligned with the social incentives. Chapter 7 discusses the issue of regulation in depth.

The choice among different financial reporting systems involves choosing among differing consequences, which affect individuals differently. Hence, some individuals may be better off under one method, and others may be better off under an alternative method. The issue is one of social choice, which involves making interpersonal welfare comparisons.[28]

6-10. IMPORTANCE TO FINANCIAL REPORTING CONSTITUENCIES

This section attempts to summarize the importance of the implications from the perspective of the various constituencies in the financial reporting environment: investors, policy makers, management, auditors, and information intermediaries.[29] This discussion faces the same difficulties cited at the outset of the previous section. As a result, the same disclaimer that was tendered there applies here as well.

Investors

The relationship between financial information and security prices can influence investors' direct demand for financial information. Security price effects are associated with other consequences. For example, changes in security prices alter the wealth of the investor and in general alter the consumption-investment opportunities available to each investor. The precise nature of the effect of security price changes on consumption-investment behavior will depend upon the personal characteristics of the investor. Security price changes can be viewed as inducing a redistribution of wealth among investors.

Investor behavior can also be affected by what information the investor possesses, by what information is fully reflected in prices, and by what information is held by others, including other investors and

---

[28] The issue is discussed at greater length in Chapter 2.

[29] Chapters 1 and 2 indicate that each of the constituencies could be further divided into subgroups. In particular, investors could be further categorized in a number of ways. To avoid repetition, the subsequent discussion will not explicitly treat this diversity. However, it is a key element to remember in any analysis of potential effects on these groups.

management.[30] These factors can potentially influence investor behavior with respect to consumption, portfolio selection, and costs incurred, including information costs and transactions costs.

The perception that prices fully reflect a rich, comprehensive information system may reduce an individual's direct demand for financial information. In such cases, the individuals act as "price takers" and are willing to adopt, as their own, the consensus beliefs reflected in prices. In one sense, they can be "free riders" with respect to the information reflected in prices, and it may be optimal for them to pursue relatively simple, costless portfolio strategies.

Conversely, the perception that security prices do not fully reflect some information can lead to adopting portfolio strategies designed to reap abnormal expected returns by exploiting the informational inefficiency. The perceived inefficiency can lead the investor to expend time and energy in searching for and interpreting such information, to pay others (e.g., information intermediaries) to provide such information, to incur transactions costs pursuing "active" portfolio management, or to adopt less diversified portfolios by investing predominantly in "underpriced" securities.

Alternatively, the perception that an information system is not fully reflected in prices may make the investor reluctant to trade in securities if it is felt that the information system is possessed by others, such as management or other investors. This concern over information asymmetry could have several effects. (1) It could lead to an attempt to extract the information from observing the behavior of those perceived to have more information (e.g., by observing the prices at which the more informed investors would be willing to trade).[31] (2) It could lead to a well-diversified, passive portfolio strategy designed to insulate the investor from trading with others who might have superior information. (3) It could cause the investor to retreat from such markets and invest in markets in which information asymmetry is of less concern. (4) It could also induce the investor to reduce the total amount of investment and to consume instead.

The potential effects of information asymmetries on investor behavior were discussed at greater length in Chapter 2. The list of potential effects is offered as illustrative and is not intended to be complete. Moreover, little is known about how important these effects are empirically, and it is not unreasonable to believe that the effects may vary across

---

[30] More precisely, investor behavior is also affected by what information is perceived to be reflected in prices and what information is perceived to be held by others, including other investors and management.

[31] The literature on "learning from prices" cited in the section on theories of market efficiency is one example of such behavior.

investors. At the present time, assertions regarding effects on individual investor behavior are largely conjectural and are empirically undocumented.

The effect of market efficiency on investor behavior is not only of concern to investors themselves but also to the other constituencies as well. As a result, market efficiency is important to these other groups in part because of its potential effects on investor behavior.

Policy Makers

Concern over the effects on investor behavior is reflected in the statements of the FASB (1976b, Chapter 2) and the SEC (1977, Introduction). The investor orientation appears to be partially motivated by concern over the welfare of the investors and the "fairness" of the security markets in which they trade. Perceived adversities and inequities may befall investors because of informational deficiencies (e.g., failure to disclose). However, the policy makers also appear to share a concern over the effects on resource allocation and capital formation [FASB (1976b), SEC (1977, Introduction)]. For example, it is contended that fuller disclosure will tend to lead to a more efficient allocation of resources because investors will be in a more informed position to judge where their funds can be used most productively and profitably, given the risks involved. It is also argued that a more favorable climate for capital formation is provided by fuller disclosure because of the effect on the perceived "fairness" of the market. Investors are said to be more willing to invest funds in the new issue market if there is greater disclosure and less risk of fraud or misrepresentation about the productive opportunities of the firm issuing the securities. Moreover, the subsequent "marketability" of the securities is said to be a function of the perceived "fairness" of the exchange markets. In other words, if the exchange market is efficient with respect to a rich comprehensive information system, investors have less concern over information asymmetries at the time they eventually sell their shares and hence are more willing to invest in the new issue market.

These arguments have not been developed rigorously and rely upon intuition. Moreover, there has been little empirical evidence of the effect of disclosure on resource allocation or capital formation. There may not be any simple relationship between the level of disclosure and the rate of capital formation. For example, increased disclosure may not necessarily lead to increased capital formation. The nature of the disclosure (i.e., the particular signal reported) may lead investors to reduce their expectations regarding future returns or to increase their assessments of risk. As a result, capital formation may be lower than it would have been had the information not been provided and reflected in security prices. In a related vein, from the perspective of "full" disclosure, there is no assurance that the level of capital formation comes "closer" to what it would be under full disclosure in moving from less disclosure to more disclosure.[32]

Market efficiency is directly related to financial reporting policy making in at least two ways. (1) The information that is fully reflected in security prices will partially determine the price effects of any given financial reporting regulation. For example, if prices fully reflect an information system, requiring disclosure of signals from that system will have no impact on prices, assuming the disclosure is expected to cause no change in the production and financing decisions of the firm (and, as a result, no change in beliefs regarding future cash flows). Of course, a price effect could occur if the disclosure is expected to alter the firm's future cash flows. However, in this situation, additional information is being provided. (2) In a related vein, if the market is assumed to be efficient with respect to publicly available information, security prices can be used to examine one aspect of the economic consequences of a proposed regulation and of the disclosures once a regulation has been implemented. A study by Dyckman and Smith (1979) on the price effects of the proposal to enact FAS No. 19, accounting in the oil and gas industry, is an example of the former. Beaver, Christie, and Griffin (1980) have examined the price effects of ASR No. 190, the SEC regulation requiring replacement cost disclosure, at the time the regulation was proposed, at the time it was enacted, and at the time when the data were first filed with the SEC.[33]

Management

Management also has an interest in market efficiency and its effects on the investor. The maximization of shareholder wealth is a commonly cited criterion for managerial choice behavior. The stewardship view implies that management has a responsibility to act in the interest of the investor and this is reinforced by the legal liability of management under legislation such as the Securities Acts of 1933 and 1934.

Management has a vital interest in the price of the firm's securities. Management compensation in the form of stock options and stock own-

---

[32] More formally, consider a ranking of information systems according to fineness (as defined in Chapter 2). From the perspective of the most fine information system (i.e., with knowledge of a signal from this information system), the level of capital formation attained under less fine information systems does not necessarily move in monotonic fashion as fineness is increased. As a result, there is no assurance that the level of capital formation moves "closer" to the level under the conditions of the most fine information, when considering increasing fineness at an intermediate level.

[33] Chapter 7 provides further examples of security price research used to examine the effects of financial reporting regulations.

ership is directly related to the performance of stock prices. Indirectly, other forms of compensation may also be affected by stock price performance. The maximization of shareholder wealth is often operationally taken to be equivalent to, or at least highly related to, the maximization of share price. The financing decisions of the firm are a prime responsibility of management. The stock price received on a new issue determines either how much proceeds are available for additional investment (assuming a fixed number of shares issued) or how much additional shares must be issued (assuming a fixed amount of desired net proceeds). In either case, the fortunes of the current shareholders are affected by the price of the new securities.

Financial reporting is considered to be a prime responsibility of management, and market efficiency is related to the effect on security prices of management choices among different financial reporting systems. Moreover, managements, competing among one another for investors' funds, have incentives to provide information to investors and information intermediaries, among others. Market efficiency has potential implications for (1) certain management decisions, such as a change in accounting methods, (2) the legal liability imposed on management for nondisclosure, (3) the choice of the level of complexity of the financial reporting system, (4) the concern of investors over moral hazard (e.g., fraud) by management, their willingness to invest funds, and hence the price which they are willing to pay for the firm's securities, (5) the concern of investors over marketability of the securities at some future time and hence the price they are willing to pay now, (6) the choice of format or form of disclosure (i.e., supplemental disclosure versus inclusion in the financial statements), and (7) the information content of accrual accounting and earnings determination, relative to other forms of financial disclosure.

Auditors

Market efficiency can influence the auditor in a number of ways. Obviously, the auditor has a responsibility to investors as the independent certifier of the financial statements prepared by management. Hence, the auditor is concerned about the effects on investors. More directly, market efficiency has potential implications for (1) the legal liability associated with nondisclosure, (2) the information content of the accrual accounting system which is the heart of the accounting system being audited, (3) the resources of the auditor allocated to issues of form versus substance, (4) the advice given to management with respect to their financial reporting decisions, such as a change in accounting method,

(5) the assessment of the potential effects of a change in reporting systems and whether or not it is a preferable one, and (6) the use of security prices as a means against which to evaluate the thoroughness of an audit.

Information Intermediaries

The information intermediary can be also affected by market efficiency. The information intermediary plays many information-related roles including that of (1) a seeker of information not already fully reflected in prices, (2) a processor, interpreter, and analyzer of information for the purposes of prediction (called *prospective analysis*), and (3) an interpretor of events after-the-fact (called *retrospective analysis*). Information intermediaries compete with one another in the gathering and interpretation of information. With respect to the first role, these intermediaries have incentives to seek out and to disseminate information. In the second and third roles the intermediaries are producers of information. Here more primitive information, such as financial statement data, is an input or factor of production. The conclusions of the analysis, interpretation, and processing are the output or product of the analysis and are a form of information.

Market efficiency can have diverse effects depending upon the mix of roles the information intermediary adopts. (1) If the information intermediary is a seeker of information not fully reflected in prices, publicly available information can constitute a competing source of information. In this sense, the information intermediary may oppose regulations for greater disclosure if it is felt that such disclosures would intrude upon the domain of the information intermediary and effectively compete with the information provided by the information intermediary. (2) To the extent that the information intermediary is a producer of information, either of prospective or retrospective analysis, financial disclosure constitutes a factor of production. As a result, the information intermediary might favor a regulation to increase the disclosure of financial information because it is tantamount to providing more of a factor of production for the information intermediary.

Market efficiency can also influence the orientation of information search or analysis. (1) As a seeker of information, the information intermediary makes a decision on which sources of information to pursue. Market efficiency can influence the sources of information sought. For example, if the market is perceived to be efficient with respect to publicly available information, an information intermediary would concentrate on gathering information that is not publicly available. The information intermediary will seek out sources that are not fully reflected in prices. (2) As a producer of information, the information intermediary can have diverse objectives. For example, the analysis could be directed at detecting mispriced securities or it could be directed at assessing the risk of different securities. If the information intermediary felt that the market was efficient with respect to a very rich, comprehensive information system, the information intermediary may choose to direct the analysis toward risk assessment rather than toward finding mispriced securities.

6-11. ACCEPTANCE BY THE CONSTITUENCIES

The current state of the art in efficient market research offers several unresolved issues concerning research design, counterevidence, and theory. The resolution of these issues could influence the degree of acceptance by the research community of market efficiency with respect to a specific information system. These factors also provide several potential reasons why the research community might express some reluctance in accepting market efficiency of various forms. What about acceptance by the major constituencies of the financial reporting environment?

As indicated previously, the services of information intermediaries are commonly sold on the basis that they can select mispriced securities. Clearly, market efficiency can be viewed as a threat to such claims. Market efficiency of the semi-strong form implies that mispriced securities do not exist with respect to publicly available data. An information intermediary who offers the services on the premise that mispriced securities can be selected based on publicly available information is unlikely to embrace semi-strong form efficiency. For example, the analyst community has typically expressed strong opposition to market efficiency.[34] Similarly, consider the position of the accountant who has a substantial investment in knowledge of accrual accounting and whose compensation is nontrivially related to such knowledge. Claims that semi-strong form market efficiency can imply that the efficacy of accrual accounting is an open issue and that many accounting issues may be capable of trivial resolution [e.g., interperiod tax allocation as suggested in Beaver (1973a)] are unlikely to be warmly received.

Each of the constituencies could be examined in detail. However, this section focuses primarily on acceptance of the efficient market research by the policy makers, the FASB and the SEC. They are used to illustrate the nature of the issues that arise in an analysis of acceptance by the constituencies.

---

[34] Of course, it would be possible to claim an ability to select mispriced securities based on nonpublicly available information. However, the current legal environment makes such claims risky and potentially exposes the analyst to legal liability. See Beaver (1976) for further discussion.

Acceptance by the FASB

The publications of the FASB have shown a considerable awareness of efficient capital markets, a willingness to consider the implications, and a willingness to sponsor research projects that employ the research methods of the security price literature. Most prominently, the FASB's _Tentative Conclusions_ [FASB (1976a)] examined the concept and its implications (see Chapter 2 and the Appendix). FAS No. 19 explicitly explored the implications of market efficiency with respect to the probable effects of the standard on the prices of firms affected by the standard [FASB (1977, paragraph 169, page 82)]. Moreover, the FASB has sponsored studies of the security price effects on their FAS No. 8 [Dukes (1978)] and FAS No. 19 [Dyckman and Smith (1979)].

The FASB has not taken a position on the efficient market hypothesis and it is not likely to for a variety of reasons. However, it certainly has demonstrated an awareness and comprehension of the concept and has made a serious attempt to incorporate such a perspective as one source of evidence in its policy-making considerations.

SEC and Market Efficiency

By contrast, the SEC has been more reluctant to incorporate such research into its deliberations. Perhaps the rationale for such reticence is similar to the reasons expressed in the introduction of the _Report of the SEC Advisory Committee on Corporate Disclosure_ [SEC (1977)], which is essentially negative in tone. Prior to examining that rationale, it would be worthwhile to explore the implications of market efficiency for the SEC under a variety of scenarios. For these purposes, the threefold distinction of weak, semi-strong, and strong form market efficiency will suffice. The following four possibilities are examined: (1) The market is not only semi-strong but also strong form efficient. (2) The market is efficient in the strong form but not in the semi-strong form. (3) The market is not efficient in either the strong form or the semi-strong form. (4) The market is not efficient in the strong form but is efficient in the semi-strong form.

Case I. (Market is not only semi-strong but also strong form efficient)

In this case, requiring public disclosure of nonpublished data would have no effect upon security prices due to informational reasons, since price "fully reflects" such data already. The effects of requiring disclosure could be related to cost reduction considerations (e.g., reducing the cost of information search by the private sector) or an alteration in portfolios held by investors. However, an informational impact upon security price presumably would not be a major motivation for disclosure regulation in such a setting. Again, this assumes no second-order effects on the production-financing decisions of the firm (see footnote 18).

Case II. (Market is strong-form efficient but not semi-strong form efficient)

This is essentially a logical contradiction since all information includes public information as a proper subset. It is represented here largely for completeness. It would be possible to argue that prices fully reflect nonpublished data but do not fully reflect publicly available data. Although this is a logical possibility, it seems empirically unlikely, since the cost of obtaining publicly available data is lower than the cost of obtaining nonpublished data. This possibility is not widely advocated.

Case III. (Market is inefficient in strong form and semi-strong form)

In this setting, presumably one rationale for requiring disclosure is the impact of disclosure upon security prices, together with its attendant impact upon investors' wealth and upon resource allocation. However, while this may be a potential motivation for bringing nonpublished data into the public domain, there is no assurance that it will have any (price) effect, since the market is not efficient with respect to publicly available data. In other words, the disclosure regulation may be ineffective because the data are not fully reflected in prices even after they are made publicly available. Hence, the SEC cannot be assured that public disclosure is an effective remedy, at least as far as prices are concerned.

Case IV. (Market is efficient in semi-strong form but not strong form)

The motivation for requiring disclosure would be essentially the same as it was in Case III above. However, it differs from the previous cases in several important respects. Relative to Case I there is now a richer set of potential consequences associated with any regulation (i.e., potential effect on price and its attendant consequences). Relative to Case III once the data are placed in the public domain, there is assurance that such data will be fully reflected in prices. In other words, requiring public disclosure is an effective remedy (at least in terms of security prices) for any perceived undesirable effects associated with the presence of nonpublicly available data.

In sum, then, Case IV in some respects offers the most friendly or most favorable climate for disclosure regulation from the perspective of market efficiency. This does not deny that there are many other considerations as well, some of which are discussed in Chapters 2 and 7. However, of the four cases cited, Case IV offers the setting in which requiring disclosure can have the maximum potential effects. Moreover,

Case IV is also the one that appears to be a reasonable description of reality based upon an overall evaluation of the empirical research discussed earlier.

Acceptance by the SEC

From the above analysis, one might suspect that the SEC has considerable incentive to contend that Case IV describes reality. In fact, by its policy of active disclosure regulation, the SEC can be viewed as acting *as if* it believes in semi-strong form efficiency but not strong form efficiency.

However, the stated policy position of the SEC makes no explicit reference to this concept. Moreover, the *Report of the SEC Advisory Committee on Corporate Disclosure* [SEC (1977)] discusses market efficiency in essentially negative tones.

> . . . The Committee believes that notwithstanding the interesting and clearly significant work done by economists and others in developing the efficient market hypothesis, the evidences that fundamental research is essentially useless are not yet, and may never be, sufficiently telling to justify the elimination of a disclosure system premised on the proposition that such research is useful and necessary. (page XXXVIII)

The above statement contains two crucial premises: (1) Market efficiency implies that fundamental research is useless and (2) the SEC disclosure system requires the assumption that such research is useful. Given these two premises, reticence by the SEC and by the Advisory Committee, who support the SEC, to accept the efficient market hypothesis is not surprising. The premises are in fact fallacious.[35] For example, a previous section of this chapter specified the role of the SEC under a variety of scenarios and concluded that market efficiency in the semi-strong form could in fact provide a "friendly" climate for mandated disclosure. However, given that the perception that such premises are valid and given that acceptance of market efficiency is equated with the demise of the SEC, it is unlikely that market efficiency will be accepted by supporters of the SEC.

In this regard, Watts and Zimmerman (1979) have offered a model to explain theory acceptance by those affected by the implications of that theory. They posit that the theory will be accepted by a group only if it is in the self-interest of that group to embrace the theory. This model has led them to characterize accounting theory in terms of a demand

---

[35] The validity of the premises are ambiguous because *market efficiency* and *fundamental analysis* are not carefully defined. However, after considerable effort, I am unable to find a *consistent* set of definitions under which both premises are valid.

for excuses. Under this view, acceptance of the efficient market hypothesis is less likely to rest on issues of research design, as discussed previously, but rather on the incentives of various parties to adopt such a view. Hence, acceptance of the efficient market hypothesis can be affected by altering the incentives of the affected groups (e.g., the SEC) or by forms of persuasion that it is in their best interests to accept the hypothesis. In this regard, consider the argument offered earlier regarding the four scenarios for market efficiency and the role of the SEC in each of the cases. In any event, the degree of acceptance by the constituencies may be largely unaffected by the sort of theoretical and research design issues that tend to influence the acceptance of a hypothesis in the research community.

6-12. CONCLUDING REMARKS

This chapter explores the definition, theory, evidence, implications, and acceptance of the concept of market efficiency. The market is efficient with respect to an information system if prices act *as if* everyone has access to that information system. In this sense, prices are said to "fully reflect" the information system. The origin of market efficiency with respect to financial information is security analysis. The empirical evidence arose in response to contentions in the financial and accounting communities that the market is inefficient with respect to certain financial statement information. The early evidence was interpreted to be consistent with the contention that security prices respond quickly and in a sophisticated manner to financial statement data. The role of anecdotal evidence, several research design issues, which introduce ambiguity with respect to interpretation of the empirical evidence, and counterevidence are discussed.

Efficient market research has a predominantly empirical tradition and largely preceded any formal, theoretical treatment of the topic. Recent research provides various theories of market efficiency. The lack of theoretical development is one reason why it is difficult to interpret empirical evidence. The theoretical and research design issues, as well as the counterevidence, could potentially influence the acceptance of various forms of market efficiency by the research community. Conditional upon market efficiency of the semi-strong form, several potential implications and nonimplications are presented, and their importance to various constituencies is discussed.

The chapter also examines the acceptance by the financial reporting constituencies, especially the policy-making bodies. It is suggested that the degree of acceptance may not rest on the theoretical and research design issues previously discussed but rather whether or not the acceptance is viewed to be in the self-interest of that particular group. However, policy-making behavior is consistent with market efficiency with respect to publicly available data but market inefficiency with respect to nonpublicly available data.

In closing, the chapter takes no position on the efficiency of the market with respect to any specific information system. The nature of empirical evidence and the interpretation is likely to change over time and be subject to continuing debate and controversy. Instead, the discussion focuses upon conceptual aspects and implications of market efficiency that continue to be relevant, regardless of the changing nature of the empirical domain.

BIBLIOGRAPHY

ARCHIBALD, T. R. "Stock Market Reaction to Depreciation Switch-Back." *Accounting Review* (January 1972), 22–30.

AXELSON, K. "A Businessman's View of Disclosure." *Journal of Accountancy* (July 1975), 42–46.

BAGEHOT, W. "The Only Game in Town." *Financial Analysts Journal* (March–April 1971), 12–22.

BALL, R. "Changes in Accounting Techniques and Stock Prices." *Empirical Research in Accounting: Selected Studies.* Supplement to the *Journal of Accounting Research* (1972), 1–38.

———. "Anomalies in Relationships Between Securities' Yields and Yield-Surrogates." *Journal of Financial Economics* (June–September 1978), 104–126.

——— and P. BROWN. "An Empirical Evaluation of Accounting Income Numbers." *Journal of Accounting Research* (Autumn 1968), 159–178.

BANZ, R. "The Relationship Between Market Value and Return on Common Stocks." Unpublished working paper, University of Chicago, September, 1979.

BASU, S. "The Investment Performance of Common Stocks in Relation to Their Price-Earnings Ratios: A Test of the Efficient Market Hypothesis." *Journal of Finance* (June 1977), 663–682.

BEAVER, W. "The Information Content of Annual Earnings Announcements." *Empirical Research in Accounting: Selected Studies,* supplement to the *Journal of Accounting Research* (1968), 67–92.

———. "Reporting Rules for Marketable Equity Securities." *Journal of Accountancy* (October 1971), 56–61.

———. "What Should Be the FASB's Objectives?" *Journal of Accountancy* (August 1973a), 49–56.

———. "Accounting for Marketable Equity Securities: Some Empirical Results." *Journal of Accountancy* (December 1973b), 58–64.

———. "The Implications of Security Price Research for Disclosure Policy and the Analyst Community." *Proceedings of the Duke Symposium on*

Financial Information Requirements for Security Analysis. Duke University, December 1976, 67–81.

―――― "Current Trends in Corporate Disclosure." *Journal of Accountancy* (January 1978), 44–52.

―――― "Reflections on Market Efficiency." *Annual Accounting Review: 1980*. Edited by S. Weinstein and M. Walker. New York: Harwood Academic Publishers, 1980a.

―――― "Econometric Properties of Alternative Security Return Metrics." Stanford working paper, 1980b.

―――― "Market Efficiency." *Accounting Review* (January 1981).

―――― A. CHRISTIE, and P. GRIFFIN. "The Information Content of SEC Accounting Series Release No. 190." *Journal of Accounting and Economics* (June 1980).

―――― AND R. DUKES. "Interperiod Tax Allocation and Delta-Depreciation Methods: Some Empirical Results." *Accounting Review* (July 1973), 549–559.

BEAVER, W., AND W. LANDSMAN. "Note on the Behavior of Residual Security Returns for Winner and Loser Portfolios." *Journal of Accounting and Economics* (December 1981), 233–241.

BERNSTEIN, L. "In Defense of Fundamental Investment Analysis." *Financial Analysts Journal* (January–February 1975), 57–61.

BOATSMAN, J. "Market Reaction to the 1976 Replacement Cost Disclosures." *Journal of Accounting and Economics* (June 1980).

BOUDREAUX, K. "Competitive Rates, Market Efficiency, and the Economics of Security Analysis." *Financial Analysts Journal* (March–April 1975), 18–24, 92.

BRILOFF, A. "Much-Abused Goodwill." *Barron's* (April 28, 1969).

―――― *Unaccountable Accounting*. New York: Harper & Row, 1972.

BROWN, P., and J. KENNELLY. "The Informational Content of Quarterly Earnings." *Journal of Business* (July 1972), 403–421.

―――― and J. WARNER. "Measuring Security Price Performance." Unpublished working paper, University of Rochester, January, 1980.

COMISKEY, E. "Market Response to Changes in Depreciation Accounting." *Accounting Review* (April 1971), 279–285.

COOTNER, P., ed. *The Random Character of Stock Market Prices*. Cambridge: MIT Press, 1964.

DOUGLAS, W. "Protecting the Investor," *Yale Review* (1933), 523–524.

DUKES, R. "An Investigation of the Effects of Expensing Research Security Prices." *Proceedings of the Conference on Topical Research in Accounting*. Edited by M. Schiff and G. Sorter. New York: New York University, 1976.

―――― *An Empirical Investigation of the Effects of the Statement of Financial Accounting Standard No. 8 on Security Return Behavior*. Stamford, Conn.: FASB, December, 1978.

DYCKMAN, T. and A. SMITH. "Financial Accounting and Reporting by Oil and Gas Producing Companies: A Study of Information Effects." *Journal of Accounting and Economics* (March 1979), 45–76.

DYCKMAN, T. and D. MORSE. *Efficient Capital Markets and Accounting: A Critical Analysis.* 2d ed. Englewood Cliffs N.J.: Prentice-Hall, 1986.

EASMAN, W., A. FALKENSTEIN, R. WEIL, and D. GUY. "The Correlation Between Sustainable Income and Stock Returns." *Financial Analysts Journal* (September–October 1979), 44–47.

FALKENSTEIN, A. and R. WEIL. "Replacement Cost Accounting: What Will Income Statements Based on SEC Disclosures Show?" *Financial Analysts Journal* (January–February 1977), 56–57.

FAMA, E. "Efficient Capital Markets: A Review of Theory and Empirical Work." *Journal of Finance* (May 1970), 383–417.

———— "Reply to 'Efficient Capital Markets: Comments.' " *Journal of Finance* (March 1976), 143–145.

FINANCIAL ACCOUNTING STANDARDS BOARD. *Tentative Conclusions on Objectives of Financial Statements of Business Enterprises.* Stamford, Conn: FASB, 1976a.

———— *Scope and Implications of the Conceptual Framework Project.* Stamford, Conn.: FASB, December 2, 1976b.

———— *Financial Accounting and Reporting by Oil and Gas Companies.* Statement of Financial Accounting Standards No. 19. Stamford, Conn.: FASB, December, 1977.

FOSTER, G. "Accounting Earnings and Stock Prices of Insurance Companies." *Accounting Review* (October 1975), 686–698.

———— *Financial Statement Analysis.* 2d ed. Englewood Cliffs, N.J.: Prentice-Hall, 1986.

———— "Briloff and the Capital Market." *Journal of Accounting Research* (Spring 1979), 262–274.

———— "Accounting Policy Decisions and Capital Market Research." *Journal of Accounting and Economics* (March 1980), 29–62.

———— OLSEN, C. and T. SHEVLIN. "Earnings Releases, Anomalies and the Behavior of Security Returns." *Accounting Review* (October 1984), 574–603.

GONEDES, N. "The Capital Market, the Market for Information, and External Accounting." *Journal of Finance* (May 1976), 611–630.

———— and N. DOPUCH. "Capital Market Equilibrium, Information Production, and Selecting Accounting Techniques: Theoretical Framework and Review of Empirical Work." *Studies on Financial Accounting Objectives: 1974.* Supplement to the *Journal of Accounting Research* (1974), 48–129.

GRAHAM, B., and D. DODD. *Security Analysis.* New York: McGraw-Hill, 1934.

GROSSMAN, S. "On the Efficiency of Competitive Stock Markets Where

Traders Have Diverse Information." *Journal of Finance* (May 1976), 573–585.

_____ and J. STIGLITZ. "On the Impossibility of Informationally Efficient Markets." Presented at the Econometric Society meetings, December, 1975.

HAKANSSON, NILS H. "Interim Disclosure and Forecasts: An Academic's Views." Berkeley: Professional Accounting Program, Graduate School of Business Administration, University of California, December 3, 1975.

IJIRI, Y. *The Foundations of Accounting Measurement.* Englewood Cliffs, N.J.: Prentice-Hall, 1967.

_____ *Theory of Accounting Measurement.* Studies in Accounting Research No. 10. Sarasota, Fl: American Accounting Association, 1975.

JENSEN, M. "Tests of Capital Market Theory and Implications of the Evidence." *In Handbook of Financial Economics,* J. L. Bickler, ed. New York: North Holland Press, 1979, chapter 2.

JOY, O., R. LITZENBERGER, and R. MCENALLY. "The Adjustment of Stock Prices to Announcements of Unanticipated Changes in Quarterly Earning." *Journal of Accounting Research* (Autumn 1977), 207–225.

KIHLSTROM, R., and L. MIRMAN. "Information and Market Equilibrium." *Bell Journal of Economics* (Spring 1975), 357–376.

KRIPKE, H. "Rule 106-5 Liability and 'Material' Facts." *New York University Law Review* (December 1971), 1062–1076.

_____ "The Myth of the Informed Layman." *The Business Lawyer* (January 1973), 631–638.

_____ "An Opportunity for Fundamental Thinking—The SEC's Advisory Committee on Corporate Disclosure." *New York Law Journal* (December 13, 1976), 1.

LEROY, S. "Efficient Capital Markets: Comment." *Journal of Finance* (March 1976), 139–141.

LIBBY, R. *Accounting and Human Information Processing Theory and Applications.* Englewood Cliffs, N.J.: Prentice-Hall, 1981.

LITZENBERGER, R., and K. RAMASWAMY. "The Effect of Personal Taxes and Dividends on Capital Asset Prices." *Journal of Financial Economics* (1979), 163–195.

LORIE, J., and M. HAMILTON. *The Stock Market: Theories and Evidence.* Homewood, Ill.: Irwin, 1973.

MAY, R. "The Influence of Quarterly Earnings Announcements on Investors' Decisions." *Empirical Research in Accounting: Selected Studies.* Supplement to the *Journal of Accounting Research* (1971), 119–163.

_____ and G. SUNDEM. "Cost of Information and Security Prices: Market Association Tests for Accounting Policy Decisions." *Accounting Review* (January 1973), 80–94.

PATELL, J., and M. WOLFSON. "The Intraday Speed of Adjustment of Stock Prices to Earnings and Dividend Announcements." *Journal of Accounting and Economics* (June 1984), 223–252.

RENDLEMEN, R., C. JONES, and H. LATANE. "Empirical Anomalies Based on Unexpected Earnings and the Importance of Risk Adjustments. *Journal of Financial Economics* (November 1982), 269–287.

RO, B. "The Adjustment of Security Prices to the Disclosure of Replacement Cost Accounting Information." *Journal of Accounting and Economics* (June 1980).

RUBINSTEIN, M. "Securities Market Efficiency in an Arrow-Debreu Economy." *American Economic Review* (December 1975), 812–824.

SEC v. BAUSCH & LOMB, INC. *Federal Securities Law Reports* (September 26, 1976), 90, 499–515.

SECURITIES AND EXCHANGE COMMISSION. *Report of the SEC Advisory Committee on Corporate Disclosure.* Washington, D.C.: U.S. Government Printing Office, 1977.

SHORES, D. "Security Returns Surrounding Earnings Announcements on the Over-the-Counter Market." Unpublished working paper, University of Washington, 1987.

SORTER, G. "An 'Events' Approach to Basic Accounting Theory." *Accounting Review* (January 1969), 12–19.

TREYNOR, J. "Efficient Markets and Fundamental Analysis." *Financial Analysts Journal* (March–April, 1974), 14.

VERRECCHIA, R. "On the Theory of Market Information Efficiency. *Journal of Accounting and Economics* (March 1979), 77–90.

WATTS, R., and J. ZIMMERMAN. "The Demand for and Supply of Accounting Theories: The Market for Excuses." *Accounting Review* (April 1979), 273–305.

Wheat Report, The. "Disclosure to Investors: A Reappraisal of Administrative Policies Under the '33 and '34 Securities Acts." New York: Brown & Co., 1969.

WYATT, A. "Efficient Market Theory: Its Impact on Accounting." *Journal of Accountancy* (February 1983), 56–65.

chapter seven

Regulation

Financial reporting takes place in a regulated environment. Chapter 1 noted that the SEC and the FASB are promulgating financial reporting regulations at an unprecedented rate. Moreover, the trend of extensive regulation is likely to continue. As a result, the quantity of regulations is at an all-time high, and the estimated life of any particular regulation is shorter than it has ever been.

Given that regulation is an important part of the financial reporting environment, this chapter explores such issues as: Why regulate? How should regulation be conducted? Who should regulate (e.g., the SEC versus the FASB)?[1] In doing so, the discussion will serve to synthesize the major concepts of the framework developed in the previous chapters.

---

[1] This chapter draws heavily upon Chapter XX of the *SEC Advisory Committee Report on Corporate Disclosure* [SEC (1977)]. An excellent review of the nature of financial reporting regulation also appears in Chapter 7 of Watts and Zimmerman (1986).

7-1. THE NATURE OF MANDATED FINANCIAL REPORTING

The regulation of financial reporting receives its impetus from the Securities Acts of 1933 and 1934, which gave the SEC statutory power to ensure "full and fair disclosure" by corporations issuing securities on an interstate basis. The Acts specifically grant the SEC the power to determine the accounting standards for reports filed with the SEC. The SEC has also interpreted its legislative authority as extending to the contents of the annual report to shareholders under the provisions of the Acts which empower the SEC to regulate the information provided in connection with proxy statements [Beaver (1978)]. Horngren (1972, 1973), among others, views the power of the FASB as being derived from the SEC. Accounting Series Release 150 delegates authority to the FASB to determine generally accepted accounting principles with respect to statements filed with the SEC.[2] This view of the FASB is adopted here. Often the illustrations refer only to the SEC. However, in general, the discussion of the rationale for regulation applies to the FASB as well as to the SEC.

Brief Review of the Financial Reporting Environment

The investment process involves giving up current consumption in exchange for securities, which are claims to future, uncertain cash flows. The investor must decide how to allocate wealth between current consumption and investment and how to allocate the funds set aside for investment among the various securities available. The investor has a potential demand for information that will aid in assessing the future cash flows associated with the securities and the firms that offer those securities. However, the investor is not acting in isolation but within a larger investment environment. This environment consists of several characteristics. (1) Investors, some perhaps with limited financial and accounting training, have the opportunity to avail themselves of the services of financial intermediaries, such as investment companies, to whom they can defer a portion of the investment process. (2) Investors, some perhaps with limited access to and ability to interpret financial information, have the opportunity to avail themselves of the services of information intermediaries, such as analysts, to whom they can defer a portion or all of the information gathering and processing function. (3)

---

[2] While the SEC has delegated such authority to the FASB, the SEC has often chosen to exercise "oversight" with respect to FASB decisions [see Horngren (1972, 1973) and Armstrong (1977), among others].

Investors have the opportunity to invest in a number of securities and to diversify out of some of the risks associated with a single security. (4) The information intermediaries compete with one another in the gathering and interpretation of financial information. (5) Managements, competing with one another for the investors' funds, have incentives to provide financial information to the investment community. (6) Investors and intermediaries have information available that is more comprehensive and perhaps more timely than the annual report to shareholders or the SEC filings. (7) Security price research suggests that security prices reflect a rich, comprehensive information system.

Under these conditions, why is it desirable to have a portion of the disclosure system contain a mandated set of disclosures?

Previous Rationale for Regulation

One approach consists of citing a litany of perceived abuses. Several questions can be raised in connection with such an approach. Were the actions in question in fact "abuses"? What one person might label "manipulation" another might label "arbitrage." In particular, what harm was inflicted as a result of such actions? Was inadequate financial reporting a contributing factor to the abuses? Will mandating financial reporting in some form deter or reduce such activities? What was the frequency of abuses relative to some measure of total activity? What are the costs associated with regulation attempting to deter such activity? These are potentially important questions because mandated disclosure tends to be imposed on broad classes of corporations, not merely on those that committed the perceived abuse.[3]

However, more fundamentally, the point is that perfection is unattainable. Any system, even a regulated one, will incur some frequency of "abuse." It is not clear that there has been a decline in the frequency of abuse since the inception of the Acts and in the presence of increased regulation. Moreover, it is as inappropriate to judge a disclosure system solely on the basis of its perceived abuses as it would be to judge the merits of a public agency, such as the SEC, solely on the basis of its perceived worst regulations. The central issue is whether or not there is some flaw in the private sector (e.g., some market failure) that leads to the conclusion that governmental regulation is a more desirable solution.

---

[3] After analyzing the perceived abuses at the time of the enactment of the Securities Act, Benston (1973, 1974) has concluded that they constitute an inadequate basis on which to justify the securities' legislation.

7-2. WHY REGULATE? (POSSIBLE RATIONALE
FOR REGULATION)

This section attempts to develop a framework for the consideration of issues regarding financial reporting regulation. In doing so, information is viewed as an economic commodity. The issue will be viewed as regulating the flow of information to the investment community. In order to examine this issue from an economic perspective, the nature of economic problems and the purpose of government with respect to those problems is discussed briefly.

Economic issues fall into two major categories: issues of efficiency and issues of equity. The first category is concerned with the most efficient means of achieving some specified result. Movement to a more efficient solution could in principle result in everyone in the economy being in a more preferred position (or at least as preferred a position) with no one being in a less preferred position (called a *Pareto-optimal solution*). The second category, issues of equity, deals with the choice among efficient solutions in which each solution will leave some individuals better off but others worse off. Issues on how wealth should be distributed among individuals in the economy is one example of an issue of equity. The government becomes involved in both types of issues. However, the rationale for governmental intervention can vary considerably depending upon the type of issue involved. Therefore, it is imperative to state the extent to which the rationale for disclosure regulation rests on efficiency or equity considerations.

In general, the government has a variety of means available to deal with these issues, including the enforcement of private contracts, the definition and enforcement of property rights, taxation, regulation, and direct ownership. The Securities Acts provide two primary means by which the flow of information to investors is affected. First is the general anti-fraud provisions; the second is the power to explicitly mandate financial reporting via the SEC filings and annual reports to shareholders.

The Securities Acts provide that it is unlawful to make a false or misleading statement or to omit a material fact in connection with the purchase or sale of a security. Laws against fraud are commonplace in the sale of a variety of commodities and they reflect concern over the pervasive problem that the quality of the product or service being sold is uncertain. Moreover, often one party to the transaction may naturally be in a position of superior information regarding the quality. Under anti-fraud provisions, certain parties to the transaction face the prospect of civil or criminal penalties when and if the quality of the commodity is eventually discovered and their behavior is deemed "fraudulent."

While the deterrence of fraud via legal liability is fairly commonplace, the presence of a regulatory mechanism that explicitly mandates the nature of what must be disclosed is a special (although not unique) feature of securities regulation. For example, neither federal nor state laws require filing a prospectus when an individual sells a home, even though the seller is in a potentially superior position with respect to information on the quality of the home.

The next sections deal with arguments that potentially provide a rationale for mandated financial reporting which by implication asserts that reliance solely on the anti-fraud provisions is inadequate.[4] The arguments fall into three major categories. (1) Financial reporting involves externalities and a form of market failure. (2) Left unregulated, market forces would lead to an asymmetrical or uneven possession of information among investors. (3) Corporate management has incentives to suppress unfavorable information.

7-3. FINANCIAL REPORTING EXTERNALITIES

An externality exists when the actions of one party have effects on other parties who are not charged (or compensated) via the price mechanism. This constitutes a form of *market failure*. While in principle it is possible to conceive of an elaborate price system that would charge or compensate the third parties for these effects, it may be undesirable to have such a system because it is too costly or simply not feasible.[5]

However, without some form of collective action, the party undertaking the action has no incentive to internalize the effects on third parties, and the actions taken may lead to an inefficiency. For example, in the classic public good analysis with positive external effects on third parties, there is an underproduction of the public good in the absence of a collective action that incorporates the third parties, who benefit from the public good but do not participate in the decision to produce or pay for it. For this reason, these third parties are often referred to as *free riders*. In this situation, the private incentives are less than the "social" incentives to produce the public good.[6]

In the financial reporting context, two examples are frequently offered. Externalities could occur when information about the produc-

---

[4] The rationale for the choice between regulation and anti-fraud provisions is discussed in Posner (1972), pp. 156–166.

[5] This is one of many possible ways of discussing externalities. It is used here because it serves to focus on the issue of "market forces" versus regulation which is a focal point of the Report of the SEC Advisory Committee on Corporate Disclosure [SEC (1977)] Introduction. Foster (1980) provides a more general discussion of the externality issue, which focuses on interdependencies without tying them to market "failures."

[6] Arrow's (1971) discussion of the incentives for invention is a well-known application of this analysis.

tive opportunities of one firm conveys information about the productive opportunities of other firms. Shareholders in the disclosing firm pay the costs of disclosure but shareholders in the other firms do not, even though they are affected by the disclosure. For example, disclosure by a firm about its success (or lack thereof) with respect to some product development may provide information to other firms about their chances of success in similar product developments. In fact, it might even obviate their having to expend resources on product developments. Thus the familiar objection to disclosure on grounds of competitive disadvantage can be viewed as one form of externality. In this setting there will be a lack of incentive to fully disclose (even though there are benefits to other firms) because the disclosing firm is not being compensated.

The second example deals with positive external effects on prospective shareholders. Investors demand information in order to assess the risks and rewards (i.e., the array of potential future cash flows) associated with alternative portfolios of securities. In making consumption and investment decisions, the investor finds information about a security useful whether or not that particular security ultimately is one of the securities in the portfolio chosen by the investor. The process of selecting the "best" portfolio inherently involves a consideration of investment alternatives (i.e., alternative portfolios). Therefore, information on securities in these alternative portfolios may be valuable at the decision-making stage, even though after-the-fact some of those securities may not be included in the portfolio chosen. In this setting, prospective shareholders do not directly pay the costs, yet they share in the benefits of disclosure (i.e., they may be free riders). If the prospective shareholders neither participate in the decision to disclose nor share in bearing the costs, there can be less disclosure than there would be under a collective agreement which included them. They would be willing to pay for additional disclosure such that everyone (both current and prospective shareholders) would be in a more preferred position (a more efficient solution would be attained).[7]

Similarly, consider a securities market in which prices reflect a comprehensive information system. Investors without effort or incurring costs are able to act as "price takers" and can adopt simple, relatively costless portfolio strategies that reflect the information. In other words, they can act as if they are adopting, as their own, the consensus or composite beliefs reflected in price, which in turn reflect a comprehensive information system. In the context of Fama's "fair game" interpretation, investors are playing a "fair game" with respect to a comprehen-

---

[7] One such collective solution is that suggested by Samuelson (1954) and was recently applied to a corporate disclosure context by Gonedes and Dopuch (1974).

sive system of publicly available information. A variation of this argument is advanced in Chapter 6 with respect to information search. Investors may benefit from information when it is reflected in prices. However, because it is reflected in prices, the direct demand and incentives to pay for it may be zero.

Care must be exercised in advancing an externalities-based argument. Earlier chapters have highlighted the potentially diverse, complex, and indirect nature of the demand for financial reporting. However, diversity, complexity, or indirectness, in and of themselves, do not necessarily lead to any form of externality or to any form of market failure. The demand for many goods and services is indirect (e.g., raw materials), and yet no externality or market failure argument is involved. In order to induce an externality or market failure, there must be something in the complexity or indirectness of the structure that produces effects or consequences that are not adequately reflected by or incorporated into the price mechanism.

7-4. ADDITIONAL CONSIDERATIONS

There are a number of additional issues to be introduced in considering an externality or public good approach to regulation.

(1) What is the materiality of the externality or public good aspect to financial reporting? Currently, little empirical evidence exists to assess the importance of potential externalities.

(2) Issues of cost must be introduced. Once costs are considered, it is no longer clear that the term *market failure* is appropriate. The private sector may in fact be adopting a cost-effective response, relative to attempting to eliminate the effects of the externalities. These include the direct costs of disclosure, the indirect costs of disclosure, and the costs of regulation. (a) The direct costs of disclosure include the costs of the production, certification, dissemination, processing, and interpretation of disclosures. (b) The indirect costs include the adverse effects of disclosure on competitive advantage (creating a disincentive to innovate or invest in product development) and legal liability, which may induce an inefficient sharing risk by management and auditors, among others. (c) The costs of regulation include the cost involved in the development, compliance, enforcement, and litigation of disclosure regulations.

(3) There are issues related to the information demanded by the regulatory agency in order to develop and monitor the regulations. In the context of disclosure regulations, the SEC attempts to determine the amount and nature of corporate disclosure that would take place and to avoid the inefficiencies induced by the externalities. In the case in which the prospective shareholders are free riders, this involves an attempt to determine their demand for information. In general, investor demand for information will be influenced by the wealth, risk preferences, and beliefs of investors. This implies a nontrivial demand for information by the regulatory agency. Economic analyses, which show the attainment of a more efficient solution via governmental regulation, typically assume perfect knowledge on the part of the regulatory body, which is obviously an unrealistic assumption. When it is too costly or simply not feasible to obtain the desired information, implementation error by the regulatory agency due to imperfect information may occur.

Individuals may not have incentives to honestly reveal their preferences for financial reporting. Individuals may understate or overstate the desirability of additional disclosure, depending upon the extent to which they perceive that their expression of preferences will be used as a basis to assess their share of the costs. A clear illustration is provided when there is no attempt to include the free riders in sharing in the costs of disclosure. Suppose that some groups are invited to participate in the process that determines the quantity and nature of corporate disclosure but are not invited to share in bearing the costs of those additional disclosures (e.g., financial analysts). In this situation, the result may be excessive disclosure instead of inadequate disclosure as suggested by the standard public good analysis. Issues of efficiency and equity are raised by such a process.

(4) There are issues that relate to the incentives of the regulatory agency itself. The economics of regulation offers two primary views of regulatory behavior.[8] The first is the "public interest" view, which states that regulatory behavior is directed toward furthering the public interest. This view implicitly assumes that the incentives of regulators are aligned so as to further the public interest and that the concept of public interest is well-defined. The second view is known as the *capture theory* and states that the prime beneficiaries of regulation are not the public (or investors, in the case of the Securities Acts) but rather those being regulated. This has led critics of the Securities Acts, such as Stigler, to argue that the primary beneficiaries of the Acts are various members in the professional investment community rather than investors at large.[9]

(5) There is the issue of alternatives to governmental regulation, such as private-sector collective agreements. For example, many goods with externalities are dealt with in the private sector. Newspapers are an example. The issue of whether to deal with the problem collectively

---

[8] The economics of regulation is reviewed in Posner (1974). Posner develops a comprehensive model of regulatory behavior, where the two primary views are special cases of his model.

[9] See Cohen and Stigler (1971, pp. 6–9).

in the private or public sector revolves around the issue of relative costs of the alternative approaches. It is argued that the government has a comparative advantage in dealing with certain types of collective agreements. In particular, when it is difficult to identify free riders or too costly to exclude them, it is intuitively felt that the comparative advantage favors governmental action.

7-5. UNEQUAL POSSESSION OF INFORMATION AMONG INVESTORS

A second major argument for disclosure regulation is that, left unregulated, market forces would lead to an uneven possession of information among investors. Selective disclosure is one example. In other words, the result would be a continuum of informed investors ranging from well-informed to ill-informed. It is further argued that such asymmetry of access to information is inherently unfair and violates the meaning of "fair" disclosure under the Securities Acts. Hence, the basis of the argument is typically one of equity rather than efficiency. Simply stated, it is only fair that the less informed be protected from the more informed.

Recent economic analysis of the demand for privately held information suggests that considerable incentives exist to expend efforts searching for and obtaining nonpublicly available information for trading purposes.[10] However, the unfairness of such a process is not self-evident.

Presumably, the analysts pass along the benefits of the information search to their clients, either directly or indirectly. In this sense, the clients of analysts become more informed investors. However, they pay for the analysts' services either directly or indirectly. As long as the services are available to anyone willing to pay for them, there is no obvious way in which harm is occurring. At the margin, investors will purchase analysts' services to that point where investors are indifferent between being more informed or less informed, given the costs of becoming more informed. In other words, the expected benefits of being more informed (e.g., in the form of expected superior returns due to better information) are equal to (or offset by) the costs incurred to obtain the additional information.[11] A common argument is that some investors

---

[10] The term *information for trading purposes* refers to the demand for information for speculative purposes. In other words, information is demanded for the purpose of earning abnormal returns due to superior information at the expense of uninformed investors. The incentives to search for such information are analyzed in Hirshleifer (1971).

[11] The process is described in greater detail in Grossman and Stiglitz (1975) and Gonedes (1976).

cannot afford to purchase the services of analysts. However, the existence of financial intermediaries makes the force of this argument unclear. Moreover, it ignores several alternatives open to relatively less informed investors. One such alternative is to partially insulate themselves from more informed traders via buy-and-hold strategies and index funds.[12] Also, the actions of the more informed may signal their information to the less informed and as a result prices may partially (in the limit, fully) reflect the information.[13]

The purchase of analysts' information can be viewed as the decision to purchase a higher-quality product (in this case, superior information). In general, quality differences exist with respect to any commodity, and usually it is not thought to be unfair when one consumer chooses to purchase a higher-quality product while another chooses a lower-quality item. The purchase of automobiles is one example, but illustrations could be provided for almost any commodity.

While selective disclosure is commonly cast as an equity issue, there are grounds for considering it on the basis of efficiency. For example, Hirshleifer (1971) provides an example in which the social value is zero to the acquisition of private information in an exchange setting.[14] If there are no costs to forming private-sector collective agreements, investors would agree among themselves not to privately seek information. Everyone who would gain in that society would no longer incur the costs of private search for information whose sole purpose is to redistribute wealth among investors via trading on superior information. In other words, the trading gains in the form of superior returns due to privately held information net out to zero across all investors. It is a zero-sum game in that every investor with superior returns is offset by other investors with inferior returns. However, to the extent that such search causes investors to incur real costs, it is not a zero-sum game, but these costs constitute dead-weight losses to investors as a whole. Investors could be better off by collectively agreeing to avoid such costs.

However, reaching and enforcing such a collective agreement might be extremely costly or simply not feasible (e.g., because of informational asymmetries). In the absence of effective enforcement, there would be an incentive to cheat on the agreement. Therefore, the SEC or the FASB may have a comparative advantage in effectively reducing private search for information. It could be accomplished by either or both of the two

[12] For a more complete discussion, see Marshall (1974) and Treynor (1979).

[13] For a more complete discussion of the ability of prices to reveal information, see Grossman (1976).

[14] Hakansson (1975) raises a related point and argues that analysts' search for information creates an inefficient redundancy in the information-gathering process that could be remedied by public disclosure. The Hirshleifer analysis is discussed more fully in Chapter 2.

major means of regulation. (1) They could preempt private search for particular information by mandating the disclosure of that information in public filings or annual reports. (2) The SEC could impose sufficient legal liability on transmittal of information from management to analysts such that information flows would be deterred (or in the limit eliminated).

This poses a dilemma. Hirshleifer's argument suggests that there is a tendency for "excessive" information, as analysts and others privately search for information and disseminate it.[15] However, this is the converse of the public good argument which implies "inadequate" information. There are opposing forces operating. In one case, the private incentives are excessive; in the other case, the private incentives fall short. To the extent the latter exists, it might be desirable to permit a certain amount of private search to compensate for the otherwise inadequate incentives to publicly disclose.[16] However, permitting too much could lead to the inefficiencies described above.

7-6. MANAGEMENT INCENTIVES TO DISCLOSE

A third major argument for disclosure regulation is that management has incentives to suppress unfavorable information. While there may be a general awareness of this potential among investors, investors would not know specifically the nature of the suppressed information. As a result, investors will be unable to distinguish quality differences among common stocks to the same extent they would under fuller disclosure. Hence, security prices will not fully reflect quality differences among stocks, and there will be uncertainty about the quality of each stock. There may be a tendency for lower-quality stocks to be selling at a higher price than would prevail under fuller disclosure and conversely for the higher-quality stocks.[17] This can lead to a phenomenon known as *adverse selection* in which the managements (and investors) of poorer-

---

[15] Once the speculative positions have been taken based on the privately held information, there will be an incentive to disseminate or "push" the information. This will result in the prices reflecting the information, and the benefits of the superior information can be realized as soon as possible. The pushing of information is discussed in Hirshleifer (1971), Demski (1974), and Marshall (1974).

[16] Both Kripke (1976) and Lorie (1974) take the position that permitting some private search is socially desirable.

[17] A lower-quality stock is one whose price is overstated relative to the price that would prevail if greater disclosures were available to investors, and conversely for a higher-quality stock.

quality stocks have greater incentives to offer additional shares for sale than the managements of higher-quality stocks.[18]

Firms can respond to this problem in a number of ways. (1) Higher-quality firms will attempt to signal their higher quality by undertaking actions that would be irrational unless they were in fact of higher quality. The effectiveness of this signaling behavior will be influenced by the extent to which the lower-quality firms can imitate the signaling behavior. Moreover, signaling may be a costly activity with no rewards beyond those of signaling. (2) Managements will offer to have their disclosure system monitored and certified by an independent party, which will lead to a demand for auditing services. (3) Management may offer warranties to shareholders whereby they will incur penalties if it is eventually discovered that unfavorable information was suppressed.[19] In fact, managements' willingness to be audited and to offer warranties can be signals in themselves. Obviously, both auditing services and warranty contracts are not costless. One of the most important costs in the warranty is that management may end up bearing "excessive" risk.

After-the-fact, it may be difficult to disentangle a deterioration in the stock price that was due to correcting inadequate disclosure as opposed to other unfavorable events. As a result, management may become an insurer for events in addition to those induced by management's disclosure policy. This may lead to an inefficient sharing of risks, relative to that which would attain if there were no uncertainty about the quality of the stocks.[20]

The anti-fraud provisions can be viewed as requiring firms to provide disclosure warranties to investors. Presumably, the legal liability reduces the incentives of management to suppress unfavorable information. The argument for governmental intervention, as opposed to private-sector contracting, is that the SEC has a comparative advantage in achieving the same result. However, while this argument forms a basis for anti-fraud statutes, it is not clear why a mandated disclosure system is desirable. In other words, why is reliance upon anti-fraud statutes deemed to be inadequate?

[18] Moreover, a *moral hazard* problem also can arise in which management changes the quality of the stock to take advantage of the information asymmetry. The moral hazard problem is discussed in Chapter 2. Obviously, adverse selection can also occur in the context of asymmetrically informed investors.

[19] This discussion heavily draws upon a branch of economic theory known as signaling theory. A paper by Ross (1979) applies this literature to the disclosure regulation context. The bibliographic references to the signaling literature appear in the Ross paper.

[20] Managers are unlikely to remain passive if such risk is imposed on them. For example, bearing this risk might alter the risk-reward tradeoffs management makes in investment decisions. They may tend to be more risk adverse because of the legal liability associated with higher risk projects.

7-7. SUMMARY OF PREVIOUS DISCUSSION

The purpose of the preceding discussion is to identify some of the issues involved in defining the role of regulation of financial reporting. Three rationales are provided for the potential desirability of the regulation. All three arguments rest on the premise that a public agency, such as the SEC, has a comparative advantage in forming collective agreements of a certain form (e.g., when the potential beneficiaries or affected parties are numerous and difficult to identify and hence when it is more costly or simply not feasible to attempt to deal with the same issue via market forces). However, it is unclear empirically whether or not these arguments are valid. Hence, in the absence of evidence, the desirability of having a regulated environment is an open issue.

7-8. HOW SHOULD REGULATION
BE CONDUCTED?

The previous sections have dealt with various aspects of the issue of why a portion of information production and financial reporting should be regulated. This section takes the existence of regulatory bodies as a given, not because such bodies are necessarily desirable but because they constitute an important part of the financial reporting environment. This section will deal with the issue of determining the content or desirability of specific proposals to regulate financial reporting.

Financial reporting regulations have several potential economic consequences which have been discussed in Chapters 2 and 6. These potential consequences include (1) wealth distribution among investors and others; (2) the aggregate level of risk incurred and risk sharing among individuals; (3) the effects on the rate of capital formation; (4) allocation of resources among firms; (5) the use of resources devoted to the production, certification, dissemination, processing analysis, and interpretation of disclosures; (6) the use of resources in the development, compliance, enforcement, and litigation of disclosure regulations; and (7) the use of resources in the private-sector search for nonpublic information. These consequences may not have the same impact among or within the different constituencies. As a result, there may not be a consensus on the desirability of a particular proposed regulation. In terms of the framework in Section 7.2, regulation of financial reporting may not only involve issues of economic efficiency but also issues of equity. The effects of a regulation, if enacted, may be analogous to redistribution of wealth among the constituencies. Hence, a tradeoff is involved as to what importance to assign to the preferences of each group. The existence of an overall objective function, such as a social welfare function, is neither clear nor is its nature well-defined [Arrow (1963)].

In addition to this conceptual issue, there is the practical problem of determining what the preferences of each group are or what the consequences are. The earlier discussion indicated that individuals may not have the incentive to truthfully reveal their preferences and may distort them in unknown ways. Moreover, the reasons given for supporting or opposing a particular regulation may not honestly reveal the individuals' motives [Watts and Zimmerman (1979)].

7-9. EMPIRICAL EVIDENCE ON THE EFFECTS OF FINANCIAL REGULATION

Many of the potential effects of reporting regulations would be difficult to assess, such as the effects on resource allocation. However, there is a class of evidence that has examined the effects of regulation on security prices.

Two early examples of studies in this category are Stigler's (1964a) analysis of the effects of the 1933 Act on the return distributions of new issues and Benston's (1973) analysis of firms affected by the initial disclosure regulations of the 1934 Act. Both Stigler and Benston concluded that the securities legislation had little or no effect on the distribution of security price returns. The findings and the interpretations placed on the findings were highly controversial and have evoked a number of criticisms.[21] The criticisms fall into three general categories. (1) The tests conducted are not appropriate tests of the effects. In other words, there was the lack of the development of a theory as to what security price return effects would be theoretically expected if the Securities Acts were or were not effective. Hence, the tests are not capable of distinguishing whether or not the legislation was effective. (2) Even assuming that the tests were appropriate, a closer or more careful analysis of the findings reveals that some effects were in fact observed in these studies. (3) Even assuming that the tests were appropriate, the research design used is not powerful enough to detect the effects. Hence, the finding of no effects may be due to inadequacies in the research design rather than the lack of any effects. The latter issue was of concern to Deakin (1976) who reexamined the period studied by Benston and concluded that there was a statistically significant effect to the 1934 Act although the estimates of the effects were small.

[21] See Gonedes and Dopuch (1974), Friend and Herman (1964), Robbins and Werner (1964), Stigler (1964b), Friend and Westerfield (1975), Friend (1975), and Sommer (1974).

A second class of studies deals with specific disclosure requirements subsequent to the passage of the Acts. Collins (1975) examines the security price behavior associated with segment reporting requirements. Hagerman (1975) investigates the effects of the 1964 amendments to the 1934 Act on bank stocks. Griffin (1977) studies the price and volume effects of sensitive foreign payments whose disclosure was encouraged by the SEC. Dukes (1978) investigates the price effects associated with disclosures under FAS No. 8, which deals with foreign currency translation. Ro (1980), Boatsman (1980), and Beaver, Christie, and Griffin (1980) examine the security price effects of the announcement and first-time disclosures of Accounting Series Release No. 190 concerning replacement cost data. The results vary with respect to whether or not a price effect was found.

An interesting variation of security price research is to examine the price effects of the announcement of the *regulation* as distinct from the price effects of the disclosure of the information required by the regulation. This permits an examination of the anticipated effects of the regulation to require an *information system*, rather than the information content of the *signals* subsequently disclosed. Dyckman and Smith (1979), Collins and Dent (1979), Lev (1979), and Haworth, Matthews, and Tuck (1978) examine the price effects of the announcement of FAS No. 19, which deals with accounting for the oil and gas industry. Beaver, Christie, and Griffin (1980) and Ro (1980) examine the price effects of the announcement proposing ASR No. 190 and the announcement of its passage.

Security price research of both types can be informative in dealing with one aspect of disclosure. With respect to the research into the price effects of disclosing the signals, the studies can provide evidence on whether or not prices behave as if such disclosure led to a systematic revision in beliefs. In other words, do prices behave as if investors perceive the signals as possessing information content? This is relevant to the extent that the rationale for disclosure is to provide information not already reflected in prices. With respect to research into the price effects of announcement of the regulation, the studies can provide evidence on the anticipated effects of the regulation as reflected in the security prices. For example, opponents of FAS No. 19 contended that it would impair the ability of "full cost" firms to access the credit market and to compete with the "successful efforts" firms. A negative price impact of announcements concerning FAS No. 19 was interpreted as consistent with the allegations of adverse effects.

Of course, price effects deal only with one aspect of the effects of financial reporting regulation. They are a proxy or surrogate for economic consequences of ultimate concern: capital formation, resource allocation, wealth distribution, and costs, among others. For example, as indicated above, if the rationale for regulation is to add to the information system that is reflected in prices (i.e., to make the market efficient with respect to a richer information system), then price effects may be a reasonable expected consequence of the disclosure. However, failure to find price effects at the time of disclosure (which is apparently the case with ASR No. 190 [Beaver, Christie, and Griffin (1980)] cannot necessarily be interpreted to imply that the regulation is valueless. For example, other effects of the regulation may have been intended or may be occurring. For example, one effect could be to provide the information via public disclosure by the corporation at a lower cost than would be incurred by the private sector's information network in seeking the same information and reflecting it in prices.

Similarly, when price effects are found, one must be careful in interpreting these effects. Although the presence of such effects may be consistent with the intent of the policy makers, it cannot be taken as *prima facie* evidence that the private-sector incentives to disclose are "inadequate." It may be that the "benefits" were perceived to be not commensurate with the "costs," such that disclosure was not worthwhile. The critical issue is to determine whether the failure to disclose was due to a misalignment of incentives in the private sector toward "inadequate" disclosure or due to a misalignment of regulators toward "excessive" disclosure.

Security price research cannot, in and of itself, answer this question. In sum, the absence of price effects is not necessarily an indictment of a regulation, and the presence of price effects is not sufficient to confirm the value of the regulation. However, security price research can provide evidence on one aspect of financial reporting regulation. As such, price effects can be a readily observable manifestation of the consequences of regulation and a reasonable implication that often naturally follows from rationale commonly offered for financial reporting regulations.

7-10. WHO SHOULD REGULATE?

This section discusses some aspects of the issue of who should regulate financial reporting—the FASB or the SEC? More precisely, how should the respective jurisdictions be defined? Traditionally, the jurisdiction of the FASB is said to be *accounting standards* and the jurisdiction of the SEC is said to be *disclosure*. However, this distinction has not been successful in describing the jurisdictional boundaries. For example, FAS No. 14 on segment reporting is viewed by many as a disclosure standard instead of an accounting standard. Moreover, many FASB standards contain disclosure provisions, as well as defining a new accounting standard. Similarly, the SEC has influenced accounting standards. Its activity in the investment credit controversy and its rejection of Standard No. 19 in the oil and gas industry are prominent examples.

Horngren (1972, 1973) offers another interpretation of the relationship between the FASB and the SEC. Horngren suggests that the SEC be viewed as central management and that the FASB be viewed as decentralized management. The SEC manages "by exception" (i.e., by oversight). Several advantages to this dual regulatory structure are cited. (1) It permits the SEC to have access to the technical expertise of the accounting profession. (2) Such services are obtained by the SEC without having to pay for them. (3) The FASB serves as a "buffer" against criticism of a regulation that otherwise would be directed at the SEC if it were the sole regulatory body. (4) There may be greater acceptance of the regulations by management and the auditors.

The other side of the coin is, of course, what are the advantages of the dual management to the FASB? There are two possibilities. (1) It provides the "cosmetic" appearance that financial reporting standards are being set in the private sector which may enhance the importance and status of the auditing profession with its clients and with other members of society. (2) It permits the FASB and the private sector, via the FASB, to have greater control or influence over the nature of the regulations. This raises the question of how much control the SEC and Congress are willing to give to the FASB. Recent statements by congressional committees [Senate (1976) and Report (1976)] have been critical of the SEC in delegating too much power to the FASB. Hence, the importance of this advantage is tenuous.

Will the FASB and private-sector standard setting survive? At one time, it was perceived that the major power of the FASB came from support of the public accounting profession itself, and its acceptance of FASB rulings was viewed as critical of the success of the FASB. However, under the view described above, the federal government (i.e., the SEC and Congress) is the prime factor in the future of the FASB. The success of the FASB will be influenced by the extent to which the FASB can promulgate regulations acceptable to the federal government, which in turn is responding to a variety of constituencies.

7-11. CONCLUDING REMARKS

This chapter explores the potential rationale for the regulation of financial reporting. The arguments rest upon the assumption that the regulatory body offers some comparative advantage in forming collective agreements on the nature of such regulations. A number of other considerations are discussed that suggest that consequences of regulation in practice may fall short of "ideal" regulation. As a result, the efficacy of regulation is an open issue. Empirical research has assessed the effects of regulation on security prices, one of the consequences of regulation. Two effects are investigated: the anticipated effects of a regulation at the time it is announced and the effects of data at the time they are reported. Although the results vary with the context examined, this empirical research may be useful in providing evidence on one aspect of financial reporting regulations.

The selection among financial reporting systems is a social choice. As such, the choice deals with such questions as: (1) What are the additional costs associated with the financial reporting regulation? (2) Are there alternative methods of dealing with the problem that might be more effective or less costly? Reliance on anti-fraud statutes and private-sector collective agreements are two possibilities. In any event, no environment, even a regulated one, is likely to drive the level of "abuse" to zero. Even if it were feasible, it is not likely that such a result would be desirable because the costs of achieving that result could be prohibitive. Implementation error by the regulators, caused by a lack of evidence on investors' demand for information, must also be considered.

Currently, there is little evidence on these questions. As a result, the desirability of financial reporting regulation is still an open question. However, the issues raised here provide a framework within which to structure future research. Notwithstanding the ambiguity with respect to the efficacy of regulation, it seems likely that extensive regulation of financial reporting will continue to be an important part of the environment.

Financial reporting regulation is a social choice because of the potentially diverse effects or consequences of regulation on the constituencies. These effects will typically entail considerations beyond those of accounting expertise. This social choice perspective naturally follows from viewing a financial reporting system as an information system in a multiperson setting. This perspective can lead to potentially dramatic changes in the nature of financial reporting, and these changes can be viewed as a form of accounting revolution.

This book has attempted to illustrate that a number of fundamental aspects of the environment are still open issues. One issue is the efficacy of accrual accounting, which is at the heart of financial accounting as it is presently structured. Another issue is the efficacy of financial reporting regulation, which is a major component of the financial reporting environment. In one sense, this uncertainty may seem frustrating; in another sense, it provides an opportunity for progress. These chapters have attempted to describe a conceptual framework within which to interpret the revolution and to possibly point to ways our knowledge of the environment may evolve.

BIBLIOGRAPHY

ANDERSON, ALISON GREY. "The Disclosure Process in Federal Securities Regulation: A Brief Review." *The Hastings Law Review* (January 1974), 311–354.

ARMSTRONG, MARSHALL. "The Politics of Establishing Accounting Standards." *Journal of Accountancy* (February 1977), 76–79.

ARROW, K. *Social Choice and Individual Values.* 2d ed. New Haven, Conn.: Yale University Press, 1963.

―――― "Political and Economic Evaluation of Social Effects and Externalities." In *Frontiers of Quantitative Economics.* M. Intriligator, ed. New York: North Holland Press, 1971.

BEAVER, W. "Current Trends in Corporate Disclosure." *Journal of Accountancy* (January 1978), 44–52.

―――― CHRISTIE, A. and P. GRIFFIN. "The Information Content of SEC Replacement Cost Disclosures." *Journal of Accounting and Economics* (June 1980).

BENSTON, G. "Required Disclosure and the Stock Market: An Evaluation of the Securities and Exchange Act of 1934." *American Economic Review* (March 1973), 132–155.

―――― "Evaluation of the Securities Act of 1934." *Financial Executive* (May 1974), 28–36.

―――― "Required Disclosure and the Stock Market: Rejoinder." *American Economic Review* (1975), 473–477.

BERNSTEIN, L. "In Defense of Fundamental Investment Analysis." *Financial Analysts Journal* (January–February, 1975), 3–7.

BOATSMAN, J. "Market Reaction to the 1976 Replacement Cost Disclosures." *Journal of Accounting and Economics* (June 1980).

COHEN, M., and G. STIGLER. *Can Regulatory Agencies Protect Consumers?* Rational Debate Seminars, American Enterprise Institute for Public Policy Research, 1971.

COLLINS, D. "SEC Product Line Reporting and Market Efficiency." *Journal of Financial Economics* (June 1975), 125–64.

―――― and W. DENT. "The Proposed Elimination of Full Cost Accounting in the Extractive Industry: An Empirical Assessment of the Market Consequences." *Journal of Accounting and Economics* (March 1979), 3–44.

DEAKIN, E. "Accounting Reports, Policy Interventions, and the Behavior of Securities Returns." *Accounting Review* (July 1976), 590–603.

DEMSKI, J. "The Choice Among Financial Reporting Alternatives." *Accounting Review* (April 1974), 221–232.

DOUGLAS, W. "Protecting the Investor." *Yale Review* (1933), 523–524.

DUKES, R. *An Empirical Investigation of the Effects of Statement of Financial Accounting Standards No. 8 on Security Return Behavior.* Stamford, Conn.: FASB, December, 1978.

DYCKMAN, T., and A. SMITH. "Financial Accounting and Reporting by Oil and Gas Producing Companies: A Study of Information Effects." *Journal of Accounting and Economics* (March 1979), 45–76.

FOSTER, G. "Externalities and Financial Reporting." *Journal of Finance* (May 1980).

FRIEND, I. "The Economic Consequences of the Stock Market." *American Economic Review* (1972), 212–219.

―――― "Economic Foundations of Stock Market Regulation." Working paper, Wharton School, 1975.

FRIEND, I., and E. HERMAN. "The SEC Through a Glass Darkly." *Journal of Business* (1964), 382–405.

FRIEND, I., and R. WESTERFIELD. "Required Disclosure and the Stock Markets: Comment." *American Economic Review* (1975), 467–472.

GONEDES, N. "The Capital Market, The Market for Information, and External Accounting." *Journal of Finance* (May 1976), 611–630.

―――― and N. DOPUCH. "Capital Market Equilibrium, Information Production, and Selecting Accounting Techniques: Theoretical Framework and Review of Empirical Work." *Studies on Financial Accounting Objectives: 1974.* Supplement to the *Journal of Accounting Research* (1974), 48–129.

GRIFFIN, P. "Sensitive Foreign Disclosures: The Securities Market Impact." Study conducted for the *SEC Advisory Committee on Corporate Disclosure* (November 1977), 694–733.

GROSSMAN, S. "On the Efficiency of Competitive Stock Markets Where Traders Have Diverse Information." *Journal of Finance* (May 1976), 573–585.

―――― and J. STIGLITZ. "On the Impossibility of Informationally Efficient Markets." Presented at the Econometric Society Meetings, December, 1975.

HAGERMAN, R. "Regulation and Accounting Principles." *Accounting Review* (October 1975), 699–709.

HAKANSSON, N. H. "Interim Disclosure and Forecasts: An Academic's Views." Berkeley: Professional Accounting Program, Graduate School of Business Administration, University of California, December 3, 1975.

―――― "Information Needs for Portfolio Choice." Presented and published as part of the *Proceedings of the Duke Symposium on Financial Information Requirements for Security Analysis.* Duke University, December, 1976, 18–46.

HAWORTH, H., J. MATTHEWS, and C. TUCK. "Full Cost Versus Successful Efforts: A Study of a Proposed Accounting Change's Competitive Impact." SEC Directorate of Economic and Policy Research, February, 1978.

HIRSHLEIFER, J. "The Private and Social Value of Information and the Reward to Inventive Activity." *American Economic Review* (September, 1971), 561–573.

HORNGREN, C. "Accounting Principles: Private or Public Sector?" *Journal of Accountancy* (May 1972), 37–41.

———— "The Marketing of Accounting Standards." *Journal of Accountancy* (October 1973), 61–66.

KRIPKE, H. "An Opportunity for Fundamental Thinking—The SEC's Advisory Committee on Corporate Disclosure." *New York Law Journal*, December 13, 1976, p. 1.

LEV, B. "The Impact of Accounting Regulation on the Stock Market: The Case of Oil and Gas Companies." *Accounting Review* (July 1979), 485–503.

LORIE, J. "Public Policy for American Capital Markets." *Federal Securities Law Reporter* (1974), 79, 646.

MARSHALL, J. "Private Incentives and Public Information." *American Economic Review* (June 1974), 373–390.

MODIGLIANI, F., and G. POGUE. "An Introduction to Risk and Return." *Financial Analysts Journal* (March–April and May–June, 1974), 68–80 and 69–86, respectively.

POSNER, R. *Economic Analysis of Law.* Boston: Little, Brown, 1972.

———— "Theories of Economic Regulation." *Bell Journal of Economics and Management Science* (Autumn 1974), 335–358.

REPORT OF THE SUBCOMMITTEE ON OVERSIGHT AND INVESTIGATIONS, COMMITTEE ON INTERSTATE AND FOREIGN COMMERCE [Representative John Moss (D-California), chairman], *Federal Regulation and Regulatory Reform* (1976).

RO, B. "The Adjustment of Security Prices to the Disclosure of Replacement Cost Accounting Information." *Journal of Accounting and Economics* (June 1980).

ROBBINS, S., and W. WERNER. "Professor Stigler Revisited." *Journal of Business* (1964), 406–413.

ROSS, S. "Disclosure Regulation in Financial Markets." *Issues in Financial Regulation.* New York: McGraw-Hill, 1979, 177–202.

SAMUELSON, P. "A Pure Theory of Public Expenditures." *Review of Economics and Statistics* (1954), 387–389.

SECURITIES AND EXCHANGE COMMISSION. *Report of the SEC Advisory Committee on Corporate Disclosure.* Washington, D.C.: U.S. Government Printing Office, November, 1977.

SENATE SUBCOMMITTEE ON REPORTS, ACCOUNTING, AND MANAGEMENT. [Senator Lee Metcalf (D-Montana), chairman], *The Accounting Establishment* (1976).

SOMMER, A. "The Other Side." *Financial Executive* (May 1974), 36–40.

STIGLER, G. "Public Regulation of the Securities Markets." *Journal of Business* (April 1964a), 117–142.

———— "Comment." *Journal of Business* (1964b), 414–422.

TREYNOR, J. "Trading Cost and Active Management." *Proceedings of*

Seminar on Investment Management: The Active/Passive Decisions. Menlo Park, Calif.: FRS Associates, September 23–26, 1979.

WATTS, R. and J. ZIMMERMAN. "The Demand for and Supply of Accounting Theories: The Market for Excuses." *Accounting Review* (April 1979), 273–305.

———— *Positive Accounting Theory.* Englewood Cliffs, N.J.: Prentice-Hall, 1986.

Wheat Report, The. "Disclosure to Investors: A Reappraisal of Administrative Policies Under the '33 and '34 Securities Acts." New York: Brown & Co., 1969.

Index

A

Abnormal expected returns, 134
Accounting income:
  descriptive differences, 73
  v. economic earnings under certainty, 65
  v. economic earnings under uncertainty, 85
  introduced, 3
  measurement error, 67–71
  shocks, 93
  under uncertainty, 85
  unexpected component, 93
Accounting revolution, 2
Accrual accounting:
  as a forecast, 98
  in an informational setting, 4
  as a method of transforming cash flows, 7
  role of, 98
  and stewardship, 2
Acts, 23
Adverse selection, 37, 186

Agency theory, 39
Aggregation, 7, 100, 156
Allocational efficiency, 157
Alpha, 31
Alter ego cash flow streams, 52
Alternative accounting methods:
  descriptive differences, 73
  evidence regarding, 112
  introduced, 67
  measurement error, 67, 72
Anecdotal evidence, 141–42
Arbitrage, 51
Auditors:
  demand for services, 40
  independence, 164
  market efficiency, 164
  regulation, 185
  role in environment, 10

B

Beliefs:
  as a determinant of security price, 133

Beliefs (*cont.*)
in a single-person setting, 24
Beta:
as a choice parameter, 32
defined, 31
evidence discussed, 125
evidence reported (*table*), 106

C

Capital asset pricing model, 32, 143
Capital formation, 42, 43, 162
Capture theory, 183
Cash flow reporting:
v. accrual accounting, 100
evidence regarding, 116
introduced, 6
Clairvoyance, 133, 158
Competitive disadvantage, 44
Complete markets:
under certainty, 50
under uncertainty, 77
Complex security, 78
Compound claim, 51
Consensus, 149–52
Consequences:
in multi-person setting (*See* economic consequences)
in single-person setting, 24
Constant dividend growth model, 60
Cost:
direct, 43, 182
indirect, 43, 182
private search, 43
regulatory, 43, 182
Cost of capital:
under certainty, 60
risky discount rate, 85
under uncertainty, 85

D

Decision theory:
components of, 23–25
introduced, 22
Demand for financial information:
direct, 10, 31
indirect, 10

Depreciation theory, 57
Descriptive differences, 67–74
Discounting:
complex claims, 78
at expected values, 79
risky discount rate, 85
Distributable income, 62
Dividend-paying ability:
introduced, 63
in relation to accounting earnings, 90
in relation to prices, 90
relationship to permanent earnings, 64

E

Earnings rate, 55
Earnings volatility, 125
Economic consequences:
discussed, 43–44
introduced, 17
regulation, 188
summarized, 17
Economic depreciation, 56
Economic earnings (*See also* economic income):
v. accounting earnings, 65
under certainty, 53, 57
desirable properties of, 57
under uncertainty, 84
Economic income (*See also* economic earnings):
defined under certainty, 56
introduced, 4
Entry price, 56
Ex ante earnings, 82
Exit price, 56
Ex post earnings, 82
Externalities, 180

F

Fair game property, 134
Fairness, 162, 183
Financial information (*See* financial reporting)
Financial intermediary, 10

Financial reporting:
  current trends in, 18
  environment (*See* financial report-
    ing environment)
  portfolio theory, 29
  regulators, 14–15
  revolution, 2
  in single-person setting, 23
Financial reporting environment:
  described, 8
  introduced, 1
  review of, 177
  summary, 16
Forecast error, 106
Fraud, 179
Free-rider, 161, 180
"Full and fair disclosure," 177
Full disclosure, 163
Fully reflect:
  defined, 135
  early use of, 134
Fundamental analysis, 132, 169
Futures markets:
  under certainty, 50
  under uncertainty, 77

G

Garbling:
  in earnings, 125
  in signals, 149
"Growth" case, 59–61

H

Historical cost accounting:
  evidence regarding, 112
  hybrid nature, 85–86

I

"Illusory" profits, 154
Information:
  asymmetry, 35, 37, 161, 182–85
  in a multi-person setting, 34–42

post-decision role, 34
pre-decision role, 34
preemptive role, 36
private search, 11, 156, 165
  in a single-person setting, 23–33
Informational efficiency, 157
Informational perspective:
  defined, 89
  introduced, 4
Information content, 104
Information economics:
  components of, 23–29
  introduced, 22
Information intermediary:
  defined, 10
  market efficiency, 165
  private search, 11, 156, 165
  prospective analysis, 165
  public good, 155
  retrospective analysis, 165
  role described, 10
Intermediary (*See* Financial inter-
    mediary; Information inter-
    mediary)
Internal rate of return, 55
Intrinsic value:
  ambiguity of, 133
  defined, 132
  nature, 133–134
  origin, 132
Invariance property, 73
Investors:
  active *v.* passive, 11
  diversified *v.* nondiversified, 10
  heterogeneity among, 9
  market efficiency, 160
  more informed *v.* less informed, 35
  professional *v.* nonprofessional, 9

L

Learning from prices, 35, 148, 161
Legal liability:
  as an economic consequence, 44
  market efficiency, 163
Litany of abuses, 178
Luck, 151

M

Management:
market efficiency, 163
regulation, 186–87
role in environment, 15
stewardship, 163
Marketability, 162
Market efficiency:
acceptance of, 166–170
anomalies, 142–44
attributes of definition, 136
defined, 130
economic consequences of, 131
evidence regarding, 138–42
forms of, 137–138
four scenarios, 167–68
illustration of theory, 149–152
implications of, 152–57
importance to, 160–65
auditors, 164
information intermediaries, 165
investors, 160
management, 163
policy makers, 162
introduced, 33
nonimplications of, 157–160
origin of, 131
theories of, 147–52
Market failure, 180, 182–83
Matching concept, 3
Materiality, 182
Mean-variance portfolio theory
(*See* portfolio theory)
Measurement error, 67–74
Mixed strategy, 36
Money pump, 51
Moral hazard:
defined, 37
regulation, 187

N

"No-growth" case:
under certainty, 58–59
Noise, 149
Normal expected returns, 134

O

Objective function, 24

P

Pareto-optimal solution, 179
Perfect markets, 50
Permanent accounting earnings:
defined, 91
evidence of, 108–112
illustrated, 93–95
v. permanent economic earnings,
98
Permanent economic earnings:
under certainty, 62–63
v. permanent accounting earnings,
98
relationship to dividend paying
ability, 63–65
Policy makers (*See also* regulators):
described, 14
market efficiency, 162
Portfolio strategy:
active *v.* passive, 11, 161
diversified *v.* nondiversified, 10
Portfolio theory:
assumptions, 29
financial reporting, 31
implications of, 31–33
introduced, 10
role of financial information,
31–33
Preferences:
as a determinant of security price,
133
in a single-person setting, 24
Present value:
under certainty, 50–53
introduced, 5
under uncertainty, 77–81
Price-earnings relationship, 105–116
Price-takers, 161, 181
Primitive claim (*See also* simple claim),
87
Private information search, 10, 165
Propriety of response, 139

Prospective analysis, 165
Public good:
  described, 180
  information intermediaries, 155
Public interest, 183

R

Random walk:
  with drift, 124
  in earnings, 94
Regulation:
  dual nature, 191
  evidence regarding, 189
  externalities, 180
  information asymmetry, 184–86
  legislative basis, 177
  possible rationale, 179–80
  previous rationale, 178
  purpose, 177
Regulators (*See also* policy makers):
  described, 14
  market efficiency, 162
Residual change in earnings, 106
Residual change in price, 106
Resource allocation, 43, 162
Retrospective analysis, 165
Risk:
  allocation of, 43, 187
  level of, 43
  management, 187
  systematic, 31
  unsystematic, 31

S

Semi-strong form market efficiency,
  137
Signaling behavior, 38, 187
Simple claim:
  under certainty, 50
  under uncertainty, 78
Single-person setting:
  components of, 23–29
  implications of, 29–31

Social choice:
  introduced, 17
  market efficiency, 160
  nature of problem, 17
Social desirability, 157
Speed of response, 139
Spot markets:
  under certainty, 50
  under uncertainty, 77
States, 24
Statistical dependency, 104
Stewardship:
  introduced, 2
  management, 163
  moral hazard, 39
Strong form market efficiency, 137
Superior performance, 150–52
Systematic return, 30
Systematic risk:
  v. earnings volatility, 125
  introduced, 31

T

Technical analysis, 132
Time adjusted rate of return, 55
Timing of response, 139
Transitory accounting earnings:
  defined, 91
  evidence of, 108–112
  illustrated, 93–95

U

Universal access, 135
Universal knowledge, 130
Unsystematic return, 30
Unsystematic risk, 31

V

Value additivity:
  under certainty, 51
  under uncertainty, 78
Value in use, 56

W

Warranty, 187
Weak form market efficiency:
  defined, 137

  evidence regarding, 132
Wealth distribution:
  as an economic consequence, 43
  effects of security prices on, 44,
    131, 160